MW01485751

Only Idle Chatter

from

Gilbert & Sullivan Austin

To Pam —

with happy memories

of our "work/play" in my

first (old time) in Austin!

from Jane Wahran

June 16, 2024

Richard D'Oyly Carte, (unnamed man), W. S. Gilbert, and Arthur Sullivan
in London, 1883

Alfred Bryan

Ralph MacPhail, Jr., Libby Weed, Bill Hatcher, and Jeffrey Jones-Ragona
in Austin, 2012

Dan Tremblay

Only Idle Chatter

from

Gilbert & Sullivan Austin

Program Notes
and
Newsletter Articles
by
Ralph MacPhail, Jr.
Artistic Director *Emeritus*

With a Foreword by
Libby Weed
President *Emerita*

2023

Copyright © 2023 by

Gilbert & Sullivan Austin

All rights reserved

ISBN: 978-1-304-85421-6

Gilbert & Sullivan Austin

P. O. Box 684542

Austin, TX 78768-4542

To all of

The Austin Savoyards

with whom I had

the pleasure of working

1998-2020

Foreword

Gilbert & Sullivan Austin is one of the many local bands of folks found around the world who delight in the innocent merriment of the Gilbert & Sullivan comic operas and seek to share that merriment with the public. GSA has enjoyed an eventful history since the first covey of G&S enthusiasts gathered in 1976 and said, "Let's put on a show!" Not a year had passed since then without informal musicales, concerts or shorter shows, and at least one grand production—that is, until a pandemic forced GSA to find other ways to enjoy and spread the charms of Gilbert and Sullivan.

Treasured and talented people have been a part of our history—onstage and behind it, in directorial positions, on the board, and in volunteer roles. But no individual has had a more significant impact on Gilbert & Sullivan Austin's vast surge in artistic quality, production values, prestige, and audience size than its Artistic Director Emeritus, Ralph MacPhail, Jr. For this reason the GSA board has long considered our introduction to Professor MacPhail by former Executive Director Robert Mellin a landmark event in our history. "Rafe," as we fondly call him, first directed for us in 1998; from that time until 2019 he stage-directed and choreographed all but four of our major productions. He was named Artistic Director in 2005.

Professor MacPhail's history prepared him remarkably for this role. He loved Gilbert & Sullivan from childhood. As director of theatre at Bridgewater College in Virginia, he staged G&S comic operas. He led Elderhostel courses on G&S, authored scholarly articles and reviews, and made presentations at wide-ranging symposia and conferences. He studied original documents such as the prompt books of W. S. Gilbert and of the D'Oyly Carte Opera Company. He was the very model of a worthy G&S director!

Very quickly GSA came to know that any G&S opera mounted on stage under Rafe's direction would be a sterling production, true to the intent of the librettist and composer, technically sound down to the smallest minutiae, and sparkling with color and exuberance. Those of us who worked closely with him also enjoyed his warm companionship at numerous gatherings. Not only was he in our estimation—"from bias free of every kind"—the finest director in the land; he was also a cherished friend and a boon companion.

This collection of Ralph MacPhail's program notes and newsletter articles published over a two-decade span provides a glimpse into his significant contributions to our literary output and also a sense of the magic he wrought on our stages and the joy he brought to our audiences. We learned a great deal from his writings, and this enabled us to appreciate the operas even more. We were charmed by his clever turns of phrase and the flash of anticipation and excitement he sparked as each show was prepared.

It is your turn to be enriched by this sampling of writings that shed light and brought rich flavor to nine of the major productions directed by Ralph MacPhail for Gilbert & Sullivan Austin, plus the shorter productions and some of his entertainingly erudite newsletter articles. As you read them, if you are like me, on several occasions you will say to yourself, "That's rich! I wish I'd known that before." And you will surely find yourself laughing aloud several times and marveling at how nimbly and precisely Professor MacPhail expresses a delightful truth. As Sir Marmaduke Pointdextre of *The Sorcerer* might say, "Enjoy yourselves, I pray!"

Libby Weed

President Emerita
Gilbert & Sullivan Austin

Contents

Introduction and Acknowledgments

"Only idle chatter" is, of course, a quotation from Gilbert & Sullivan's *Patience*. Sham "Idyllic Poet" Reginald Bunthorne uses it to describe his affected verbiage—best delivered, he sings, by lying "upon daisies" and discoursing "in novel phrases" of his "complicated state of mind." I'm afraid that the chair in front of my computer is anything but a bed of flowers, I'm not very adept at novel phrases, and I certainly have never had a very complicated state of mind.

But when Sue Ricket Caldwell became editor of the Gilbert & Sullivan Society of Austin's *Newsletter* in 2008 and asked for an article for each issue, Bunthorne's "only idle chatter" came to mind as a guiding principle. The purpose of these articles would be to create interest in the forthcoming production: to encourage readers to audition, to participate in backstage and front-of-house activities, and to purchase tickets. So the articles needed to be "accessible" to readers without a prior knowledge of Gilbert & Sullivan and their works—and interesting as well as to Savoyards with varying degrees of such knowledge. This same principle had been at the forefront when I, as staging director, began writing program notes for the productions, which needed to create interest, provide background, and set the stage.

So the texts reprinted in the following pages don't break new ground in Savoy opera scholarship. I do hope, however, that readers with any degree of knowledge of and experience with Gilbert & Sullivan will find articles of interest—and find also perhaps a surprise or two. They appear substantially as they were originally published; however, I've taken the liberty silently to correct errors, update web links as needed, and delete references to then-current events and other articles in the issues in which they appeared.

This project came about during the COVID-19 pandemic. Gilbert & Sullivan Austin (as the society had been renamed) was, like so many other performing groups, forced to close down production. With that came some reorganization. I became Artistic Director *emeritus*, and without a "grand production" to plan, had the idea to gather these articles and pro-

1

gram notes into a book to benefit the organization, specifically the scholarship fund, and at the same time help assuage the temporal and emotional gaps brought about by my change in status.

Sue Caldwell got me started by sending digital copies of the texts as they appeared in the *Newsletter* (in 2020 re-christened *The Austin Savoyard*). I'm afraid her willingness may have brought about more than she bargained for because her wide knowledge of Microsoft Word and desktop publishing has been called upon frequently in the past months. I really can't thank her enough for her expertise and patience, and for her tastefully illustrating a number of the articles with images she selected from the Gilbert & Sullivan Archive when they first appeared.

I also acknowledge this incredible online resource with thanks. All Savoyards should be grateful for the Gilbert & Sullivan Archive.

Another change in GSA leadership came about during this period when the long-serving President of GSA, Libby Weed, stepped down. Libby had been a valued "first reader" of many of these articles, and her enthusiasm and support combined with corrections and suggestions were always much appreciated. When I asked Libby if she would be willing to write a foreword to this book, she (though very ill) responded with delight. I am pleased to note that Libby lived to know that the GSA Board of Directors, under President Diane Radin, renamed the GSA scholarship in Libby's honor—something that happened after Libby's very kind and generous foreword had been submitted and was resting safely on my hard drive. All Austin Savoyards miss Libby Weed and are grateful for her many contributions to the growth and success of the organization.

So I am very pleased to acknowledge my indebtedness to Sue and Libby, and also to a number of their (and my) colleagues, including President Diane Radin, who along with CFO and Treasurer David Wieckowski and Production Chair and Bursar Michael Meigs endorsed the project when it was "pitched" to them over a capital lunch in Austin during the summer of 2023. GSA Legal Counsel Charles Smaistrla was consulted on copyright matters in the preparation of this book. GSA's Videographer David Little prepared the lovely cover for this publication (and also all of the GSA program cover designs, used as dividers, inside it).

I am also grateful to Mr. Ian Martin, General Manager of the D'Oyly Carte Opera Trust in London, for permission to reprint an article of mine from a decades-old issue of *The Savoyard*, and to Dr. John Goddard, former President of the (now inactive) Gilbert & Sullivan Society of

Northwest Louisiana, for permission to reproduce the program covers and notes for the Society's productions of Gilbert's *Rosencrantz and Guildenstern* and *Sweethearts.*

Late in the editing process Arthur Robinson offered to read the entire book "in proof," and his fresh eyes saved more than a few of my errors, typographical and factual, from appearing in print, for which I'm grateful while acknowledging that any remaining errors are mine and mine alone. But little did I realize when accepting Arthur's offer to proofread that this book would also benefit from his deep knowledge of printed Savoy opera lore, and that he would lead me to much corroborative detail regarding sources of "common knowledge," oft' repeated quotes, and other information. I have acknowledged Arthur's many and welcome contributions in the notes at the end of the book and here thank him again most sincerely for giving verisimilitude to my idle chatter.

I wish to thank others who have assisted in many various ways: my loving wife, Alice Hoffman MacPhail, for her patience and support; Lynne Bastian and Alexander D. MacPhail for helping with MS Word arcana; Andrew Crowther, for several dives into Gilbertian bibliographical rabbit-holes; Robinson McClellan of the Morgan Library and Museum for searching for an elusive letter; Carol Davis and Lynne Greene-Brooke for a bibliographical mystery's solution; my "collector pals," Harold Kanthor, J. Donald Smith, and David Stone, for responding to inquiries; Andrew Crowther, Jeffrey Jones-Ragona, Diane Radin, and Gayden Wren for their "blurbs" on the back cover; Gina Dwyer of Idea Box Creative for uploading the cover for the book after combining David Little's lovely graphic wizardry. I am also deeply grateful to Marc Shepherd for uploading of the text for publication.

Finally, the dedication (on page v) is an expression my appreciation of and affection for the companies that brought to life the productions for which the following articles were written; by "Austin Savoyards" I include casts, orchestras, backstage and front-of-house personnel, and GSA's hard-working boards of directors. I will ever treasure memories of them and my decades-long association with this remarkable organization.

Ralph MacPhail, Jr.
Bridgewater, Virginia
September-December 2023

2010 Grand Production

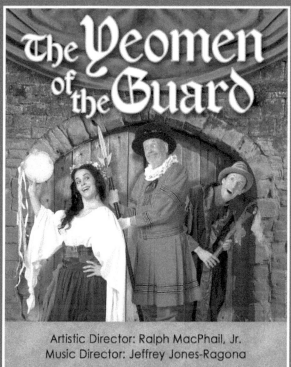

The Yeomen of the Guard

Artistic Director: Ralph MacPhail, Jr.
Music Director: Jeffrey Jones-Ragona

June 10-20, 2010
Travis High School Performing Arts Center
Austin, Texas

Introducing *The Yeomen of the Guard*

Our summer production for 2010 was originally produced in London by Richard D'Oyly Carte in 1888, near the end of the quarter-century-long Gilbert & Sullivan partnership. *The Yeomen of the Guard* is more serious in tone than the usual Savoy opera, for Sullivan had for years been begging Gilbert for plots of "real human interest and probability" where music (according to the composer) would have a more important part in communicating emotion to the audience. (No magic talismans or lozenges, please!)

Gilbert gave Sullivan what he craved—and included plenty of humor in it, too. The librettist admitted that the inspiration for *The Yeomen of the Guard* came from seeing a poster for the Tower Furnishing Company while standing in Uxbridge Station awaiting a train into the City. Here, he thought, would be a location for an opera that would meet Sullivan's requirements: quintessentially English, "The Tower" was a centuries-old palace and fortress and prison (with, actually, a number of towers), and with many a tale "grim and gory" of real-life imprisonments, intrigues, and executions.

Opportunities for pageantry abounded, with a male chorus composed of the Tower Warders in their scarlet uniforms. But not all of the citizens of the tower were military. Since the Tower of London was also a garrison, the warders' families were also in residence, along with support personnel—*perfect* for a mixed chorus.

But what to call it? An early idea was *The Tower of London*. Other possibilities were *The Beefeaters* and *The Tower Warders*—these last two perhaps more accurate than the final title. Why? Well, that's a subject for a future column.

We know that Gilbert visited the Tower of London while working on his libretto, for the Tower, then as now, was one of London's most popular tourist attractions. He probably also re-read William Harrison Ainsworth's popular and oft' reprinted 1840 novel *The Tower of London* (I'm reading it now), and perhaps thought back on a couple of his "Bab" Ballads. Contemporary reviewers of the original production noted that Gilbert was also familiar with Edward Fitzball's libretto for William Vincent Wallace's opera *Maritana* (1845). These sources of inspiration will also be discussed in a future article.

For now, let us say that both Gilbert and Sullivan considered *The Yeomen of the Guard* their finest joint work. Why? The answer to that will be the subject of yet another column! In the meantime, read the libretto and listen to a recording. You can start by Googling the title Gilbert & Sullivan finally selected for what became next summer's show.

Auditions for
The Yeomen of the Guard

*T*he Yeomen of the Guard* was Gilbert's favorite collaboration with Sullivan—and Sullivan's with Gilbert. It has plenty of Gilbertian humor, but also its serious side, which makes it unique in the Savoy opera canon. My purpose this month is to provide information for auditionees concerning the auditions and also concerning the wonderful show slated for production this summer.

Music Director and Conductor Jeffrey Jones-Ragona and I request that auditionees memorize a song from Gilbert & Sullivan or something similar and provide a copy of the music for the auditions accompanist.

If *The Yeomen of the Guard* is not in your library, you can download the libretto from The Gilbert & Sullivan Archive (use *The Yeomen of the Guard* tab at gsarchive.net). You can also download *some* printed music from the opera from this website, read a plot synopsis, or download audio files.

The Chorus is composed of the **Chorus of Yeomen of the Guard** (seven gentlemen, two of which, a tenor and baritone, have brief soli) and the **Chorus of Citizens** (four gentlemen, two having brief dialogue, and eleven ladies, none with solos or speaking lines). **The Citizen Males** can be of assorted ages and body types; **the Yeomen Men** should project military bearing, and should ideally grow beards—and be able to march. **The Women Citizenry** can be of assorted ages and body types. **Two children**, ages 8-12, will also be cast, one of which should be male.

The Yeomen of the Guard has wonderful roles and singing opportunities:

Sir Richard Cholmondeley (pronounced "Chumley") (bass-baritone, in his 60s or 70s) is the Lieutenant (*Leftenant*) of the Tower and in command. A stern taskmaster with limited sense of humor, he claims our sympathy for having saved Colonel Fairfax "from the pestilent dangers which threaten human life outside" the Tower.

Colonel Fairfax (tenor). In his early middle years. Fairfax is the military hero around whom the plot swirls. Condemned to death for a crime he didn't commit, he is dashing and brave, but easygoing, and ready to die—though more than willing to escape his execution!

Sergeant Meryll (bass-baritone) is an older man, a retired soldier with many a memory of a life in battle. Staunch and true, but not the sharpest bayonet in the arsenal. He is clever and willing to risk all in helping to set Fairfax free.

Leonard Meryll (tenor) is the Sergeant's son, who appears early and late in the opera but who is then impersonated on-stage (and in his absence) by Colonel Fairfax through most of the opera. Must sing well a difficult tenor part in his one trio.

Jack Point (light baritone), a wand'ring jester, with a bag of old jokes that don't work very well. Must move and dance well, be agile and nimble, playful, but must also exhibit pathos and sentimentality. Whether he falls insensible at the end of the opera due to unrequited love for Elsie—or dies of a broken heart—is one of The Great Questions in Gilbert & Sullivan—and one that Shall Be Answered!

Wilfred Shadbolt (bass-baritone), the Head Jailor and Assistant Tormentor of the Tower, is lugubrious, ugly—well, in fact something of a slob—unshaven, and also something of a professional sadist. Frequently played as middle-aged, but he considers himself younger—he's also a swain for Phoebe, though his affection is not reciprocated.

Elsie Maynard (dramatic soprano), 17 years old, a strolling singer and partner to Jack Point. Her mother's illness leads her to a plot-initiating decision to marry a condemned prisoner (Colonel Fairfax). Elsie is something of a vixen (for tormenting Point, who genuinely loves her). She must sing and dance very well.

Phoebe Meryll (mezzo-soprano), a pert little flirt, warmhearted, but plucky and clever. Opens the opera (unique in G&S) with a spinning song solo. Strong actress required. She is Sergeant Meryll's daughter and Leonard's sister.

Dame Carruthers (contralto), housekeeper of the Tower. Grim, born and bred "in the old keep," stern, granite-hearted (sometimes) but sympathetic. "Of a certain age."

Kate (lyric soprano) is Dame Carruthers' niece. She is also the twelfth member of the women's chorus; no soli but some important ensemble singing.

❖

Some Musical Rarities from
The Yeomen of the Guard

*T*he Yeomen of the Guard has its secrets. Did you know that two soli for major characters were cut, one before the opening night and one after? Each song arguably helps to more fully round out its singer—but gone they've been, usually, for well over a century. Did you know that Sullivan set thrice that tenorian favorite, "Is life a boon?"—and at Gilbert's behest? Did you know that the original production had soli for a Third and Fourth Yeomen in addition to the First and Second? Do you know what is probably the "real" reason for the Sergeant Meryll/Dame Carruthers duet, "Rapture, rapture," at the end of the opera?

All of these numbers will be featured at the Musicale on Sunday, March 7, at 3 pm in the sanctuary at Genesis Presbyterian Church. For now, here's a brief preview.

The loutish, love-sick Wilfred Shadbolt, Head Jailer and Assistant Tormentor at the Tower of London, originally had a song, which began:

> When jealous torments rack my soul,
> My agonies I can't control,
> Oh, better sit on red hot coal
> Than love a heartless jade.

He goes on to compare his jealousy with the Tower's bone-breaking rack, and possibly gains some audience sympathy in the process.

I've often wondered if the song was cut because of a somewhat pedestrian lyric, and a somewhat pedestrian setting—or because of its sadism—or perhaps because it included perhaps the most sensuous lyric in all Gilbert & Sullivan:

> The bird that breakfasts on your lip,
> I would I had him in my grip,
> He sippeth where I dare not sip,
> I can't get over that.
> The cat you fondle soft and sly,
> He lieth where I may not lie.
> We're not on terms, that cat and I.
> I do not like that cat.

Gilbert cut it before opening night—but it will be sung at our next musicale in March.

Sergeant Meryll's song wasn't cut until after opening night. It doesn't advance the plot or tell us anything about the good sergeant that we don't learn elsewhere. I like it better than I used to—probably because through it we learn something about the fast passage of time as perceived by a gentleman of a certain age as he reflects on Leonard, his son, who has "come to join the Tower Warders":

> A laughing boy but yesterday,
> A merry urchin blithe and gay,
> . . . .
> Today a warrior all sunbrown,
> Whose deeds of soldierly renown
> Are all the boast of London town,
>   A veteran tomorrow!

The lyric also reflects a father's pride in the accomplishments of his son:

> When at my Leonard's deeds sublime,
> A soldier's pulse beats double time,
>   And brave hearts thrill
>   As brave hearts will
>   At tales of martial glory.
> I burn with flush of pride and joy,
> A pride unbittered by alloy,
> To find my boy—my darling boy—
>   The theme of song and story!

Well, this superannuated stage director and father understands Meryll's "proper pride"!

One of the most famous tenor songs in G&S is Colonel Fairfax's first-act aria. Ariel Rios sang it at a recent musicale—and we shall hear it again—but twice. Sullivan actually composed it three times, and we will hear it once as Sullivan originally composed it the second time (the first setting does not survive), and then as he composed it once again—again at the behest of his collaborator, who didn't think the original settings were "quite right" and "upbraided."

Years later, Gilbert was asked for a quotation from the Savoy operas for Sullivan's memorial, and he selected the opening words of this song:

> Is life a boon?
>   If so, it must befall
>   That Death, whene'er he call,

Must call too soon.

(This inscription can be read on the monument any day of the week in London outside the Riverside Entrance to the Savoy Hotel in the Embankment Gardens.)

Gilbert & Sullivan further cut the first act by tightening the Finale. The one we're familiar with today features soli by the First and Second Yeomen lauding Leonard Meryll's heroics through rhetorical questions, but Gilbert originally had declarations instead of questions for two other Yeomen:

> 3RD YEOMAN.   You, when brought to execution
>   Like a demigod of yore,
>   With heroic resolution
>   Snatched a sword and killed a score. . . .
> 4TH YEOMAN.   Then escaping from the foemen,
>   Bolstered with the blood you shed,
>   You, defiant, fearing no men,
>   Saved your honour and your head! . . .
> FAIRFAX. (*aside*)   True, my course with judgement shaping,
>   Favoured, too, by lucky star,
>   I succeeded in escaping
>   Prison-bolt and prison bar!
>   (*aloud*) Oh! the tales that are narrated
>   Of my deeds of derring-do
>   Have been much exaggerated,
>   Scarce a word of them is true!

(When Gilbert proposed this cut to Sullivan, he reminded his collaborator that he was suggesting cutting his words, not Sullivan's music!)

Jeffrey and I have not decided just which of these numbers to restore to the production in June. The arguments pro and con are many and varied—and some convincing!

But we know that we will include the rollicking but oft'-cut duet for Dame Carruthers and Sergeant Meryll at the end of Act II. It features one of Gilbert's favorite words ("Rapture, rapture"!), and not only does it "soften" Gilbert's dénouement of four principal characters ending up in two "forced marriages," but there is another and rather pragmatic reason for its inclusion. That reason? (Shhh! It's a secret. It gives Fairfax and Elsie more time to change for their wedding!)

Sum Up Some History—Clear Up Some Mysteries

In Act II of *The Yeomen of the Guard*, jester Jack Point tells jailor Wilfred Shadbolt (who aspires to jester-hood): "I will teach thee all my original songs, my self-constructed riddles, my own ingenious paradoxes; nay, more, I will reveal to thee the source whence I get them." That source is Point's handbook, *The Merrie Jestes of Hugh Ambrose*.

Since our show this summer is grounded in English history, I will teach thee all of my esoteric understandings of the history of the Tower of London and its lore, my self-digested learnings based on decades of reading and research, my own ingenious conclusions based on the writings of scholars, ancient and modern; nay, more, I will reveal to thee the source whence I get them. That source is *The Gilbert & Sullivan Lexicon* of Harry Benford*.

> *The Yeomen of the Guard* "is set in the Tower of London during the reign of Henry VIII (1509-1547)."
>
> "The Tower of London is a fortress dating back in part to William the Conqueror. Located on the north bank of the Thames, it occupies about eighteen acres and includes more than a dozen individual towers. Rich in history and bloodshed, the Tower is a centerpiece of British history."
>
> "**Yeomen:** In England a yeoman was originally a man who owned and farmed his own land. The term later came to be applied to archers and cavalry soldiers recruited from among the nation's farmers and countrymen. The Yeomen of the Guard was originated in 1485 as a bodyguard for the monarch. Until 1548, their duties included service at the Tower of London. Ever since that date a similar group, called the Corps of Yeomen Warders, has had that specific duty. The Tudor uniforms worn by the two corps are almost identical and this causes the two to be confused. . . ."
>
> "**Tower Green:** An open square within the Tower of London. Most public executions took place on Tower Hill, just outside the walls of the Tower. Especially important prisoners, however, were executed in the relative privacy of Tower Green.

---

* Harry Benford's *The Gilbert and Sullivan Lexicon* is now online. See GSOpera.com/lexicon.

Anne Boleyn and Catherine Howard were accorded that privilege. Why should Colonel Fairfax be so honored? To simplify staging, I presume."

"**Little Ease:** A narrow place of confinement; specifically the name of a dungeon cell in the White Tower." (The white tower is the imposing, free-standing building in the center of the complex, and, I believe, the oldest. It is the one usually visualized by people when hearing "the Tower of London.")

"**Beauchamp [pronounced 'BEE-chum']** Tower: One of the main towers in the Tower of London [. . . ,] it was built around 1300 and remained nameless until 1397, when Thomas Beauchamp, Earl of Warwick, was imprisoned there. . . . Rudolph Hess, Hitler's henchman, spent time there, too."

"**Cold Harbour:** Another tower in the Tower of London. . . . it was used as the queen's residence during the time of Henry VII. . . . the tower was demolished in about 1670."

"**Halbert:** A medieval weapon combining an ax blade and spear on a long handle. . . . The word is more commonly spelled 'halberd.'" (Production Manager Bill Hatcher has done a lot of research on halbert/ds, and Chris Buggé is making a dozen of them for our show.)

"**St. Peter's:** . . . the garrison church of St. Peter ad Vincula, which was within the Tower, adjacent to Tower Green. . . . the original church was built by Henry II in about 1185 in penance for the murder of Thomas à Becket. It was rebuilt in 1306 and again (after a fire) in 1512." *This* is the incarnation you can visit today. Or tomorrow.

One character in *The Yeomen of the Guard* and his position are also worthy of note in our limited space:

"**Sir Richard Cholmondeley:** The most important thing to know about Sir Richard is that his family name is pronounced 'Chumley.' You may also want to know that there really was such a person in command of the Tower during the time of Henry VIII. Extensive wrangles have developed over Gilbert's intent in using the name. Was he using the character or just the name? No one knows; nor need we be much concerned. Let us press on."

"**Lieutenant ['Lef-TEN-ant']** of the Tower: The lieutenant served under the constable of the Tower. The constable was Henry VIII's chief security officer throughout the greater London area. The lieutenant of the Tower was in charge of day-today operation of the Tower itself, the most important stronghold in the nation. As a royal appointment, it was an exceedingly important and prestigious post."

The above represent only a small percentage of lore, rich and rare, to be found in Harry Benford's *The Gilbert & Sullivan Lexicon*. I encourage you to learn more about the Tower of London, which remains one of the top tourist attractions in the city, by reading further, by visiting the Tower itself when next in London—and of *course* by seeing this summer's production in June!

"We, Gilbert and Sullivan, Have A Song to Sing, O!"

In *The Complete Annotated Gilbert and Sullivan*, Ian Bradley notes that the duet for Jack Point and Elsie Maynard in Act I of *The Yeomen of the Guard* "is, perhaps, the best-loved of all Gilbert and Sullivan's songs."

I've never tried to decide on the one *I* like best, but I think "I have a song to sing, O!" would rank in my favorite 25—or *maybe* favorite dozen. Or baker's dozen.

The lyric is a complex one, with each verse building on the one before it by an additional two lines. Because of this, it has frequently been compared in style to the old nursery rhyme, "The House that Jack Built."

The story of Sullivan's difficulty in setting the lyric has been told often, but never better than by Gilbert himself. William Archer first quoted Gilbert's recollection of how this well-loved duet came about:

. . . The verse always preceded the music, or even any hint of it. Sometimes—very rarely—Sullivan would say of some song I had given him, "My dear fellow, I can't make anything of this"—and then I would rewrite it entirely—never tinker at it. But, of course, I don't mean to say that I "invented" all the rhythms and stanzas in the operas. Often a rhythm would be suggested by some old tune or other running in my head, and I would fit my words to it more or less exactly. When Sullivan knew I had done so, he would say, "Don't tell me what the tune is, or I shan't be able to get it out of my head." But once, I remember, I did tell him. There is a duet in

The Yeomen of the Guard beginning:

> I have a song to sing, O!
> Sing me your song, O!

It was suggested to me by an old chantey I used to hear the sailors on board my yacht singing in the "dog-watch" on Saturday evenings, beginning:

> Come, and I will sing you—
> What will you sing me?
> I will sing you one, O!
> What is your one, O?

and so on. Well, when I gave Sullivan the words of the duet he found the utmost difficulty in setting it. He tried hard for a fortnight, but in vain. I offered to recast in another mould, but he expressed himself so delighted with it in its then form that he was determined to work it out to a satisfactory issue. At last, he came to me and said, "You often have some old air in your mind which prompts the metre of your songs: if anything prompted you in this case, hum it to me— it may help me." Only a rash man ever asks me to hum, but the situation was desperate, and I did my best to convey to him the air of the chantey that had suggested the song to me. I was so far successful that before I had hummed a dozen bars he exclaimed, "That will do—I've got it!" And in an hour he produced the charming air as it appears in the opera. I have sometimes thought that he exclaimed "That will do—I've got it," because my humming was more than he could bear; but he always assured me that it had given him the necessary clue to the proper setting of the song.

Here is Gilbert's last verse of this duet as it appears in Act I:

ELSIE.	I have a song to sing, O!
POINT.	Sing me your song O!
ELSIE.	It is sung with a sigh
	And a tear in the eye,

> For it tells of a righted wrong, O!
> It's the song of the merrymaid, once so gay,
> Who turned on her heel and tripped away
> From the peacock popinjay, bravely born,
> Who turned up his noble nose with scorn
> At the humble heart that he did not prize:

> So she begged on her knees, with downcast eyes,
> For the love of the merryman, moping mum,
> Whose soul was sad, and whose glance was glum,
> Who sipped no sup, and who craved no crumb,
>   As he sighed for the love of a ladye!
>
> ALL.   Heighdy! Heighdy!
>   Misery me, lackadaydee!
> His pains were o'er, and he sighed no more,
>   For he lived in the love of a ladye!

By the end of the opera, we learn that the lyric is more than just a lovely duet by an itinerant jester entertaining a crowd with his partner. Elsie the "merrymaid" is happily united with Colonel Fairfax (her "lord"), and Jack Point is left, sad and alone, his jokes against love for Elsie and matrimony long forgotten. Originally Gilbert had Elsie sing:

> It's the song of a merrymaid, peerly proud,
> Who loved a lord and who laughed aloud
> At the moan of the merryman moping mum,
> Whose soul was sad and whose glance was glum, [etc.].

But at the first revival of *The Yeomen of the Guard* at the Savoy in 1897, nine years after the première, Gilbert softened Elsie's "farewell" to Jack Point considerably—and the words invariably leave audiences with lumps in throats if not tears in eyes—as they lead to a conclusion unique in Gilbert & Sullivan:

> It's the song of a merrymaid, nestling near,
> Who loved her lord—but who dropped a tear
> At the moan of the merryman, moping mum,
> Whose soul was sad and whose glance was glum,
> Who sipped no sup, and who craved no crumb,
>   As he sighed for the love of a ladye!

Arthur DiBianca as Jack Point and Michelle Haché as Elsie

I have a song to sing, O!

*T*he Yeomen of the Guard was originally produced in London by Richard D'Oyly Carte in 1888, near the end of the quarter-century-long Gilbert & Sullivan partnership. The show is more serious in tone than the usual Savoy opera, for Sullivan had for years been begging Gilbert for plots of "real human interest and probability," where music (according to the composer) would have a more important part in communicating emotion to the audience. (No magic talismans or lozenges—and easy on the topsy-turvy humor, please!) He had also been receiving admonitions from the musical establishment to eschew the trivialities of the comic-opera stage, especially since becoming *Sir* Arthur Sullivan, and channel his musical energies into more exalted spheres. Queen Victoria herself had recently suggested that Sullivan compose a "grand opera," which, she told him, he would "do so well."

" . . . the grim old fortalice . . . "

Gilbert gave Sullivan what he craved—and included plenty of humor in it, too. The librettist admitted that the inspiration for *The Yeomen of the Guard* came from seeing a poster for the Tower Furnishing Company while standing in Uxbridge Station awaiting a train into the City: its logo featured a scarlet-uniformed Beefeater. Here, Gilbert thought, would be a setting for an opera that would meet Sullivan's requirements: quintessentially English, "The Tower" was a centuries-old palace and fortress and prison, with many a tale "grim and gory" of real-life imprisonments, intrigues, and executions. It is not generally recognized that, as Ian Bradley noted in his *Complete Annotated Gilbert & Sullivan*, Gilbert also tapped into a "wave of patriotism and nostalgia which swept Britain in the wake of Queen Victoria's golden jubilee" in 1887.

"Tower Warders,/ Under orders"

Opportunities for pageantry abounded, with a male chorus composed of the Tower Warders in their scarlet uniforms. But not all of the citizens of the Tower were military. Since the Tower of London was also a garrison, the warders' families were also in residence, along with support personnel—perfect for a mixed chorus.

But what to call it? An early idea was *The Tower of London*. Other possibilities were *The Beefeaters* and *The Tower Warders*.

We know that Gilbert visited the Tower of London while working on his libretto, for the Tower, then as now, was one of London's most popular tourist attractions. He probably also re-read William Harrison Ainsworth's popular and oft' reprinted 1840 novel *The Tower of London*, and perhaps thought back on a couple of his "Bab" Ballads dealing gleefully with prisons, torture, and beheadings.

Contemporary reviewers of the original production noted that Gilbert was also familiar with Edward Fitzball's libretto for William Vincent Wallace's opera *Maritana* (London, 1845), which was in turn based on a plot element in Victor Hugo's drama *Ruy Blas* (Paris, 1838), where an imprisoned, condemned knight, Don César de Bazan, marries a gypsy, escapes, and returns disguised as a monk. (Jules Massenet would, in 1872, compose an opera titled *Don César de Bazan*.)

"Oh, a private buffoon is a light-hearted loon . . . "

Gilbert turned Don César into Colonel Fairfax, and the gypsy girl Maritana of the English opera into "strolling singer" Elsie Maynard. He gave her a partner, the jester Jack Point. In creating this "man of jollity," Gilbert, using a time-honored custom of characterizing "fools" on stage, filled Jack's dialogue and lyrics with sentiments that could (should?) be taken seriously—for Gilbert's own, in fact. (Listen carefully to Point's lyrics to "I've jibe and joke" in Act I and "Oh! a private buffoon" in Act II, and you'll hear Gilbert lamenting the lot of the professional humorist!)

Gilbert called his work a "New and Original Opera," deleting the customary additional descriptor before the word "Opera." Sullivan orchestrated the overture, written in strict symphonic form, himself, instead of delegating the task of stringing together a medley of tunes from the opera to an assistant. Gilbert also broke tradition and opened his opera with two solos delaying the expected chorus. But what a chorus it is! When the Yeomen appear on stage the entire ensemble sings one of Sullivan's signature "double choruses," and audiences realize that it was worth waiting for. As the story develops and moves toward its ending, it is clear that both librettist and musician were aiming for that higher sphere. Certainly the ending has no parallel in their other joint works, musically *or* dramatically.

". . . the best thing we have done." W. S. Gilbert

As for the Queen's suggestion that Sir Arthur Sullivan write a "grand" opera—he did, three years later. *Ivanhoe*, with a libretto by Julian Sturgis, opened at D'Oyly Carte's new, custom-built Royal English Opera House in 1891—and quickly faded as Gilbert & Sullivan revivals played merrily not far away on the West End at their spiritual home, the Savoy, and on tour—and would continue to do so for nearly a century under the D'Oyly Carte banner.

The revivals of *Ivanhoe* since the first run in London can be counted on the fingers of one hand, and the first professional recording was finally released in 2010 (on the *Chandos* label).

The Yeomen of the Guard, however, has *never* to this day been out of the active repertory, has been recorded many times, and has delighted generation after generation of theatergoers, music lovers, and audiophiles. Gilbert and Sullivan themselves considered *The Yeomen of the Guard* their finest joint work, Sullivan telling an interviewer for the *Strand Musical Magazine* that the work was his "favourite opera."

As we've rehearsed this lovely show, we think we've discovered a number of reasons why. We hope you will enjoy discovering your own as we, with greatest pleasure, offer our production to you.

❖

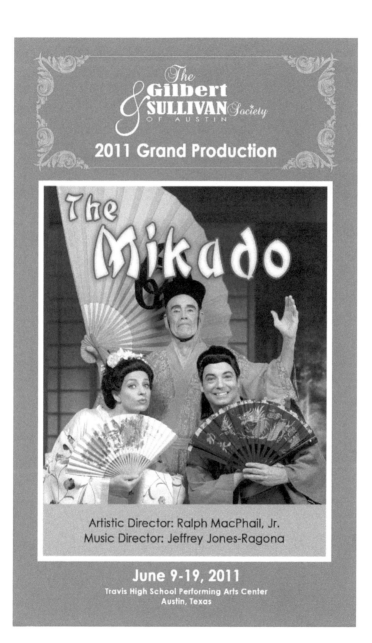

The Gilbert & SULLIVAN Society OF AUSTIN

2011 Grand Production

The **Mikado**

Artistic Director: Ralph MacPhail, Jr.
Music Director: Jeffrey Jones-Ragona

June 9-19, 2011
Travis High School Performing Arts Center
Austin, Texas

The Mikado: **The Masterpiece**

"**M**asterpiece" is one of those words like "awesome": it's thrown around frequently, sometimes without a lot of thought. It's an important word in our language, it seems to me, and consequently it should be used with care. It should not be wasted in describing anything less than a work that fits one of these three definitions from the Second College Edition of *The American Heritage Dictionary*:

> 1. An outstanding work of art or craft.
> 2. The greatest work of an artist or craftsman.
> 3. Something superlative.

We all have our favorite Gilbert & Sullivan operas. I will tell anyone who asks that *The Mikado* is not one of my three favorites. I will also admit that *The Mikado* has brought more delight to more people than perhaps any other work written for the lyric stage. It is the most frequently performed and adapted of the Savoy operas. It has no doubt been performed numerous times every day of every year over the past century.

I will also admit (argue, even) that *The Mikado* is the *masterpiece* (all three definitions) of the Gilbert and Sullivan collaboration.

What makes The Mikado *the Gilbert & Sullivan masterpiece?*

I think that one can analyze *The Mikado* from any direction and find that Gilbert & Sullivan were at the top of their form. It is a mature work, written in the middle of their collaboration, at a time of relative good-will and trust. Here are some brief observations from one who has probably spent too much of his life studying the opera—and who's directed six productions of it since 1977:

The Mikado **is brilliantly plotted**, with every entrance and exit motivated and carrying the story forward.

The Mikado **is filled with masterful Gilbertian lyrics,** ranging from patter to lyrical, nonsensical to philosophical, topical to universal.

The Mikado **has a magnificent Sullivanian score of musical "hits"**—a score characterized by a rhythmic brilliancy, tuneful ebullience, and orchestral felicity.

***The Mikado* is populated with memorable characters.** If some have names that sound like English "baby-talk," the characters more than do their names justice!

***The Mikado* is colorfully exotic in costume and set,** but at the same time the opera is grounded not far from Big Ben.

***The Mikado* is brilliantly satirical**—with satire that reads and plays as if it were "written today to entertain us today."

And *The Mikado* is wildly funny!

The great twentieth-century Savoyard Martyn Green had a wonderful answer when asked which of his parts he enjoyed playing the most. He always said, "The one I'm playing now—unless it's the one I'll be playing next."

I loved working on *Iolanthe* a year ago and *The Yeomen of the Guard* this past summer. I eagerly anticipate directing *Patience* again in 2012, but for now, I can't wait to get started on ***The Mikado***, for it really *is* the masterpiece of Gilbert and Sullivan.

The Mikado's Secrets

I n the last issue, I discussed reasons *The Mikado* might be regarded as the Gilbert & Sullivan masterpiece. The reasons I gave were no secrets. This time, I'd like to tell you some of the secrets that hide within the libretto.

By "secrets," I don't mean word games. (For instance, do you know where the "hidden character" Ray Zaralla appears in the libretto? His name is spoken by one of the Titipudlians. But *where*?) Rather, by *The Mikado*'s "secrets" I refer to some of the facts that few people know about the comic opera—and a couple that *no one* knows—as far as *I* know.

For instance, did you know that Gilbert tried to cut the Mikado's song before opening night? 'Tis true (and is beautifully dramatized in Mike Leigh's brilliant film *Topsy-Turvy*). Gilbert's reasons aren't known, but a good guess would be that he feared that the song's list of people worthy of punishment was too similar to Ko-Ko's famous "little list" song in Act I. (But of course the number remained, thus adding "My object all sublime" to the list of lines frequently quoted from *The Mikado*—the list that includes "I've got a little list.")

Speaking of "I've got a little list," did you know that the original position for it was later in Act I, after the letter arrives from the Mikado threatening dire consequences if someone isn't beheaded within one month? The original first line, "As it seems to be essential that a victim should be found" was changed to "As some day it may happen that a victim must be found" when the song was shifted to earlier in the act, after "Behold the Lord High Executioner" and Ko-Ko's introductory speech (which is—something that people often overlook—more obsequious and timid tailor-like sales-talk than something one would expect from a blood-thirsty Lord High Executioner!).

Did you know that Yum-Yum's brilliant aria, "The sun, whose rays" ("The moon and I") was originally sung in Act I? 'Tis true: it came after "So please you, Sir, we much regret" and an expanded introductory speech and before Nanki-Poo's entrance and dialogue leading to the kissing duet. (Or, for that matter, did you know that that kissing duet was originally twice as long, with a full second verse and chorus for the two?)

Did you know that Pitti-Sing's solo at the start of the Act II finale ("For he's gone and married Yum-Yum") did not originally exist, and the original finale started with Nanki-Poo and Yum-Yum singing "The threatened cloud has passed away"?

Have you ever noticed that when Sullivan set the soprano's name to music, he invariably put the accent on the *second* "Yum," but when it's spoken in dialogue, the accent is invariably placed by actors on the *first*?

Two more secrets—so secret that no one that *I* know knows the answers. The first: The Lord Chamberlain's license-deposit copy (submitted on March 11, 1885, to secure copyright and pass the censor) was assembled from galley proofs of the Chappell libretto—until the lyric for "There is beauty in the bellow of the blast" (the last number before the Act II finale). From this point on the libretto is in Gilbert's hand. Why? The only plausible answer is because the ending was changed at least *three days* before the opera was first performed, on March 14, 1885. I have discovered evidence that this ending was being worked on as early as February 16th, but I'm not ready to reveal "corroborative detail." My discovery only tells me that the resolution of the plot was up in the air nearly a full month before the première, and we know from the Lord Chamberlain's copy that it was finally decided about three days before opening night. Nothing survives, as far as I know, to suggest the *original* ending of the opera. How I'd like to know what *that* was!

One final mystery: D'Oyly Carte copyrighted a work in America called *Titipu; or, The Lord High Executioner*, according to records at the Library of Congress. However, this title has never been discovered in business papers, press reports, or correspondence relating to the creation of the opera. Was this an attempt to foil those pesky American pirates who were always eager to present their own productions without paying royalties in those pre-international copyright days? No one knows (as far as *I* know).

Now as for that elusive fellow Ray Zaralla: If you've not found the reference to him in the standard libretto of *The Mikado*, and if you find yourself lying awake with a dismal headache trying to think of where he appears, here's a hint: he may have been the brother-in-law to that much-easier-to-find hidden character—this one in *Iolanthe*—named William (Billy, for short) Maywish.

And if you want an even *better* hint, just send a begging e-mail to RafeMacPhail@Yahoo.com.

Onward to Titipu!

Auditions for *The Mikado*

With keenest anticipation I look forward to returning to Austin for auditions for *The Mikado*—and for helping our wonderful Society to celebrate a remarkable 35 years of production.

The Mikado is usually regarded as the masterpiece of Gilbert & Sullivan and is arguably the most popular comic opera ever written. It has been translated and adapted more frequently than any other of the G&S works, and has probably been performed more frequently than most of the rest of them put together. My purpose here is to provide information for auditionees concerning the auditions and also concerning the hilariously funny and incredibly tuneful and popular show we will present this summer. And I hope that much of what follows will also be of interest to members who will *not* be auditioning.

Music Director and Conductor Jeffrey Jones-Ragona and I request that each auditionee memorize a song from Gilbert & Sullivan or something similar that will show their voice and range to best advantage. *It is also mandatory to provide a copy of the music for the auditions accompanist.* I will ask people auditioning for principal roles to read from the libretto with me.

If *The Mikado* is not in your library, you can download the libretto from The Gilbert & Sullivan Archive (gsarchive.net). You can also download some printed music from the opera from this website, read a plot synopsis, or download audio files. And there's a *lot* more there, too!

The Chorus is composed of the **Chorus of Japanese Noblemen** (12 gentlemen, one of whom ["Go-To"] has a brief solo, and who MAY sing the Act II "Merry Madrigal") and the **Chorus of School-Girls** (12 vivacious ladies, all "eighteen and under," though their age will probably range considerably above that limit). **Two children** (pre-teens) will also be needed for the non-speaking, non-singing roles of Ko-Ko's Axe-Bearer and The Mikado's Attendant.

The Mikado has classically memorable roles, incredible singing opportunities, and requires actors who can sing well as well as singers who can act well. And boy—is it a *romp*!

The Mikado of Japan (bass or "dark baritone"). He appears only in the second half of the second act, but all of the action swirls around his edict against flirting, which turns this delightful activity into a capital crime. Larger than life and bloodthirsty (he likes to find punishments that fit crimes), with a BIG voice, he is cowed only by the redoubtable Katisha.

Nanki-Poo (tenor). He's the Mikado's son, who fled his father's court rather than marry the terrifying harridan Katisha. He can sing all sorts of "ballads, songs, and snatches" and dance a hornpipe. He also loves Yum-Yum and knows how to tell her (and show her!). He is also clever when it matters most—when his life is on the line. Strums a lovely samisen, too!

Ko-Ko (light baritone). This timid tailor was made Lord High Executioner of Titipu after he was convicted of flirting, which essentially stopped executions because he would be unable to execute another until he'd cut his *own* head off. Ko-Ko is a little dynamo of energy, frantically trying to stay ahead of plot complications in order to preserve his own life—and he, too, loves Yum-Yum. Never in dramatic literature was there a more amusing love triangle!

Pish-Tush (baritone). This noble lord has an important, expository solo in Act I and participates in a good number of ensembles. Something of a foil to Ko-Ko and Pooh-Bah, Pish-Tush helps the others negotiate the maze of plot complications. His part in the Act II madrigal, depending on his voice, is sometimes sung by Go-To—and this may happen in our production.

Pooh-Bah (bass-baritone). One of Gilbert's greatest creations, Pooh-Bah was, as he admits, "born sneering." He holds all of the municipal offices in Titipu (other than Lord High Executioner), and accepts the salaries attached to them—and bribes at every opportunity. Traditionally a LARGE man, his physique matches his [self-]importance. Pooh! Bah!

Go-To (bass). Go-To is a member of the male chorus who has a single question in recitative early in Act I before Nanki-Poo's introductory song, and he *may* speak Pish-Tush's line before and sing his part in the madrigal in Act II.

Yum-Yum (soprano). Just eighteen years old and home from school for the "hols," Yum-Yum's in love with Nanki-Poo even though she's betrothed to her guardian Ko-Ko. She's beautiful and knows it—and can sing beautifully about it. Still, like many a Gilbertian soprano, she knows which side of the bread holds the butter, and has second thoughts about marrying Nanki-Poo when burial alive will be one of her wedding gifts.

Pitti-Sing (mezzo-soprano). If Yum-Yum is delicious, her sister is indeed a pretty thing. Sings well, too. Filled to the brim with girlish glee, Pitti-Sing is Yum-Yum's sister and is also Ko-Ko's ward. She is a saucy little thing, and gives Katisha what-for in the Act I finale. Her role is one of the great soubrette parts in all of Gilbert & Sullivan.

Peep-Bo (mezzo-soprano). The third of the famous "three little maids," Peep-Bo is a little minx who seems to have a bloodthirsty streak—especially in her dialogue with Yum-Yum in Act II. She wonders, with the other girls, "What on earth the world can be?"

Katisha (contralto). Another of Gilbert's greatest creations. She's a frightening though not grotesque harridan "of a certain age," spurned by Nanki-Poo, and looking for love. Her two solos make her a three-dimensional character of somewhat tragic dimensions, but she also has her fair share of comic opportunities.

I think there's only one G&S activity more fun than seeing one of their operas performed on stage—and that's actually *working* on one. If you need a little push to encourage you to audition, please consider this it. Jeffrey and I do all we can to make the auditions fun and relaxed.

Please encourage a friend or two to audition so that even *more* can share the delight of Gilbert & Sullivan.

See you in Titipu!

The Mikado: Several Secrets in Sullivan's Score

In an earlier column, I wrote about several "secrets" in the history of *The Mikado* and in Gilbert's libretto. I thought this time it would be fun to turn our attention to "Sullivan's secrets."

It has often been noted that *The Mikado*, while set in Japan, is as English as fish 'n' chips. This is certainly true of most of the music, but Sullivan *did* do his Japanese homework. When working on his score, he called on Algernon B. Mitford, formerly of Her Majesty's Foreign Office with a stint in Japan (and author of *Tales of Old Japan*), and got a piece of authentic Japanese music to use as the Mikado's entrance music. Mitford gave him a march composed in the Meiji era called "Ton-yare Bushi." In addition to taking down the tune, Sullivan transcribed the lyric phonetically, presumably gave it to his collaborator, and Gilbert then incorporated it into his libretto, labeling it—in quotation marks—'*March of the Mikado's troops.*' Here are the words:

> Miya sama, miya sama,
> On n'm-ma no mayé ni
> Pira-Pira suru no wa
> Nan gia na
> Toko tonyaré, tonyaré na?

A rough translation is, "O! Prince, what is that fluttering in front of your horse?" The second verse, which is not used in *The Mikado*, answers this musical question: "Don't you see—this is the royal banner—entrusted to me that I may defeat the enemies of the Crown. Don't you see?"

Not only does this authentic Japanese music, composed on the pentatonic scale, herald The Mikado, but it heralds *The Mikado,* too, for the composer featured it early in his overture to the work.

Sullivan may have been the first Western composer to use the "Miya sama" tune, but not the last. Giacomo Puccini also used a quotation from it in *Madama Butterfly* thirteen years after *The Mikado* was written.

The Mikado has other musical secrets. Gilbert said, late in his career, that he never had to explain a joke to Sullivan. What he *didn't* say was that Sullivan often brought his own sense of humor to his scores. Here are some examples:

The vocal line to the words "Behold the Lord High Executioner" is a quotation from an old song with roots perhaps in the seventeenth century. An 1835 version with music and lyrics by Henry Russell, called "A Fine Old English Gentleman," was certainly recognized by original audiences. By using this tune, Sullivan builds on Gilbert's joke by comparing Japanese tailor/executioner to a benevolent old squire in the English countryside. Here's the third verse of Russell's song:

> When winter cold brought Christmas old,
> He opened house to all,
> And, though three score and ten his years,
> He featly led the ball;
> Nor was the houseless wanderer
> Then driven from the hall,
> For, while he feasted all the great,
> He ne'er forgot the small—
> **Like a fine old English gentleman,**
> All of the olden time.

Sullivan put other musical jokes into *The Mikado*. I remember reading years ago that there was originally a musical rest after "Freed from its genius tutelary" in "Three Little Maids." At a rehearsal for a revival, the composer sketched in a little "bassoon gurgle," telling his players that he'd been wanting to do that for years. Listen for it—it's still there—and note also how the music of the *entire trio* seems to giggle over with girlish glee!

When you hear The Mikado suggest that music-hall singers be forced to attend

> . . . a series
> Of masses and fugues and 'ops'
> By Bach, interwoven
> With Spohr and Beethoven,
> At classical Monday Pops

listen carefully, and you'll hear a quotation from Bach's "Great" Fugue in G minor in the orchestra.

The next musical number in the opera, "The Criminal Cried," tells of a *faux* execution with corroborative if fictional detail provided by Ko-Ko, Pitti-Sing, and Pooh-Bah. And it is filled with musical jokes. Listen for the instrumental "shriek" in Ko-Ko's verse, and for a decapitated head thudding to the ground after Pooh-Bah insists "that head was dead."

But Sullivan's best and most subtle musical joke is in the middle verse, when Pitti-Sing asserts that, as he was decapitated, the victim "whistled an air, did he": originally Sullivan inserted a snatch from a widely known tune from a child's piano exercise immediately after these words—but he later changed it to a quotation from the well-known English war-song, "The Girl I Left Behind Me."

Here are the lyrics to the first verse:

> The hours sad I left a maid
> A lingering farewell taking
> Whose sighs and tears my steps delayed
> I thought her heart was breaking
> In hurried words her name I blest
> I breathed the vows that bind me
> And to my heart in anguish pressed
> The girl I left behind me.

My friend Bill Hyder recently stated succinctly Sullivan's motivation in selecting this well-known tune, "The Girl I Left behind Me": "Consider the story Pitti-Sing is telling: A criminal was about to be executed. He caught the eye of 'a beautiful maid' (Pitti-Sing can't be accused of modesty!). It gave him courage, but he knew he wouldn't see her again, so he 'whistled an air'—and what an appropriate title Sullivan chose!"

When Gilbert asserted, after Sullivan's passing, that when working with his most famous collaborator "he never had to explain a joke," what he *didn't* say is that, quite often, Sullivan made his own jokes the way he knew best—through his music.

Lexicographic Gleanings for *The Mikado*

One of the many delights of Gilbert & Sullivan is appreciating librettist William Schwenck Gilbert's mastery of the English language and especially his vocabulary, which, like Katisha's circulation, just may be "the largest in the world."

And nobody has studied Gilbert's vocabulary more than Harry Benford, long-time Faculty Adviser to The University of Michigan Gilbert

& Sullivan Society and author of the invaluable *Gilbert and Sullivan Lexicon*, now online at GSOpera.net.

Harry was kind enough to allow me to skim a baker's dozen of his explanations of terms from *The Mikado* to share with you.

Pre-Adamite (Pooh-Bah claims to be "of pre-Adamite ancestral descent"): "Brewer [in his *Dictionary of Phrase and Fable*] informs us that this was the name given by Isaac de la Peyrère to a race of men whom he thought to have existed before the days of the Garden of Eden. He thought that only Jews are descended from Adam and Eve and that Gentiles derive from Pre-Adamites."

Ablutioner (Pooh-Bah accuses Nanki-Poo of being a "very imperfect ablutioner"): "Pooh-Bah seems to imply that Nanki-Poo needs a bath, which at first seems out of character for a G&S tenor. But remember that he has been traveling for a month, or nearly, and without so much as a pocket handkerchief to mop his brow or dust his sandals. Then, too, there are just so many words that rhyme with *executioner*."

Guy ("the lady from the provinces, who dresses like a guy" is on Ko-Ko's little list): "This refers to the effigies of Guy Fawkes that are burned each November 5 in Britain to celebrate his lack of success in blowing up the Houses of Parliament in 1605. . . . [Jane W.] Stedman notes that the phrase 'was also current in Gilbert's day as meaning someone grotesque or ridiculously dressed—in this case the lady dresses inappropriately in attempting to look fashionable.' [J. Stuart] Bradshaw assures us the expression is still in use in England. Some observers think Gilbert had in mind the American slang term for a man. The term was in those days not well known in England . . . , so I doubt the validity of the proposal."

Genius tutelary (The Three Little Maids claim to be freed from the "genius tutelary" of their "ladies' seminary"): "The OED [Oxford English Dictionary] . . . says regarding *genius*: 'With reference to classical pagan belief: The tutelary god or attendant spirit allotted to every person at his birth to govern his fortune and determine his character . . . ; also, the tutelary and controlling spirit similarly connected with a place, an institution, etc.' To this we may add that *tutelary* pertains to guardianship."

Marine Parade (Yum-Yum says that Nanki-Poo "is the gentlemen who used to play so beautifully on the—on the—" and Pitti-Sing reminds her that she seems to be searching for the term "Marine Parade"): "In seaside resort cities, a waterfront street or promenade, usually with the beach on one side and major hotels, shops, etc., on the other. Since few American audiences understand the term, Pitti-Sing might substitute some familiar words such as *board walk*. I admit this would spoil Yum-Yum's dumb reference to a musical instrument, but that's a badly strained joke that might well be left out anyhow." [I don't often disagree with Harry, but—bah!]

Lucius Junius Brutus (Nanki-Poo characterizes his father, the Mikado, as "the Lucius Junius Brutus of his race"): "A Roman consul who lived about 500 B.C. He condemned his own two sons to death when they were caught in a plot to restore the villainous Tarquinius to the monarchy. . . . [Daniel] Knight adds that Lucius Junius Brutus's name has become synonymous with duty above all."

And for yam I should get toco (Yum-Yum fears this if she embraces Nanki-Poo since she's engaged to Ko-Ko): "For today's audiences this is one of the most confusing expressions in the entire G&S canon. Let's start with *toco*. The OED . . . defines this as slang for chastisement or corporal punishment. There is good evidence that it was a common expression in Victorian England. . . . In some editions, incidentally, the word is spelled "toko." [Eric] Partridge [in his *Dictionary of Slang and Unconventional English*] has an entry: '*Toco for yam.* To be punished.' It goes on to say that the expression, which dates back as far as 1860, is analogous to the Biblical stone for a loaf of bread. More explicitly, you can take it to mean 'For doing something pleasant I should be punished.' I think we can conclude that the term was generally understood in the vernacular of the day, but mystifies people today. Whoever is playing Yum-Yum can substitute 'that' for 'yam' and accompany 'toco' with a finger drawn across her throat. If people still don't understand, it's their own fault for not owning a copy of this book." [This substitute of "that" for "yam" appears in the G. Schirmer score, so that's the way the line is usually sung in American productions. But *not* in Austin—since 1998.]

Happy Dispatch (Nanki-Poo threatens to "perform the Happy Dispatch with this dagger" if he can't marry Yum-Yum): "A euphemism of *Hara-Kiri,* from *hara* meaning 'belly' and *kiri* meaning 'cut.' It refers to suicide by disembowelment as formerly practiced, with due ceremony, by the highest classes in Japan when in disgrace. [Daniel] Knight adds that the suicide's family was also required to die with him unless a special writ was obtained from the emperor. The practice went out in the late 1800s."

Parliamentary Trains (One of the Mikado's punishments is to make railway car graffiti scribblers "ride on a buffer, In Parliamentary trains"): "In 1844 the British Parliament decreed that each workday every railroad company had to run at least one train in each direction, with stops at every station, and run at least twelve miles an hour. The law was changed in 1883, but those minimum-fare parliamentary trains were still slow and uncomfortable."

   <u>Monday Pops</u> **(Another of the Mikado's punishments is to force "music-hall singers" to listen to music "At classical Monday Pops")**: "Popular concerts. [Arthur] Jacobs explains the term as being short for 'Classical Monday Popular Concerts.' They were established in 1858 by the music publishing house of Chappell and were held in St. James's Hall, on the site of the present-day Piccadilly Hotel. . . ."

   <u>Snickersnee</u> **(Ko-Ko, in his lie about a beheading that never happened, tells the Mikado that he "drew" his "snickersnee")**: "An old, jocular word for a long knife or small sword; the term is from the Dutch *snik and snee*, a sailor's knife. It has also been ascribed to the musical chord emitted by a well-swung vorpal blade. . . ."

   <u>Niger</u> **(Ko-Ko, agreeing with Katisha, assures her that he likes "to see a tiger From the Congo or the Niger, And especially when lashing of his tail!")**: "The general region of northwest Africa drained by the Niger River. Many critics have complained that tigers are not native to the Congo, Niger, or any other regions of Africa. Not only that, but *Niger* does not rhyme with *tiger*. Ko-Ko's education (a dropout Ph.D. in tailoring) obviously was not of the highest order. Gilbert, presumably, was only kidding."

   <u>Tom-tit</u>: **(Ko-Ko sings an affecting tale to Katisha about this bird who committed suicide due to unrequited love)**: "A bird of the tit family, all being cute little chickadee-like rascals. Brewer . . . and the noted ornithologist Michael Walters . . . both agree that *Tom* implies not male, but small, as in Tom Thumb. This being so, was Gilbert careless when referring to 'a little tom-tit'? In any event, the context clearly implies a small male bird."

   If you're not familiar with Harry Benford's *Gilbert and Sullivan Lexicon*, perhaps you will realize from reading these entries that it is probably the most entertaining reference work ever written. It is truly indispensable to any Savoyard's library—and it's now available to all on the internet.

   Now put this newsletter aside, take out a piece of paper, and number from one to thirteen. . . .

Our Object All Sublime . . .

B efore rehearsals began for this production of *The Mikado*, my friend and fellow Gilbert & Sullivan enthusiast William Hyder wrote from his home in Maryland:

> I'm sure you'll do it right—throwing away this musty old traditional rubbish and utilizing all the resources of modern stagecraft and dance, not to mention philosophy. Have you noticed that the libretto of *The Mikado* foreshadows the existentialism of Martin Heidegger? *Ko-Ko* represents the tragic nature of being in a finite world, and the anguish that oppresses man as he senses the inevitable limits of life (represented by *The Mikado*). Then *Pooh-Bah* obviously symbolizes the many other existents and conditions to which man must relate, and *Katisha* is the embodiment of the "resolute decision" which Heidegger advocates as the method of asserting one's essence and destiny—and which *Ko-Ko* reluctantly embraces at the end of the show.
>
> Work with me along these lines, . . . and we'll get the fun out of G. & S. yet.

Well, of course Bill was kidding, for he knows that the Gilbert & Sullivan Society of Austin would want to keep the fun *in* G. & S. by working along traditional lines—lines which are *not* rubbish and which do not *have* to be musty. We both know that *The Mikado*, the most popular of fourteen comic operas written by Gilbert & Sullivan between 1871 and 1896, has continued to delight audiences since its première in London at the Savoy Theatre in 1885. *Why* does it continue to do so? Certainly one important reason is the sparkling musical score composed by Sir Arthur Sullivan. But Sir William S. Gilbert should also be given his due. The opening night critic from *The Theatre*, an important monthly, wrote: "The text of *The Mikado* sparkles with countless gems of wit . . . and its author's rhyming and rhythmic gifts have never been more splendidly displayed; as for the dialogue, it is positively so full of points and hits as to keep the wits of the audience constantly on the strain."

Nearly fifty years later, G. K. Chesterton substituted "satire" for "wit," and, I believe, hit on the major reason for the continuing popularity of Gilbert's libretto: "There is not, in the whole length of *The Mikado,* a single joke that is a joke against Japan. They are all, without exception, jokes against England, or that Western civilization which an Englishman knows best in England."

And Gilbert's British satire of 126 years ago seems very fresh today—even to Americans in the early twenty-first century. Now it is true that we've updated the "lady novelist" reference in Ko-Ko's little list song, and that we've changed Nanki-Poo's address abroad from Knightsbridge (the location in London of a Japanese exhibition which helped to inspire *The Mikado*) to—well, you'll find out. But Gilbert himself sanctioned these particular places for topicalities. Except for these changes and several other traditional interpolations to the printed libretto (and a couple of contemporary "pestilential nuisances" added to Ko-Ko's song just for fun), this *Mikado* is the *Mikado* written by W. S. Gilbert in 1885.

One reason for the freshness of the book is the fact that a number of the lines have become permanent expressions in our language. Just as a legendary lady once remarked that Shakespeare's plays are made up of quotations, here you'll discover that various Gilbertian characters first gave us "I've got a little list," "The flowers that bloom in the spring," and "To let the punishment fit the crime."

Another reason for the continuing popularity of *The Mikado* is the fact that Gilbert's jibes transcend the era in which they were born. Most of us have a "little list" like Ko-Ko's, and our imaginations are as adept as the Mikado's at devising punishments for people whose actions rub us the wrong way. Perhaps most of us know a pluralist Pooh-Bah; and this worthy's line, when hesitating to condescend to the Three Little Maids, "They are not young ladies, they are young persons," sounds surprisingly like contemporary political correctness. Certainly Ko-Ko seems to be a supreme example of The Peter Principle: in Act II, everyone learns that the timid tailor turned Lord High Executioner has indeed been promoted to his level of incompetence!

Our "object all sublime," then, has been to offer a traditional *Mikado*, one that stands on its own intrinsic merits and does not have to be re-written, jazzed, swung, rocked (all of which *have* been done, by the way), or weighted down with the philosophy of Heidegger. The original *Mikado* has been "ever joyous, ever gay" for a century and a quarter. Wild "concept" productions "never will be missed," and we hope that you will find this offering "a source of innocent merriment, of innocent merriment"!

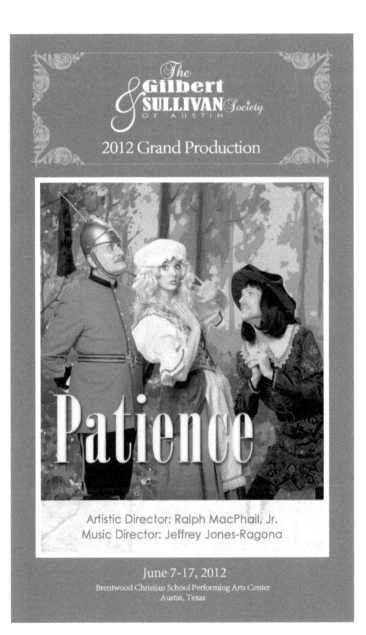

The Gilbert & Sullivan SULLIVAN Society
OF AUSTIN

2012 Grand Production

Patience

Artistic Director: Ralph MacPhail, Jr.
Music Director: Jeffrey Jones-Ragona

June 7-17, 2012
Brentwood Christian School Performing Arts Center
Austin, Texas

An Introduction to *Patience*

"**L**et me confess" (as Bunthorne sings in recitative in Act I of *Patience; or, Bunthorne's Bride*), this Gilbert & Sullivan's hit show of 1881 has always been one of my favorites. It is true that my list of favorites has become considerably longer in recent years following our productions in Austin of *Iolanthe* and *The Yeomen of the Guard*, but *Patience* is *still* near the top of the list.

Anyone who's been around the arts for any length of time would *have* to love *Patience*, the story of a simple dairy-maid so naïve she "cannot tell what this love may be" that has consumed the other girls ("rapturous maidens," as Gilbert calls them) in the village. It's the object of the maidens' love that puzzles Patience and delights us: Reginald Bunthorne, a "fleshly poet," with his too-too precious poetry, his velvet knee-breeches and floppy beret, and his professed fondness for lilies, muted colors, and "all one sees that's Japanese."

But when Bunthorne himself sings "Let me confess," he admits that he's an "aesthetic sham," and his passion is not "high aesthetic art" but rather "a morbid love of admiration" by the young girls—and *this* motivates his enigmatic vocabulary, precious posing, and artsy artifice.

All goes well for him until a rival poet appears on the scene, just after Patience has agreed to marry Bunthorne as an act of unselfishness (which, she's told, true love must be). And caught in the swirl of changing alliances are the staunch Lady Jane and a male chorus of Dragoon Guards who just don't "get it" when it comes to poetry—but who are willing to adopt the outward appearance of these two poets to "get the girls."

You don't have to be in and of the arts to appreciate Gilbert's satire on affectation, of course. I remember wearing an ascot occasionally in college—so, *so* cool! And if you've ever adopted the hair style of the current teen idol, worn the fashions of the latest pop-culture phenom, or used the expressions of current TV stars, you will appreciate what Gilbert was writing about. (And maybe wince a little, too, at the recollection! Those ascots!)

Combine Gilbert's wit and lyrics and situations with Sullivan's irresistible melodies, ensembles, and choruses, and you have a wonderful show, filled with color and humor and delight—and one that might even make some of us working on it wince a bit when we think of younger days.

The libretto can be read in any library (or at any computer: just search on the Gilbert & Sullivan Archive, where you can also find the music). CDs and DVDs are available at reasonable cost through on-line retailers.

Jeffrey and I directed *Patience* at St. Stephen's School back in 1999, and we're looking forward to auditions in early March for the coming production. It's a *delightful* show!

❖

"Short Article by Rafe on *Patience*"

M y title comes from Sue's "Newsletter Schedule." She wants it short, so I'm going to pass the buck, with your cooperation, and make this something of a take-home quiz. (Each of these questions could be the subject for a long article.) Your copy of the libretto or the score will be helpful for some of the questions, or, if they're not handy, surf over to gsarchive.net/patience/html/index.html for a copy of the libretto. (The *Patience* page itself at the Archive may also be helpful.)

1. During its original run in 1881, Richard D'Oyly Carte transferred *Patience* from London's Opéra Comique to a new theatre built especially for the Gilbert & Sullivan productions. What is the name of this theatre? What distinguished it at the time from any other public building in the world? What policies did D'Oyly Carte adopt that made the theatrical experience more pleasant (and less expensive) for his patrons? Even though *Patience* might be legitimately called the first _____ Opera (named after the theatre), *Iolanthe* might *more* legitimately called the "first" of these operas. Why?

2. In the original production, the aesthetic poet Bunthorne was made up and costumed with elements reflecting a well-known painter and a well-known poet. Name the artist and the poet and discuss how they were represented in Bunthorne's appearance.

3. Archibald Grosvenor, another poet in *Patience*, reads two of his poems ("Gentle Jane" and "Teasing Tom") to the maidens in Act II. Which Victorian poet was his (or Gilbert's) "model" for these verses: Lewis Carroll, Oscar Wilde, Algernon Swinburne, or Coventry Patmore? Support your answer.

4. Bunthorne's poem in Act I, "Oh, Hollow! Hollow! Hollow!" is *not* a hunting song. In fact, it might be regarded as a rather (for Gilbert in the Savoy operas) scatological poem! What supports this analysis? How does Angela's enthusiastic appraisal of the poem after its recitation relate to the images in the verse? Do you think Gilbert was pushing the envelope of propriety with Angela's comment? Discuss.

5. A seldom appreciated and surprising theme runs through *Patience* equating love with pain. This theme is not as graphically expressed as it is in what I understand is an extensive body of underground

Victorian literature—but it's hard to deny that it's in the libretto. Cite examples.

Good luck!

Finished! At last! Finished!

(And just under 400 words, Sue.)

Audition Notes on *Patience*

Patience is a high-spirited send-up of artistic affectation. Originally it poked fun at the pre-Raphaelite "brotherhood" in London of the 1870s and '80s, but Gilbert's wit transcends the original target, and Sullivan's tunes have remained ever funny, martial, sentimental, poignant—whatever the moment in the plot demands. My purpose here is to provide information for auditionees concerning the auditions and also concerning the hilariously funny and incredibly tuneful show we will present this summer. If you're planning to audition, please read this in its entirety. And even if you're not, you may find it interesting!

Music Director and Conductor Jeffrey Jones-Ragona and I request that each auditionee memorize a song from Gilbert & Sullivan or something similar that will show their voice and range to best advantage. *It is also mandatory to provide a copy of the music for the auditions accompanist. No* a cappella *auditions will be heard. An accompanist will be provided, but singers will be welcome to bring their own if they wish.*

If *Patience* is not in your library, you can download the libretto from The Gilbert & Sullivan Archive (gsarchive.net). You can also download some printed music from the opera from this website, read a plot synopsis, or download audio files. And there's more, too!

Patience is filled with fun-to-act roles, incredible singing opportunities, and requires actors who can sing well as well as singers who can act well. And nowhere was Gilbert more trenchant (and amusing) in his satire of artistic affectation or Sullivan more tuneful. (*Patience,* of course, has another of those wonderful Act I finales—one of the best, in fact.)

42 Only Idle Chatter

THE CHORUS is composed of the **Chorus of Dragoon Guards** (12 gentlemen, resplendent in scarlet and gold uniforms, who know how to march and perform facing movements) and the **Chorus of Rapturous Maidens** (12 languid and limp ladies, over-the-top in their expressions of unrequited love, dressed in "aesthetic draperies" of muted colors, playing "archaic instruments," and speaking with the latest "aesthetic slang," which is "too, too utter"!).

Colonel Calverley (bass or "dark baritone"). He is commanding officer of the Dragoons, stuffy, lacking a sense of humor, "in charge," and with two challenging patter-songs in Act I, so he must also have excellent diction. A large man. Dances in Act II.

Major Murgatroyd (baritone). A rather small part with excellent comic possibilities, such as his leg cramp that gives him so much trouble when he tries to imitate the aesthetic poets! Dances in Act II.

Lieutenant, the Duke of Dunstable (tenor). An aristocratic soldier, who joined the army because he wearied of toadies. He finds military a good change-of-pace from aristocratic living. Dances in Act II.

Reginald Bunthorne (light baritone). One of Gilbert's great comic creations, Bunthorne is a sham "aesthetic poet," who affects the

dress, behavior and writing abilities of a poet in order to get the admiration of the village maidens. The opera centers on Bunthorne's quest for the love of the village milkmaid, Patience, and he is content to change his ways in order to get it. He finds out as so many others do that the path to true love doesn't run smooth—and in fact, *his* is bumpy indeed. The sub-title of *Patience* is *Bunthorne's Bride*—but who (or what?) ends up as his bride?

Archibald Grosvenor (high baritone). He's also a poet: "the Apostle of Simplicity." He loved Patience when but a tot, and Patience loved him, but his path to true love crosses Bunthorne's, and for a while it's equally bumpy. He has better fortune, however, than his rival, even if he has to cast off his poetic trappings and become "an every-day young man" in order to claim his bride.

Mr. Bunthorne's Solicitor (silent role). He appears in the Act I finale to run the raffle (Bunthorne attempts to raffle himself off as a bridegroom to one of the maidens since he can't have Patience!), and in the Act II finale. He has no speaking or singing, but a mobile face and good acting skills are musts.

The Lady Angela (mezzo-soprano). An important singing and acting role, she rather sets the tone for the lovesick maidens. Lovely singing and a good comic sense are essential.

The Lady Saphir (mezzo-soprano). Another aesthetic maiden, a follower. Something of a scholar and user of arcane expressions. A good actor and singer.

The Lady Ella (soprano). Still another aesthetic maiden, with a short but dynamic solo as a part of the opening chorus, calling for a beautiful and strong singing voice.

The Lady Jane (contralto). Another of Gilbert's great creations, the part calls for a commanding contralto voice and a great sense of humor. She's one of those aging females, but loves to sing about her fading charms and growing proportions while accompanying herself on a 'cello. She loves Bunthorne, too—much to his chagrin.

Patience (lyric soprano). She is a simple and naïve dairy-maid who has no idea "what this love may be" that's so captured the rapturous maidens, but when she learns that it's her duty to love, she sets forth to fall in love with all her heart. Alas, the road on which she sets forth is that same bumpy one that Bunthorne and Grosvenor are using, and—well, her perseverance is rewarded.

    I've often said that there's only one G&S activity more fun than seeing one of their operas—and that's actually *working* on one. If you need a little push to encourage you to audition, please consider this it. Jeffrey and I do all we can to make the auditions fun and relaxed.

    And then please encourage a friend or two to audition so that even *more* can share the delight of Gilbert & Sullivan. This show's a *hoot*!

Spring Fever in Far-Off Bridgewater

Here I sit, in my Gilbert & Sullivan room in Bridgewater, Virginia. The flowers blooming outside my windows (lilacs, daffodils, iris, dogwoods, forsythia) do, indeed, breathe promise of merry sunshine, and also the promise of another trip to Austin—just four weeks from tomorrow (though you're reading this a couple of weeks later).

    Work's already begun on *Patience*, of course. Jeffrey Jones-Ragona and I cast a wonderful roster of actor-singers for this summer's show weeks ago, and his music rehearsals are well under way. President

Libby Weed and that incredible GSSA board have been making plans, raising money, organizing publicity, and otherwise preparing to put *Patience* into production—on a brand-new stage, in fact: the one at Brentwood Christian School off North Lamar.

I toured this new facility while in town for auditions in February/March, and it's a beauty! It's very modern and has what I call a "lima bean (kidney bean?) arrangement" of seats. There are about 400 of them, and they're arranged on a broad arc so that every seat is ideal. And of course it has an orchestra pit, something that Jeffrey and I and many others have been longing for since we left St. Stephen's School in 2004. (The parking for this new theatre is convenient, too.)

Production Manager Bill Hatcher has been in almost daily contact by phone and e-mail, finding props, finalizing the contract with Malabar of Winnipeg, Canada, for our costumes, lining up a strong roster of production personnel, and working on the staging-rehearsal schedule (a huge job, because we try to work around conflicts, call only artists needed, and use everyone's time well).

Jeffrey's contracting the orchestra, David Little's juggling props, costumes, and people in preparation for the photo-shoot—and here I sit, heart in Austin but kept at bay by the set of curious chances that characterize my close-yet-so-far relationship with GSSA.

Other enticing e-mails report that Janette Jones is planning another of her unique musicales, and I'm pleased that I'll be in town for it—and delighted that she's asked me to participate, for I've always wanted to shake hands with Oscar Wilde. . . .

In an earlier column, I quoted Bunthorne's "Let me confess," and I feel another confession coming on: When I sat down to write this, I was planning to explain just *why* I've considered *Patience* one of my favorite Savoy operas for now over forty years. But I have a problem: I've run out of space!

So I've no room to extol Gilbert's wonderful lyrics, comic situations, memorable characters, and satirical send-up of artistic pretension. I've no room to wax eloquently on Sullivan's score, which came early in the collaboration and builds on the English-speaking-world-wide successes of *H.M.S. Pinafore* and *The Pirates of Penzance*: that incredible Act I finale, those quirky duets and trios (and quintet!) of Act II, and Patience's ballad that always makes me feel guilty. (Read the lyric to "Love is a plaintive song" and see why I always think of Alice when I hear it—Alice who lets me run away from home for over a month at a time to indulge my love for these wonderful comic operas with a company such as GSSA that invariably brings them to the stage with beauty—visual, aural, and emotional—with lots of laughs and perhaps even a tear or two, too.)

But I'm out of space, and besides that my eyes are drawn outside once more on this sunny afternoon. The flowers that bloom in the spring have nothing to do with this case, I suppose, but if I stop here I can go for a little walk, rejoicing in this lovely day in Virginia and anticipating delightful early summer of roses and wine in Texas—with friends and colleagues I hold dear.

See you soon!

Patience **and Oscar**

One of the features of the recent *Patience* musicale, devised so creatively by Janette Jones, was an appearance by Oscar Wilde. So as I prepared my remarks as emcee for the afternoon, I tried to focus on this brilliant Irish wit, poet, and dramatist and his part in the evolution of what became the sixth Gilbert & Sullivan collaboration, *Patience; or, Bunthorne's Bride.*

As I thought about it, it seemed to me that Oscar has everything to do with *Patience,* and yet, today—nothing. How topsy-turvy! How Gilbertian!

Gilbert's original idea for his plot had its "genesis," as he put it, in his 1867 "Bab" ballad, "The Rival Curates," in which two Anglican clergymen, Clayton Hooper and Hopley Porter, vie for the attention of their village maidens. (Gilbert earlier had borrowed this idea for *The Sorcerer,* in creating Dr. Daly, Vicar of Ploverleigh, who yearned for younger days when he was much admired by the young ladies.)

But as Gilbert worked, he felt "hampered" (his word) by the idea of clergymen, concerned that such a plot might lead to a "charge of irreverence" (also his words).

Gilbert was no doubt familiar with Oscar Wilde, a young Irishman, recently arrived in London from Oxford. Wilde enjoyed capturing attention, and he did this in the way he dressed, his epigrammatical conversation, and his love for flowers, blue china, and *Japonaiserie.* He became the face of the so-called "aesthetic movement," a group of artists (painters, novelists, designers, poets, critics) yearning for the days when art could be appreciated for its own sake. They were rebelling against the materialistic and utilitarian functions of art in mid-Victorian England.

Wilde's "peculiarities" were lampooned by George DuMaurier in his *Punch* cartoons, where Wilde-like characters were pictured worshipping blue china, devoted to lilies and Japanese *tchotchkes*, and describing things as "utter" or "too too precious."

DuMaurier, and later Gilbert & Sullivan, were not lampooning the Pre-Raphaelite brotherhood as much as the faddish way in which popular culture adopted the speech, dress, and mannerisms of the Pre-Raphaelites, much as teenagers today might speak the slang, wear the garb, and otherwise walk the walk and talk the talk of the latest pop idol.

Patience, with rival poets named Reginald Bunthorne and Archibald Grosvenor instead of those rival curates, had its première at the Opéra Comique in London. (It was in the same dim, stuffy, subterranean theatre where Richard D'Oyly Carte had produced *The Sorcerer, H.M.S. Pinafore,* and *The Pirates of Penzance.*) The "Entirely New and Original Aesthetic Opera" opened on April 23, 1881.

Oscar Wilde was only 25 at the time, having achieved nothing substantial except for his "aesthetic pose," but Wilde is the one personality from the "aesthetic movement" who remains in our collective memories.

Long before *Patience,* D'Oyly Carte had a dream: to build a theatre expressly for English light opera, and the construction of this theatre was completed during the opening run of *Patience* at the Opéra Comique.

Patience was transferred to the new Savoy Theatre and opened on 10 October 1881 (about six months after the première). The Savoy was an innovative public building, the most striking innovation being that "the electricity" was laid on throughout, the first public building *in the world* to be so wired.

The new and softer glow of incandescent bulbs that replaced the harsh and oxygen-eating gas lights meant that the sets needed to be repainted and the costumes reconstructed for this innovative new theatrical "space."

D'Oyly Carte, ever the showman, didn't keep his innovation a secret. Tickets were at a premium, for even before *Patience*, opening-night reservations for Gilbert & Sullivan productions were highly sought. The first night at the Savoy was a glittering social occasion, as usual, but there was one special playgoer in the stalls that night.

This was none other than Oscar Wilde Himself, wearing his trademark velvet suit. Asked later about *Patience*, he said, "Caricature is the tribute that mediocrity pays to genius." When later asked if he'd ever (quoting from *Patience*) "walked down Piccadilly with a poppy or a lily in his medieval hand," he replied that he'd accomplished something more difficult: he convinced people he actually *had* done so!

Oscar subsequently accepted a proposal by impresario Richard D'Oyly Carte, and went to America on a lecture tour as *Patience* ran in London. Cynics said D'Oyly Carte sent Wilde to these shores as "a sandwich-board boy for *Patience*"—and the cynics were probably right!

In the United States, Oscar Wilde gave his lecture on home décor—to Society matrons and to coal miners and to all sorts of audiences in between; best of all, he dressed like Bunthorne in *Patience*, and his outrageous pronouncements in countless interviews garnered him newspaper coverage wherever he went. Two of my favorite Wildean *bon mots* date from this trip: when he landed in New York, he told the customs official that he "had nothing to declare but his genius." And when asked by reporters about his voyage, he admitted that he "was disappointed with the Atlantic Ocean"!

Meanwhile, as Oscar toured the United States, *Patience* made its première in America and ran merrily on at the Savoy in London.

It was literally the first of the Savoy Operas and ran for a remarkable 578 performances!

Gilbert was more than a little concerned about how the opera would "go" when it was revived twenty years later at the Savoy in the first decade of the twentieth century. Sullivan and D'Oyly Carte were both dead, Wilde had been disgraced (though his plays would continue to live as monuments of comedy—and do so even to this day), and the Pre-Raphaelite brotherhood and their "rapturous groupies" had long since abandoned their yearnings. As Gilbert put it, "The aesthetic movement was as dead as Queen Anne."

But as Gilbert himself wrote, "The old opera woke up splendidly." Modesty probably precluded his saying why, but the reason is of course that he "builded better than he knew," and every generation can appreciate *Patience* for its satire on affectation.

Which brings me back to the point I was trying to make at the start. *Patience* has its existence thanks to Oscar Wilde, but today's audience need not realize this. In fact, many today think of Oscar as the author of "The Ballad of Reading Gaol," *The Picture of Dorian Gray,* and a play usually regarded as one of the finest of *all* English comedies, *The Importance of Being Earnest.*

But had Oscar not left Ireland, or had not come down to London from Oxford, or had not become so flamboyant—so outrageous, even—long before he established his literary reputation—it's very likely that *Patience* would have been about two rural Anglican curates—or perhaps not have been written at all.

❖

Patience in Perspective

Welcome to "The Inner Brotherhood"!

Last summer the Gilbert & Sullivan Society of Austin explored one manifestation of the craze for "things oriental" in London during the 1880s, and this summer we take a look at another English mania that incorporated this "longing for all one sees that's Japanese." The opera is, of course, *Patience; or, Bunthorne's Bride*, which opened at the Opéra Comique in London on April 23, 1881, and was transferred, several months later, to Richard D'Oyly Carte's new theatre, the Savoy, the first theatre (in fact, the first public building) in history to be lit entirely by "the electricity."

Although it is not as well-known as *The Mikado*, *Patience* nevertheless usually ranks high on Gilbert & Sullivan enthusiasts' lists of favorites.

Why? Well, there's Sullivan's glorious score, of course. And Gilbert's satirical, metrical, and topsy-turvy humor. But the irony is that *Patience* had the potential to be the most topical and most quickly dated—and forgotten—of all of the Savoy operas. Theatregoers in 1881 thought that Gilbert meant the velvet-frocked Bunthorne to be a parody of a soft young apostle of æstheticism recently down from Oxford—Oscar Wilde. Grosvenor represented another poet, they thought— Algernon Swinburne. Patience's dress was based on Luke Fildes' painting, "Where Are You Going, My Pretty Maid?" while Lady Jane's was modeled on Whistler's "Princesse du Pays de la Porcelaine." Gilbert's groupings (the librettist staged his own works) may have reminded Pre-Raphaelite enthusiasts of other well-known paintings: the Twenty Lovesick Maidens were discovered grouped like those in Burne-Jones's "Triumph of Love," and the procession in the Act I finale with Bunthorne garlanded was very like Leighton's "Triumph of Cimabuë." It was all very *yearning*, very "greenery-yallery, Grosvenor Gallery," very topical—

and thus very likely to be consigned to obscurity as the fad for "æstheticism" faded.

But Gilbert, as he did in his other collaborations with Sullivan, builded better than he knew. "When it was revived after a lapse of nineteen years," he wrote in 1902, "the 'æsthetic craze' was as dead as Queen Anne, and no little anxiety was felt by the management of the

Savoy Theatre as to how the piece would be received. However, we were not a little surprised and relieved to find that the allusions to the absurdities formerly connected with the mania had lost nothing of their normal significance. The revival ran merrily for eight months." And 110 more years have seen

countless additional revivals of *Patience* on the lyric stage, each attesting to the universality of Gilbert's libretto. We still have our Bunthornes and Grosvenors—and lovesick maidens—to say nothing of dragoon guards! Gilbert's æsthetic poets, with their lovesick followers, have passed among us in recent memory as hippies, valley girls, and rock stars, to say nothing of _____ and _____. (The task of filling up the blanks I'd rather leave to *you*!) In fact, whenever we find our friends, our children—or even ourselves—affecting the dress or language or behavior of the popular cultural icon of the moment, we might glance over our shoulder and squint with embarrassment: isn't that Bunthorne chuckling behind us?

❖

The Gilbert & Sullivan Society of Austin

presents

November 11, 2012
Worley Barton Theater at
Brentwood Christian School
Austin, Texas

Entertaining Austin Audiences Since 1976

"I'm Not Making This Up, You Know!"

My title, which is also the title of Anna Russell's autobiography, comes from the English comedienne's signature routine: her hilarious explication of Wagner's "Ring" cycle. But I'm pressing her famous declaration into service here to provide some background to the November 11 Musicale.

I first heard of Anna Russell in high school, when a friend, who knew of my enthusiasm for Victor Borge, introduced me to "The Queen of Musical Parody" by lending me one of her long-playing records. It contained neither "The Ring" nor "How to Write Your Own Gilbert & Sullivan Opera," but I remembered this recording in the mid-1960s when the lure of the Savoy operas beckoned, and I learned *of* this routine, which (I read somewhere) evidently enraged the blue-haired ladies of London's Gilbert & Sullivan Society after it was recorded in 1953.

I found the LP as a newlywed while in the Army in Baltimore: *Anna Russell Sings! Again?* (a sequel to *Anna Russell Sings!*), and listened to it many times while making a transcription of every very funny word. The routine makes fun of mostly *H.M.S. Pinafore*. It is set in New York among the social elite, "The Great 400," and the characters include a patter baritone named Clodbelly Bunion ("The Rich Tycoon"); the lowly-status tenor, John Smith, who's in love with the socialite Pneumonia Vanderfeller; and a former nursemaid (named "Dandelion"!) who mixed up some babies a many years ago and thus straightens the road to true love for the tenor and soprano at the end. While telling the tale, Miss Russell makes fun of patter songs (with an obligatory encore!), tenor arias "in 6/8 time, accompanied on a stringed instrument," sweet English soprano warbling, a madrigal, a revelatory plot-resolving contralto number, and finally a finale—where "everyone has a little sing, with a free-for-all at the end." The result was that I ended up with a typescript, and also memory of every word of the routine. I also located a copy of *The Anna Russell Songbook*, which contained most of the music. (It's missing "The Madrigal.")

In 1983, I directed a production of *Patience* at Barksdale Theatre outside Richmond, Virginia, and one of the delights of the 12-week run was a post-show cabaret about every four weeks in which the company would entertain one another after the show. We had men wearing aesthetic maidens' costumes and wigs singing songs from *Patience* using high voices, serious opera arias, folk songs. I even did my magic show at one. But for one of these cabarets, I decided to press A. R. into service, and with Alice's help dressed up in drag (wig, dress, stockings, shoes— complete with my then-signature handlebar moustache!), and with a box full of hats, lip-synced the G&S routine with the 1953 LP recording providing the audio.

Just a year later, I learned that Miss Russell would be appearing at the Kennedy Center Opera House in Washington, D. C., as a part of her "First Farewell Tour," but before I could make a reservation, the performance was sold out. We made the three-hour drive anyway, Alice, Alexander, and I, "on spec," hoping to get standing-room admission— which we did. She was wonderful, telling her audience that some of them knew the routines better than she did, so if she had any memory lapses, to just yell out the next line! During the intermission, a mom, dad, and little daughter left, and we three MacPhails slipped down into their seats. She started off the second half with "How to Write Your Own Gilbert & Sullivan Opera."

After this memorable evening, I wrote Miss Russell a fan-letter, confessing to her that I'd lip-synced the G&S routine, and asking for an autograph quotation from it for my scrapbook to go with my original Gilbert and Sullivan letters. After four months, including one address correction (her agent's address in the KenCen program was incorrect, so I had to find a Manhattan phone book at the college library), I received a thick envelope from—Australia. The "Anna Russell" of the return address was hand-written (an autograph!). Inside was a two-page, hand-written letter, explaining the delay. She also wrote, "It certainly doesn't bother me that you 'lip synced' the G&S. I have seen people lip sync lots of my numbers over the years, but never the G&S. I should very much like to have seen that."

She continued: "My retirement is becoming a bit of a laugh. I started my 'World Farewell Tour' last Nov in San Francisco, & it keeps evolving before me much faster than I am getting it done. As you see I am now on the Australian lap with 16 concerts next month & they keep adding new bits in the gaps. At this rate I'll go up at 96 in spontaneous combustion in Minsk." After a bit more airy persiflage, this wonderful lady signed off: "The best of luck with your productions in the future. Sincerely, Anna Russell." (A second autograph!) And the third page contained the requested quotation (which is reproduced below)—and autograph number three:

> To Ralph MacPhail Jr.
>
> "His political connections have become so highly publicized
> He's forced to be respectable, the poor Tycoon."
>   Clodbelly Bunion
>
> Very best wishes
>
> Anna Russell.

Since receiving this envelope, I've often thought that if she always treated her fans the way she treated me, it's no wonder she had such a successful career for over three decades on the concert stage.

Anna Russell almost made it to 96. She died in 2006, shortly before her 95th birthday—but in Australia, not in Minsk.

Janette Jones and Co. will, at the next Musicale, show the routine Miss Russell recorded in Baltimore in 1984 just days after we saw her at the KenCen. Janette will be joined by some well-loved Austin Savoyards to demonstrate just what Anna Russell is making fun of. The script, which I secured from friends at the Valley Light Opera in Amherst, Massachusetts, was originally devised and produced by Glen Gordon.

You'll *really* get a kick out of it. And I hope you enjoyed my story. Truly, I didn't make it up, you know!

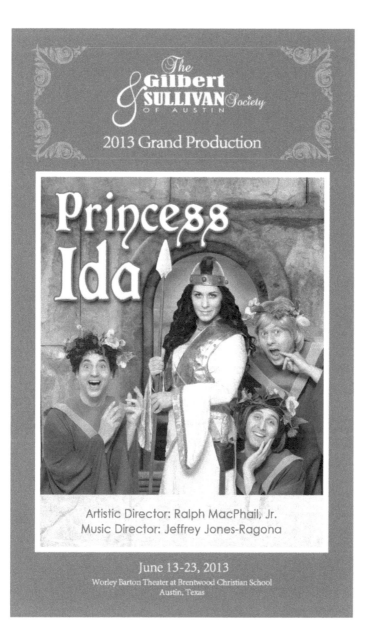

The Gilbert & SULLIVAN Society OF AUSTIN

2013 Grand Production

Princess Ida

Artistic Director: Ralph MacPhail, Jr.
Music Director: Jeffrey Jones-Ragona

June 13-23, 2013
Worley Barton Theater at Brentwood Christian School
Austin, Texas

Princess Ida: Mighty Maiden with a Mission—and A Mighty Melodic Comic Opera, Too

This summer the Gilbert & Sullivan Society of Austin will complete the cycle of the 11 frequently-produced Savoy operas with *Princess Ida; or, Castle Adamant*. True it is that numbers from this most melodic and amusing of shows have frequently graced our musicale programs, and while acknowledging that a semi-staged concert production was offered several years ago at Westminster Manor, this will be the first fully staged production not only by GSSA but, as far as we've been able to determine, the first full production ever to be staged in Austin.

And I couldn't be more excited about it! *Princess Ida* was first produced in London by Richard D'Oyly Carte in 1884, one in the succession of his hits that began in 1875 with *Trial by Jury*. That venerable one-act, of course, makes fun of the British legal system; in succession came Gilbert's tilts at the aristocracy (*The Sorcerer*), Her Majesty's Royal Navy (*H.M.S. Pinafore*), Robert Peel's "bobbies" (*The Pirates of Penzance*), the "aesthetic movement" (*Patience*), and the House of Lords (*Iolanthe*).

What next? Well, women's education for one thing (but as we shall see, that wasn't all). Sullivan had been objecting to Gilbert's topsy-turvy plots and situations, and hankering for a story of "real human interest and probability." That he got, even if Gilbert had to dip into his library of previously written plays for inspiration—and more than a little dialogue as well.

Gilbert's main source was his own "Respectful Per-Version" of Alfred, Lord Tennyson's long poem, *The Princess, A Medley* (1847); his burlesque was produced at the Olympic Theatre in 1870. *The Princess* was presented in five acts, written in blank verse with new lyrics for well-known musical numbers added, and laced with excruciating puns—all typical of the burlesque tradition out of which grew the Gilbert & Sullivan operas during the first decade of the collaboration.

In 1870, women had few opportunities for higher education in England. Between 1870 and 1884, however, the picture changed: Girton and Newnham Colleges opened in Cambridge, and Oxford boasted Somerville and Lady Margaret Hall. The University of London was not far behind; two years before *Princess Ida* opened, Westfield College, the U. of L.'s first women's college, was established. (In my library I have a book entitled *Castle Adamant in Hampstead: A History of Westfield College 1882-1982*.)

In *Princess Ida*—and both Tennyson's poem and Gilbert's 1870 burlesque—the title character has established a women's university from which all men are barred—even chessmen (well, in Gilbert's!). "Man," they are taught, "is Nature's sole mistake!" Princess Ida and her small faculty, along with a hundred female students, sequester themselves at Castle Adamant, one of her father's country houses, and ambitiously soar "towards the Empyrean heights/ Of every kind of lore" "in search of wisdom's pure delight."

Enter Prince Hilarion and his two pals. Hilarion had been betrothed to Ida at the early age of one (when he was twice her age: two), and he's determined to breach the battlements of Castle Adamant to claim his bride by storming "their bowers/ With scented showers/ Of fairest flowers/ That we can buy."

They do—in Act II—but without flowers; instead they disguise themselves as female students—and homely ones at that. But along the way Hilarion & Co. and the academics of Castle Adamant delight the audience with an incredibly lovely sequence of musical numbers that is frequently called "the string of pearls."

In addition to women's education, *Princess Ida* also aims its shaft at mindless macho militarism, the oratorios of Handel, grand opera—and even Darwin and his controversial *Origin of Species* (1859). I've no space to discuss the intricacies of the plot (a luncheon on-stage, an heroic rescue of Ida from drowning, a fight or two, and a Victorian male strip-tease—of suits of armor), the clever characterizations, the *three* colorful sets, the multiple costumes. You can certainly read more by going to the Gilbert & Sullivan Archive on-line—and listen to some of the music as well. More detail in my next column.

In the meantime, both of Gilbert's plays are available online (at the Gilbert & Sullivan Archive). Project Gutenberg will yield Tennyson's *The Princess*. Lulu Books sells a volume with both of Gilbert's plays *and* an abbreviated version of the Tennyson poem; search on "*The Princess and Princess Ida*" at Lulu.com.

A large cast of principals and a chorus of 12 ladies and 12 gentlemen will be our goal at auditions.

Which character in *Princess Ida* is often considered to be a Gilbertian self-portrait? Which number occasionally prompted the D'Oyly Carte to hire a "grand opera guest artiste" when performing the work in London? Which number sounds like the music was written by the composer of *Messiah*? Which two speeches show Gilbert's familiarity with *Hamlet* and "the Scottish play" (even *if* the librettist professed to disdain Shakespeare)?

Delights lie ahead as we progress towards those empyrean heights. Do plan to join us on the climb!

An Introduction to Characters and Audition Notes on *Princess Ida*

*P*rincess Ida* is a high-spirited send-up of feminism, the very idea of females needing higher education—and so much more. As I mentioned in the last column, Charles Darwin and his *Origin of Species* come into Gilbert's sights, and the dramatist also "aims his shaft" (to *just miss* a metaphor) at grand operatic conventions and the style of G. F. Handel; and if some might think that Gilbert is too hard on the ladies, just look at his men, whether they be intellectually challenged tenors, a world-class misanthrope, or mindless militants who blindly follow orders into war.

My purpose here is to provide information for auditionees concerning the auditions and also concerning the funny, lovely, and challenging characters in the show we will present this summer. If you're planning to audition, please read this in its entirety. And even if you're *not*, please read it anyway: I hope you will find it interesting—and that it will give you a foretaste of the delights coming in June.

Music Director and Conductor Jeffrey Jones-Ragona and I request that auditionees <u>memorize</u> a song from Gilbert & Sullivan or something similar that will show their voice and range to best advantage. *It is also mandatory to provide a copy of the music for the auditions accompanist. No a cappella auditions will be heard. An accompanist will be provided, but singers will be welcome to bring their own accompanist if they wish.* The Society welcomes newcomers with delight.

If *Princess Ida* is not in your library, you can download the libretto from the Gilbert & Sullivan Archive at gsarchive.net, where you will also be able to read a plot synopsis, see vintage images, and download audio files.

Princess Ida is filled with roles that are fun to play; it has incredible singing opportunities (needed will be *two* principal tenors, *two* principal sopranos, and *three* principal bass-baritones), and the work requires actors who can sing well as well as singers who can act well. It is the only Gilbert & Sullivan opera with dialogue in blank verse. It is also the only one of their works set in three acts.

THE CHORUS is composed of the men: **Soldiers and Courtiers of King Hildebrand** (12 gentlemen, resplendent picturesque costumes); and the women: **Courtiers of King Hildebrand in Act I and "Girl Graduates" of Princess Ida's University in Acts II and III)** (12 females, including the supporting principals in Acts II and III, Sacharissa, Chloe, and Ada, with a costume change for all between Acts I and II and for some between II and III).

Here are brief character sketches, with a nod of gratitude to the writings of William Cox-Ife, Peter Kline—and a certain W. S. Gilbert (see the list of references, below*):

KING HILDEBRAND (Bass-Baritone): "A bluff and domineering monarch." A big voice is needed by a singer who can sing patter clearly and dominate the stage when he's on it. He's "a peppery kind of King, Who's indisposed for parleying" when action can accomplish his goals. Hilarion is his son, and Hildebrand *will* insure that Hilarion claims Princess Ida; he takes King Gama and his sons into custody until this can be accomplished, thus leading to Act II.

HILARION (Lyric Tenor): "Hildebrand's handsome young son." This is a demanding part with two important solos. Like father, like son: he is somewhat lacking in a sense of humor—but sings beautifully! He was betrothed to Princess Ida "at the extremely early age of one" (when he was two) and the basic plot of the opera concerns his attempt to claim his bride, though she has sequestered herself with her female students in a country estate belonging to *her* father (King Gama) and teaches her charges to "abjure tyrannic Man." (See "Cyril" and "Florian," below.)

CYRIL (Tenor): "Happy-go-lucky friend of Hilarion, with an eye for the girls." This second tenor has more of a sense of humor than the first (Hilarion). The part can even be sung by a high baritone. Cyril has a memorable "kissing song" in Act II, and with Florian and Hilarion, has a number of ensemble turns with his buddies. (See "Florian, below.)

FLORIAN (Baritone): Also a happy-go-lucky pal of Hilarion and a flirt, but less so than Cyril (and with more humor than Hilarion). See "Cyril," above. The three young rakes also disguise themselves in academic robes as females once in Castle Adamant and have a show-stopping trio—with one of those incredibly amusing G&S dances. (How *well* I remember this sequence performed by the old D'Oyly Carte at the Kennedy Center in 1976.)

KING GAMA (Light Baritone): "An embittered King; twisted in mind and body." The role typically played by a comedian or "patter baritone"; Gama is traditionally portrayed as an elderly hunchback, with a twisted leg and stick. His Act I song is usually regarded as a Gilbertian self-portrait, however negative—and his Act III solo is cut from the same cloth. *This* king lacks Hildebrand's diplomacy: Gama says what he thinks—and it isn't very pleasant—but *very* funny! He appears only in Acts I and III.

ARAC (Bass): Son of Gama, "warrior, imposing, and thickheaded." Arac and his brothers are soldiers (see "Guron" and "Scynthius," below) and are dumb as bricks—and they should ideally be BIG hulking brutes! Arac has important solo contributions to the show; the other two do not (other than an occasional solo line), but contribute to funny trios. Arac's second solo is a spoof of Handelian oratorio singing, supported by his brothers, so he must have a big voice.

GURON (Bass-Baritone): Big and imposing and also a son of Gama, Guron does not have the vocal demands of Arac (see above); he has little solo singing and few spoken lines, but can create a memorable appearance in his ensembles with Arac and Scynthius. (See Scynthius, below.)

SCYNTHIUS (Bass-Baritone): Gama's third son, Scynthius is another big, hulking brute. With Arac and Guron (see above), he participates in memorable ensembles throughout (but has little solo singing), and all three do a show-stopping Victorian "strip-tease" of armor before The Big Fight in Act III.

PRINCESS IDA (Dramatic Soprano): Gama's beautiful daughter. "Principal of Castle Adamant, the girls' college, where men are an anathema." This is the most challenging soprano role in Gilbert & Sullivan vocally, and the acting demands are heavy, too. Playing her antipathy toward all man‍kind is a challenge, and she has an incredible dramatic scene toward the end when her students abandon her and her cause. Her singing throughout must dominate, and she has a long speech in blank verse welcoming her "new students" and stating her goals for their enlightenment.

LADY BLANCHE (Contralto): "Professor of Abstract Science at Castle Adamant. A domineering woman, very jealous of Princess Ida, and whose one ambition is to become Principal." She has plenty of ensemble singing and dialogue. A forceful, ambitious woman, she's also Melissa's mother. She's not as lovable as some of the other "older woman" roles in Gilbert & Sullivan, but is important and dominating. (SPOILER ALERT: She even accomplishes her goal at the end!)

LADY PSYCHE (Soprano): "Professor of Humanities, whose academic training is not proof against the charms of Cyril." Dignified without being pompous, intellectual from a baby, Psyche is also susceptible to the charms of men. She has a delightful solo to sing—about "Darwinian man"! A lovely little "nerd," who knew as a child that a buttercup was called "ranunculus bulbosus," who gave away the conjuror's secrets at parties (little beast!), and who also "tackled visitors with 'You don't know Who first determined longitude—I do—Hipparchus 'twas—B.C. one sixty three!'"

MELISSA (Mezzo-Soprano): "Lady Blanche's daughter. A really saucy young [lady], who finds nothing repulsive about 'the monster called man'"—especially when she sees one for the first time. Has some short musical solos. Never having seen men before, she notes that Hilarion, Florian, and Cyril's cheeks "have not that pulpy softness which One gets so weary of in womankind: Their features are more marked— and—oh, their chins! How curious!" (Was five o'clock shadow ever more amusing?)

SACHARISSA (Soprano): Girl graduate/student at the university, she has a single line to sing and scattered dialogue lines and sings in all of the ensembles of the female chorus. She's threatened expulsion for bringing chessmen inside Ida's university, only to plead that "I meant no harm; they're only men of wood!" She's reminded, however, that "They're men with whom you give each other mate"! Tsk-tsk. . . . (This performer will also sing in the Chorus of Act I.)

CHLOE (Female Chorister—Speaking Part): Another girl graduate/student at the university. Has about four speaking lines and sings in all of the ensembles of the female chorus. When in Act III Princess Ida asks Chloe where the rifles are that are needed to repel the male invaders, she responds, "We left them in the armoury, for fear That in the heat and turmoil of the fight, They might go off!" (This performer will also sing in the Chorus of Act I.)

ADA (Female Chorister—Speaking Part): Still another girl graduate/student at the university, with but one speaking line, in response to Ida's request to speak with her Bandmistress before battle: "Please you, ma'am, the band Do not feel well, and can't come out today!" She, too, sings in all of the female chorus ensemble sections. (This performer will also sing in the Chorus of Act I.)

I've said perhaps too often that there's only one G&S activity more fun than seeing one of their operas—and that's actually *working* on one. If you need a little push to encourage you to audition, please consider this it. Jeffrey and I do all we can to make the auditions fun and relaxed.

Please encourage a friend or two to audition so that even *more* can share the delight of Gilbert & Sullivan. Do plan to audition for Austin's first fully staged production *ever* by *any* group of *Princess Ida; or Castle Adamant*!

*References

William Cox-Ife, *How to Sing Both Gilbert and Sullivan* (London: Chappell & Co., Ltd., 1961).

W. S. Gilbert, *The Savoy Operas: I* (London: Oxford University Press, 1962).

Peter Kline, *Gilbert & Sullivan Production* (The Theatre Student Series) (New York: Richards Rosen Press, Inc., 1972).

Deadlines—Deadlines—Deadlines!

'Tis April 5, and I've known for months that Sue Caldwell is expecting, by the end of today, a column from Bridgewater for the *Newsletter*. I suppose it's human nature to wait until the last moment, and Sue's been around long enough to know not to expect early submissions—from me, anyway.

As I was reflecting on this (it was more fun to so reflect than to sit down and *write*), it occurred to me that deadlines—*lots* of them—are faced by all of us who are involved in theatrical production.

I know I need to be ready to start staging *Princess Ida* at the first rehearsal following the GSSA Musicale on May 12. Am I ready—never having directed this show before? Not by a long shot. But I finished staging—on paper—Act I before I left my desk yesterday. "No worries," as the kids say. There's still plenty of time. . . .

But while this date looms, there's some satisfaction in having already met earlier deadlines. This is the fourth column on *Princess Ida*, and the earlier three were filed on time. Our efficient Production Manager Bill Hatcher has met more deadlines than I can count—and tossed more than a few my way ("Have you a Flow-chart? Staging Sequences? Rehearsal Blocks?"). Months ago, Jeffrey and I, at Bill's urging, worked at selecting a score to use for the show (the standard score is published only in England and doesn't include the dialogue) so they would be on hand by auditions. Done.

Bill's also pulled from me a prop list (however preliminary), set plans (in time for a production meeting in Austin the Saturday following auditions), and costume information, 'most all of this in 2012. As late as yesterday we were wrestling on how to divide the Men's Chorus in Act I into Soldiers and Courtiers (they're all Soldiers in Acts II and III), and just two days ago we decided to make the Daughters of the Plough in Acts II and III supernumeraries (quite apart from the Ladies Chorus). Why was it important to make these decisions now? Because according to contract from our costumiers, the Malabars in Winnipeg, we have to submit this information 45 days prior to the production. *They* have *their* deadlines to meet, too.

The resourceful Bill has also managed to rent some interesting props for the Girl Graduates to use in their studies in Act II from our friends at the Gilbert & Sullivan Society of Seattle. They're already in Austin and ready to use in rehearsal—one less thing to worry about.

But we've both been worrying about the huge broadswords needed by Arac, Guron, and Scynthius in Act I. Bill suggested I contact my friend Mary Metz, M.B.E., of the Gilbert & Sullivan Society of Houston. According to an e-mail I saw this morning, Houston leading lights Steve and Barbara Robbins (who have seen some of *our* shows) are checking the warehouse today to see if they will be available. Here's hoping. [Later: They found them. And they will shortly be on their way to Austin.]

Tonight I'll be in Bridgewater, but I'd really love to be in Austin, for our incredible media relations guy, David Little, will be meeting with Michelle Haché, Holton Johnson, Derek Smootz, Michael Borysow, and photographer Brenda Ladd to shoot the production logo photograph that will grace posters, postcards, the website, and our playbill/program's cover. It won't be too early to get this done, David will tell you. And he has a list of *additional* self-imposed deadlines for other strategies to let all of Austin know that *Princess Ida* will be The Show to See in June.

Last night, President Libby Weed sent me and several others a draft of a fundraising letter to look over. (What *would* we do without e-mail?) And this is just one example of the work that's been going on by our hard-working and dedicated Board of Directors as they raise funds, line up personnel, write contracts, enter into agreements, plan publicity stunts, sponsor informal concerts, write for grants, and meet so many other deadlines that my grey matter swirls when thinking about them.

Jeffrey will be starting music rehearsals later than usual, necessitated by the Austin Lyric Opera schedule, but this will be a first *Princess Ida* for him, too, and you know as well as I do that he will be more than prepared for *his* first rehearsal: deadline, April 30.

Bill Hatcher has also been working this week (and earlier) at securing air travel for me and Alice. He's always on top of his deadlines, but on this matter he's been waiting for prices to drop, and when they did earlier this week, he swooped down (if you can do this by computer) and nailed our flights (to mix a metaphor).

Michael Meigs has found a car for my use (*thank* you, R. B. Rudy!), and Michael's even going to let me use *his* car—after he leaves the country. Dates for taking delivery of and switching vehicles are all worked out, as are the dates for my (and Alice's) stay with the ever-hospitable Russell and Kay Gregory.

Chris Buggé responded to Bill's invitation to build three tables for Act II of *Princess Ida*. We don't need them for performances only—we also need them *early* for rehearsals (since they need to be of a special size, be moved by the cast, and be sturdy enough to be stood upon), starting in early May. Chris made one, sent me a photo for approval (e-mail again!), which was immediately forthcoming. I wouldn't be surprised if he's already completed the other two, too. Deadline more than met—and one less thing to be concerned about.

And while Chris was building tables, Bill was foraging for stools (we'll need over a dozen—and need them for rehearsals, too—no waiting to the last minute).

Bill has also published the rehearsal schedule, after wrangling the cast's conflicts (a *huge* job), and now all company members know when they will be needed for rehearsal and can thus plan their lives around our exciting project.

If you've read this, you will know that I met my deadline (well, if I were late, Sue would never tell you), as did the other contributors to this issue. Sue has met her own subsequent deadlines of compiling the submissions into a coherent and attractive issue, circulating them multiple times to her informal editing/proofreading committee, editing based on our picky feedback and adding photographs, and finally firing the finished document through cyberspace to the printer. The printer has deadlines as well, for production and mailing.

There! I'm about done. I need to run this through the spell-check and read it one mo' time, and *then* I can get back to my blocking book.

But not before pressing [SEND].

P. S. Mission accomplished—deadline met!

"Useful Knowledge Everywhere One Finds" [1]

The Gilbert & Sullivan partnership almost dissolved before *Princess Ida* was written.

During the run of their preceding work, *Iolanthe*, composer Arthur Sullivan received the honor of knighthood from his most important fan, Queen Victoria. And then the composer's friends and the musical establishment went to work, admonishing Sullivan that there are some things that Arthur Sullivan could do that Sir Arthur Sullivan *shouldn't*—things such as writing comic operas. His gifts should be employed, they thought and said or wrote, on loftier endeavors: symphonies, cantatas, "grand" operas.

To worsen this situation, librettist William S. Gilbert had proposed a new work based on a magic lozenge—a pill that would turn any character taking it into the kind of person they *pretended* to be. This had no appeal to Sullivan, who saw the characters as mechanical puppets, and provided little scope for musical characterization as human beings.

So it looked as if the partnership, which had brought fame and fortune to the two men, was at an end. Their string of successes, which added so much delight to the musical and dramatic worlds of the day, was about to be cut. *Trial by Jury*, *The Sorcerer*, *H.M.S. Pinafore*, *The Pirates of Penzance*, *Patience*, and *Iolanthe* made Gilbert & Sullivan household names. As Gilbert later said, they had become as much an institution as Westminster Abbey.

We have *Princess Ida* thanks to prescient producer Richard D'Oyly Carte's five-year contract, which required Gilbert & Sullivan to write another comic opera for the Savoy Theatre on six months' notice.

Gilbert saved the day by setting his "lozenge plot" aside and proposing a new subject, a subject that appealed to the composer for its characters and opportunities to compose on a grander scale than before. The new work was to be called *Princess Ida*. But, in truth, the subject was anything but new.

Gilbert had proved himself with his earlier successes a master of—well, if not self-plagiarism, then at least at using ideas from earlier works: his short stories, his "Bab" ballads, and even libretti for his earlier short musical entertainments. The genesis of *Princess Ida* is to be found in his 1870 burlesque of a long poem by the poet laureate, Alfred, Lord Tennyson, which was published in 1847, *The Princess*. Gilbert's "perversion" (as he called it) of Tennyson's poem follows the basic characteristics of burlesque, a popular form of musical theatre of the mid-nineteenth century: their plots were based on well-known stories and plays; the dialogue was in rhymed-couplets and heavily laced with positively *excruciating* puns. The musical numbers were new lyrics set to pre-existing melodies from popular culture and the operatic stage. It was not quite respectable, for one of the greatest features for the males in the audience was the use of breeches (or trouser) roles: handsome young men were played on stage by pretty young women in tights—in an era when a glimpse of stocking was looked on as something more than shocking!

In fact, when Gilbert & Sullivan started writing, they determined to raise the level of musical theatre by *avoiding* such cross dressing, unrealistic diction, and silly stories. Sullivan would provide *original* music, and Gilbert would provide *coherent* plots and avoid the pun-laden couplets that characterized the diction of burlesque. It is impossible today however, to ignore the earlier dramatic form when trying to understand the roots of Savoy opera, and perhaps *Princess Ida* can be productively seen as an acknowledgment of the influence of burlesque on the evolution of Gilbert & Sullivan opera.

Even in 1870 (a year before he first teamed with Sullivan—for *Thespis*), Gilbert was trying to improve on convention and raise the literary quality of burlesque: he wrote *The Princess* in blank verse instead of rhymed couplets, and while puns were still very much in evidence, they were fewer than usual. However, he had no composer: his lyrics were meant to be sung to pre-existing melodies. He retained the five-act structure, and the patrons' expectations at the Olympic Theatre, for which the piece was written, required that Prince Hilarion and his two friends, Cyril and Florian, be played by women—in tights!

It was to this 14-year-old burlesque that Gilbert turned when Sullivan demanded something different. Gilbert re-used much of his blank-verse dialogue, but wrote new lyrics for the musical situations. He reduced the five acts to three (still one more than the hitherto customary two).

It is rather Gilbertian, however, that while the librettist updated his dramatic form, and, in his lyrics, benefited from years of experience in writing for Sullivan, his subject matter stayed the same, for one of the main subjects of both plays is the concept of higher education for women.

In 1870, women had few opportunities for higher education in England. Between *The Princess* of 1870 and *Princess Ida* of 1884, however, the picture changed: Girton and Newnham Colleges opened in Cambridge, and Oxford boasted Somerville and Lady Margaret Hall. The University of London was not far behind; two years before *Princess Ida* opened, Westfield College, the U. of L.'s first women's college, was established.

In *Princess Ida*—and both Tennyson's poem and Gilbert's 1870 burlesque—the title character has established a women's university from which all men are barred—even chessmen (well, in Gilbert's!). "Man," they are taught, "is Nature's sole mistake!" Princess Ida and her small faculty, along with their female students, sequester themselves at Castle Adamant, one of her father's country houses, and ambitiously soar "towards the Empyrean heights/ Of every kind of lore" "in search of wisdom's pure delight."

Enter Prince Hilarion and his two pals. Hilarion had been betrothed to Ida at the early age of one (when he was twice her age: two), and he's determined to breach the battlements of Castle Adamant to claim his bride by storming "their bowers/ With scented showers/ Of fairest flowers/ That we can buy."

They do—in Act II—but without flowers; instead they disguise themselves as female students—and homely ones at that! But along the way Hilarion & Co. and the academics of Castle Adamant delight the audience with an incredibly lovely sequence of musical numbers that is frequently called "the string of pearls." Clearly, with *Princess Ida*, Sullivan had the story and the characters he craved, and he gave them some of his finest music.

In addition to women's education, *Princess Ida* also aims its shaft at mindless macho militarism, misanthropy, the oratorios of Handel, the conventions of grand opera—and even the studies of Darwin and his controversial *Origin of Species* (1859)! Listen carefully, and you'll also hear allusions to Shakespeare, a Gilbertian predecessor whom the librettist professed to detest.

While working on this lovely show, we've discovered many delights for both eye and ear: the music and the humor, of course, are there as always in Gilbert & Sullivan, but *Princess Ida* is perhaps closer to being both opera and fairy tale than any of their other works. There are multiple choruses with multiple costumes, three sets, and many opportunities for movement and interesting groupings.

We should be grateful that, nearly 130 years ago, Sullivan found a lozenge too distasteful to swallow and forced Gilbert to turn his attention elsewhere and write a different libretto—one that pokes fun at both men and women but in the end affirms that universal influence, "the sway of love," in a final finale that is unique in the Savoy operas.

At its heart, perhaps, *Princess Ida* is a fanciful (and at times quite literal) battle of the sexes. Who will win? No "spoiler-alert" is necessary here. All will be revealed in good time.

But here's a hint: When my friend William J. Brooke wrote the story of *Princess Ida* for children, he ended it this way: ". . . Ida learns that her biggest struggle is with herself and only by giving up can she allow herself to win. In the Battle of the Sexes, the only way to survive is not to fight; and the only victory is when both sides surrender completely. That's called love."

So who will win? Since we have *Princess Ida* to see and hear, we *all* will!

"Useful Knowledge Everywhere One Finds" [2]

The Gilbert & Sullivan partnership almost dissolved before *Princess Ida* was written.

In 1883, composer Arthur Sullivan was knighted by Queen Victoria. The composer's friends and the musical establishment admonished him that there are some things that Arthur Sullivan could do that Sir Arthur Sullivan *shouldn't*—things such as writing comic operas. His gifts should be employed, they thought, on loftier compositions.

Meanwhile, librettist William S. Gilbert had proposed a new work based on a magic lozenge that would turn any character into the kind of person they *pretended* to be. This had no appeal to Sullivan, who saw in the plot little scope for musical characterization and development.

We have *Princess Ida* thanks to producer Richard D'Oyly Carte's five-year contract, which required Gilbert & Sullivan to write another comic opera for the Savoy Theatre on six months' notice.

Gilbert set his "lozenge plot" aside and proposed a new subject, one that appealed to the composer for its characters and opportunities to compose on a grander scale than before. But in truth, the new work, *Princess Ida*, was anything but new.

The genesis of *Princess Ida* is to be found in Gilbert's 1870 burlesque of a long poem by Alfred, Lord Tennyson (published in 1847), *The Princess*. Gilbert's "per-version" of the Poet Laureate's poem was a burlesque, a popular form of musical theatre of the mid-nineteenth century in which plots were based on well-known stories and plays, and dialogue was in rhymed-couplets and laced puns. The musical numbers were new lyrics set to pre-existing melodies. It was not quite respectable, for one of

its distinctive features was "trouser roles": young men were played on stage by pretty young women in tights—shocking!

In fact, early in the Gilbert & Sullivan partnership, the collaborators determined to raise the level of musical theatre by *avoiding* such cross dressing, unrealistic diction, and silly stories. And they *did*, with *H.M.S. Pinafore, The Pirates of Penzance, Patience,* and other successes.

Even in 1870, Gilbert was trying to improve on convention and raise the literary quality of burlesque: he wrote *The Princess* in blank verse instead of rhymed couplets, and while puns were still very much in evidence, they were fewer than usual. However, he had no composer: his lyrics were meant to be sung to pre-existing melodies. And the burlesque required that Prince Hilarion and his two friends Cyril and Florian be played by women—in tights!

It was to this 14-year-old burlesque that Gilbert turned when Sullivan demanded something different. He re-used much of his blank-verse dialogue, but wrote new lyrics for the musical situations—and he retained his basic satirical subject: higher education for women.

In 1870, women had few opportunities for higher education in England. Between *The Princess* of 1870 and *Princess Ida* of 1884, however, the picture changed: Girton and Newnham Colleges opened in Cambridge, and Oxford boasted Somerville and Lady Margaret Hall. The University of London was not far behind; two years before *Princess Ida* opened, Westfield College was established in the capital.

In *Princess Ida*—and both Tennyson's poem and Gilbert's 1870 burlesque—the title character has established a women's university from which all men are barred. "Man," they are taught (in *Princess Ida*), "is Nature's sole mistake!" In addition to women's education, *Princess Ida* also aims its shaft at mindless macho

militarism, misanthropy, Handel and grand opera singing—and even at Darwin and his controversial *Origin of Species*. Listen carefully, and you'll also hear allusions to Shakespeare!

The result is a comic opera that pokes fun at both men and women but in the end affirms that universal influence, "the sway of love," in a romantic final finale that is unique in the Savoy operas.

At its heart, perhaps, *Princess Ida* is a fanciful (and at times quite literal) battle of the sexes. Who will win? No "spoiler-alert" is necessary here. All will be revealed in good time.

But here's a hint: When my friend William J. Brooke wrote the story of *Princess Ida* for children, he ended it this way: ". . . Ida learns that her biggest struggle is with herself and only by giving up can she allow herself to win. In the Battle of the Sexes, the only way to survive is not to fight; and the only victory is when both sides surrender completely. That's called love."

So who will win? Since we have *Princess Ida* to see and hear, we *all* will!

The Gilbert & Sullivan Society of Austin

Trial by Jury

Artistic & Stage Director: Ralph MacPhail, Jr. • Music Director: Jeffrey Jones-Ragona

First Presbyterian Church
Austin, Texas

February 23, 2014

Trial by Jury

*T*rial by Jury premièred on March 25, 1875, at the Royalty Theatre in London. It was the first Gilbert & Sullivan opera produced by Richard D'Oyly Carte and is the only one-act work the duo wrote, although they had written others with other collaborators. It is also their only through-composed work—a true opera (without dialogue)—although they called it a "dramatic cantata."

It is a cliché but no exaggeration to say that *Trial by Jury* took London by storm, affirming D'Oyly Carte's feeling that English comic opera could be more successful than the usual musical theatre of the age which was frequently composed of adaptations of French works (with all of the Gallic sexiness excised). (*Trial by Jury* was, in fact, originally an afterpiece for a production of Offenbach's *La Périchole*.)

In 1877, D'Oyly Carte launched his own company devoted to English comic opera, and over the next two decades produced another dozen works from Gilbert & Sullivan, all of which continue to hold the stage with countless productions each year by groups such as ours. Pay careful attention to *Trial by Jury,* and you will discover the seeds for the distinctive style and characteristics of their later works.

We hope you will enjoy this "chamber" production—fully staged and sung, with grand piano accompaniment, costumes, props, and the suggestion of a set—as we sing so merrily, "trial-la-law"!

The Story

*H*ark, the hour of ten is sounding we hear as the Usher tries to bring order from the Great British Public to the courtroom, and separates the spectators from jurors in preparation for a trial for breach of promise of marriage. He encourages the Jury to adopt his own bias (*Now, Jurymen, hear my advice*) just before the arrival of the Defendant, Edwin (*Is this the Court of the Exchequer?*), who explains his roving eye with the ladies (*When first my old, old love I knew*). The Jury agrees that they were cut from the same cloth (*Oh, I was like that when a lad!*) but assert they have become respectable. All welcome the Judge, who tells all how he came to his exalted position. He had a roving eye, too, and it helped! (*When I, good friends, was called to the bar*) The Jury take their oath (*Oh, will you swear*) before the entrance of the Bridesmaids (*Comes the broken flower*) and the Plaintiff, Angelina (*O'er the season vernal*). She quite captivates the Jury *and* the Judge. The Plaintiff's Counsel then presents her case (*With a sense of deep emotion*) which is supported by Angelina's tears (*That she is reeling*). All threaten the Defendant, leading Edwin to present his defense (*Oh, gentlemen, listen, I pray*), suggesting he would thrash and kick his wife, since he is "such a very bad lot," especially when drinking. After objections, the entire ensemble considers this *A nice dilemma*. The Plaintiff declares her love for this rake, asking the jury to consider her distress when assessing "the damages Edwin must pay," which leads the Judge to consider making Edwin tipsy as a way to determine the truthfulness of his defense. All but the Defendant object, leading the Judge to solve the impasse in an unexpected but delightfully humorous way, and all sing of *joy unbounded*.

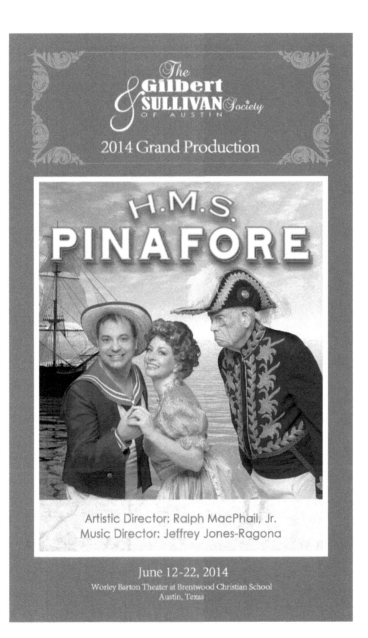

What's in a Name?
(Sometimes, a lot, actually . . .)

When Little Buttercup enquires about the identity of a certain lovesick sailor aboard H.M.S. *Pinafore*, the Boatswain answers:

> That is the smartest lad in all the fleet—
> Ralph Rackstraw!

The bumboat woman replies:

> Ralph! That name! Remorse! Remorse!

I hope you'll experience no remorse in deciding to read this column, which will concern itself with the names of the various characters in Gilbert & Sullivan's first international hit and still a firm favorite with Savoyards everywhere, *H.M.S. Pinafore.*

And while the name of the opera is so familiar to many that they don't even notice its irony, I want to focus on the names of the *characters* rather than on their ship.

Let's start with Sir Joseph Porter, K.C.B. After all, Gilbert did, listing him first in his *Dramatis Personæ* because Sir Joseph is 1) a male and 2) of highest professional rank among the characters (though not the highest in social rank; this topsy-turvy state of things needs a column devoted to it alone).

What does Sir Joseph's name tell us? He's a knight of the realm, a Knight Commander of the Bath (K.C.B.) in fact. Harry Benford tells us in his *Gilbert & Sullivan Lexicon* (www.GSOpera.com/lexicon) that K.C.B. is "one of the highest orders of knighthood" and notes that literal knightly bathing as ritualistic purification dates from as early as the 11th century. *I* think Gilbert was making a sly joke in bestowing this order on Sir Joseph, First Lord of the Admiralty, "the lord who rules the water."

But there's more! Sir Joseph's knighthood throws his family name into eclipse. But surely Gilbert's selection of "Porter" (a doorkeeper, a luggage carrier, a cheap beer) was not an accidental choice for a world-class parvenu such as Sir Joseph.

Hebe, "Sir Joseph's First Cousin," has a name defined in the *OED* as "youthful, prime," and as Martyn Green also points out in his *Treasury of Gilbert & Sullivan,* "she usually is"! (In fact, Hebe in Greek mythology was the Goddess of Youth, the daughter of Zeus and Hera.)

"Little Buttercup" is one of the most famous characters in all Gilbert & Sullivan (and has one of the most famous songs), but only careful program readers know that Gilbert gave this peddler woman and former nurse a "real" name as well: Mrs. Cripps. While working on this column, I did an online search on "cripps"—and found this definition: "A large error. A mistake with large consequences." If you know what I know of what *Mrs. Cripps* knows, this is a surprisingly apt appellation for the lady, which Gilbert makes clear in Little Buttercup's revelation at the end of *H.M.S. Pinafore.* (This online source [www.urbandictionary.com] says this definition is "Derived from Dave Cripps - chief disastoror [sic] extraordinaire. 'Oh no, I've done a right Cripps here.'" Scholarly integrity leads me reluctantly to admit that this definition probably evolved a century after *H.M.S. Pinafore* was launched and that "cripps" does not appear in the *OED.* Let's decide to call it topsy-turvy irony. [And the *West Side Story* gang is called the Crips—with but one p.])

Gilbert loved the sea, and his financial success led to the purchase of yachts which he enjoyed sailing. It shouldn't be surprising then to find that many of his sailors aboard H.M.S. *Pinafore* have names that are also names of various parts of a ship's rigging: Dick *Deadeye*, Bill *Bobstay*, Bob *Becket*. (Hie thee to www.GSOpera.com/lexicon for corroborative detail.)

But what of Ralph *Rackstraw*'s family name? It doesn't appear to have the same legitimate etymological pedigree of those of his fellow sailors. The indefatigable Harry Benford notes, however, that "rack" appeared in a 1921 seaman's manual as "slang for a berth." It's not too large a leap to assume that straw made such a berth more comfortable.

As for Ralph's first name, we know that Gilbert meant for it to be pronounced "Rafe" for Buttercup rhymes "Ralph" with "waif" in her revelation at the end. I have a small file (somewhere!) on various theories of how "Ralph" came to be pronounced "Rafe" in England, but none are entirely satisfactory. (I *do* know, however, that I became "Rafe" while directing a production of *H.M.S. Pinafore* near Richmond, Virginia, in 1981—"a many years ago," as Mrs. Cripps sings.)

Finally, let's look at that name of the eponymous ship. W. S. Gilbert originally called his work *H.M.S. Semaphore* (which rhymes, of course, with "one cheer more"). This change was suggested by Arthur Sullivan, the librettist's composer.

It was a most apt substitution. Life aboard H.M.S. *Pinafore* was as topsy-turvy as anything Gilbert ever created (a kind captain, a polite crew, immaculate cleanliness, no profanity with civility to all, etc.). How delightful that instead of naming his ship after a mode of naval communication, Gilbert *and Sullivan* named it after a Victorian child's smock!

Saluting Sir Joseph

S ir Joseph Porter, K.C.B., First Lord of the Admiralty, is arguably the most iconic character in the Gilbert & Sullivan operas: his "fore and aft," white plumed headgear, embroidered tunic, white satin breeches, white stockings and buckled shoes suggest the essence of Gilbert & Sullivan.

Certainly Sir Joseph has a lot to answer for to *me*, for 'twas he who drew me into the delights of Gilbert & Sullivan. I first saw him represented on stage when I was about 13 at Swanson Junior High School in Arlington, Virginia. An abridged version of *H.M.S. Pinafore* was presented in April (I still have a program!), with Carter Scruggs playing Sir Joseph, and it was he I saw the following Monday morning with the request to borrow "his music" (I didn't know to ask for a "vocal score") because I wanted to read the words about the funny man who "polished up the handle on the big front door."

We might call it "Gilbertian" that this iconic character is one of the most misunderstood of all of Gilbert's creations, at least by us Yanks. First of all, he's often called an "admiral." But being First Lord of the Admiralty is to be a member of the Prime Minister's cabinet—it is *not* to be a member of H.R.H.'s Royal Navy. Think Secretary of the Navy in this country, and you will appreciate the distinction. (My friend Bill Hyder cautioned me years ago to beware of Sir Josephs wearing epaulettes on their uniforms, for this indicates that both the costumer *and* the director don't understand the distinction, for only a military man would wear epaulettes.)

In fact, Sir Joseph's "Court Dress" is a part of the joke: A "first sea lord" would no more wear his ceremonial finery when boarding a ship than would he have an admiring crowd of sisters, cousins and aunts that attend him wherever he goes!

This leads us to the biggest misunderstanding we Americans have of Sir Joseph, which is central to Gilbert's plot in *H.M.S. Pinafore* and to his theme. Read his lyric to "When I was a lad" carefully, and you will see

that Sir Joseph Porter's roots are lowly—perhaps as low as Ralph
Rackstraw's. It was through his industry that he rose professionally (office
boy to junior clerk to articled clerk to partnership in a law firm to Member
of Parliament). Sounds like the "American Dream," doesn't it?

In this country, we accept such upward mobility as a birthright,
and just after Sir Joseph explains his rise he closes with a joke that really
obscures the bigger joke. The first joke:

> Stick close to your desks and never go to sea,
> And you all may be Rulers of the Queen's Navee!*

The bigger joke that we fail to grasp is that Sir Joseph is Captain
Corcoran's superior *professionally*, but very much his inferior *socially*.
Remember that Josephine, the Captain's daughter, sings of her "papa's
luxurious home, hung with ancestral armour and old brasses" when
debating with herself about whether to give up her accustomed life of
luxury to marry a penniless sailor.

And when Sir Joseph condescends to the Captain in Act II, telling
him that "love levels all ranks," the Captain is happy to swallow all this
because his daughter is to be the bride of a Cabinet Minister—an "Elysian
prospect," he says.

All this makes the dénouement all the more trenchant. If Buttercup
is telling the truth and if she did indeed switch the "patrician" Rackstraw
and lowly Corcoran in childhood's happy hour, we see Sir Joseph's true
stripes when confronted by this inconvenient truth. As he says to the just-
fallen Corcoran: "I need not tell you that after this change of your
condition, a marriage with your daughter will be out of the question."
Corcoran replies, quoting Sir Joseph's earlier assertion, "Don't say that,
your honour—love levels all ranks."

"It does to a considerable extent, but it does not level them as
much as that," replies to Sir Joseph, whose first cousin Hebe quickly steps
forward and offers herself as his bride. "Nothing could possibly be more
satisfactory," for the class distinctions are maintained, as they are for
Corcoran and Buttercup. The dénouement for Ralph (now captain) and
Josephine (soon to be the captain's wife instead of the captain's daughter)
is also romantically satisfactory (assuming Ralph will take possession of
that ancestral home!). In fact, the new social relationship of Josephine and

---

* This joke is even larger when we realize that Gilbert based Sir Joseph on
W. H. Smith, Disraeli's First Lord of the Admiralty in 1878 who had
"never been to sea." (A discussion of this needs a column of its own—but
I'm well out of space!)

Ralph offers a new definition of topsy-turvy: Josephine is marrying "up" and Ralph "down."

As the sextet of principals sing of their happy ending, Gilbert & Sullivan reprise *five* of the opera's catchiest tunes, the audience leaves with a feeling of elation at the resolution, and it's only later (if at all) some may start to ask pesky questions, such as: Do you mean to say that Josephine is in love with a man old enough to be her *father*? And, Can Buttercup *really* be in love with a person she nursed when she was young and charming?

But back to Sir Joseph for a moment—and a little homework assignment: on stage and on recordings he frequently makes a little-recognized "mistake" in delivering a famous lyric as Gilbert wrote it. I'll leave it to *you* to find the frequent misquotation (it's but a single word), but here are two hints: 1) it's in the first verse of his most famous song (I'm guessing that many readers can recite it by heart—and perhaps even make the mistake themselves); and 2) the "misquotation" is near at hand.

I am grateful to my friend Gayden Wren for contacting me after the last *Newsletter* appeared to correct my statement that Crips is the name of one of the gangs in the musical *West Side Story*. As Gayden gently reminded me, Crips is the name of an actual gang; the fictional gangs in *WSS* are the Jets and the Sharks.

Audition Notes on *H.M.S. Pinafore*

H.M.S. Pinafore is one of the three most popular of the Gilbert & Sullivan operas, and its initial success on both sides of the Atlantic in the late 1870s put the musical partnership firmly in the consciousness of the English speaking world. It is a shortish opera by later standards, but its unflagging tunefulness, its delightful humor, its characters and their stories, and its Buttercup's-basketful of now familiar expressions that have entered the English language have all ensured its being kept alive by performing groups: it never fails to delight.

My purpose here is to provide information for auditionees concerning the auditions and also concerning the characters in the show we will present this summer. If you're planning to audition, please read this in its entirety. And even if you're *not*, please read it anyway: I hope you will find it interesting—and that it will give you a foretaste of the delights coming in June!

Music Director and Conductor Jeffrey Jones-Ragona and I request that auditionees *memorize* a song from Gilbert & Sullivan or something similar that will show their voice and range to best advantage. *It is also mandatory to provide a copy of the music for the auditions accompanist. No a cappella auditions will be heard. An accompanist will be provided, but singers will be welcome to bring their own accompanist if they wish.*

If *H.M.S. Pinafore* is not in your library, you can download the libretto from the Gilbert & Sullivan Archive (gsarchive.net), where you will also find additional material, read a plot synopsis, see vintage images, and download audio files. Go to GSOpera (gsopera.com/opera/51/lexicon) for other good information on the work.

H.M.S. Pinafore is filled with roles that are fun to play, and several of them have serious sides—and challenges—too; the work is familiar to many, and thus deserving (as is all of Gilbert & Sullivan) of careful characterization and effective singing and acting. But it will be new to many others, too. *H.M.S. Pinafore* was my own introduction to G&S, and many others have told me the same. The show has probably brought more fans to Gilbert & Sullivan than any of their other works.

THE CHORUS is composed of the men: **The Able Seamen (sailors) serving aboard H.M.S. Pinafore** (14 gentlemen, of various ages, idealized seamen in brilliant white uniforms and occasionally dark blue pea jackets); and the women: **Sir Joseph Porter's sisters, cousins and aunts** (14 females, idealized Victorian maidens of various ages, in Victorian finery and millinery designed for traveling).

Here are brief character sketches, with a nod of gratitude to the writings of William Cox-Ife, Peter Kline, and to a certain W. S. Gilbert*:

The Rt. Hon. SIR JOSEPH PORTER, K.C.B (*First Lord of the Admiralty*) **(Light Baritone)**: "The civilian cross that the Royal Navy has to bear."[1] "The Monarch of the Sea"—but one who's never (no, never!) been to sea. He wants to marry Captain Corcoran's daughter Josephine. Sir Joseph is from humble beginnings, but swaggers about in his Court dress, believing that "A British sailor is any man's equal—excepting mine"[2]—that is, he's a snob and does little to endear Josephine to him. "He is as lacking in a sense of humor as he is in human feeling, and yet he attempts both."[3] But he's very funny, and invariably endears himself to audiences!

CAPTAIN CORCORAN (*Commanding H.M.S. Pinafore*) **(Baritone)**: "The Captain is a genuinely attractive man who loves his daughter, respects his crew, and admires his superiors."[3] He's the ranking officer aboard-ship and hopes to climb socially if he can get his daughter to marry Sir Joseph. A topsy-turvy version of the usual naval commander, he is polite to his crew, and they return the favor. There is, however, in his past a deep secret that only Little Buttercup knows—until the final minutes of the opera when its revelation leads to the inevitable happy conclusion.

RALPH RACKSTRAW (*Able Seaman*) (Tenor): Ralph is a "simple sailor with an amazing, but quite respectable vocabulary."[1] He's in love with Josephine though beneath her in social standing; when she refuses her love, he almost commits suicide by blowing his brains all over the deck, but Josephine reveals her love, and they plot an elopement that very night. This, however, is revealed to the Captain by the dastardly Dick Deadeye, and Ralph is sent to the brig. Buttercup reveals her secret, however, and the two lovers are reunited with "joy [and] rapture unforeseen."[2] (By the way, you're not going to *believe* this, but "Ralph" is pronounced "Rafe" in the opera: it has to be—for Gilbert rhymes it with "waif.")

DICK DEADEYE (*Able Seaman*) (Bass): Although Dick is "able," he suffers from physical shortcomings, including a humped back, a withered arm, and a dead eye. He is "the villain of the piece," and not "a popular character,"[2] as he himself admits. He's "an old, battered, embittered sailor, with a stern conviction of what's right."[1] He betrays Ralph and Josephine's elopement to the Captain. If one listens to what he says he invariably speaks common sense, however cynical—even if it conflicts with our sympathies toward the other characters.

BILL BOBSTAY (*Boatswain's Mate*) (Bass-Baritone): "The Petty Officer *par* excellence."[1] Friend of Ralph and respected by his fellow sailors, and is full of good cheer and *bonhomie*. Has a great solo in Act II: "He is an Englishman!" The Boatswain hangs out with the Carpenter's Mate.

BOB BECKET (Bass-Baritone or Bass): (*Carpenter's Mate*): Friend of Ralph and the other sailors; joins Ralph and the Boatswain for the wonderful trio, "A British tar": "Not very bright, especially when it comes to sightsinging!"[1] He has no solo spoken speeches in dialogue.

TOM TUCKER (*Midshipmite*) (Non-speaking, non-singing): The part is traditionally played by a child (male or female, but appearing to be male) about ten years old. He's an officious little mite, superintending the sailors, and appears at various times throughout the opera. His "real" name was always listed in D'Oyly Carte programs as "Master Fitzaltamont," which was done because printing deadlines preceded his recruitment at local venues. *Our* Middy will have his or her real name in the program!

MARINES (Non-speaking, non-singing): Two military men dressed in scarlet and white uniforms, they add pageantry to Sir Joseph's entrance in Act I, take Rafe to his dungeon cell in Act II, and appear again in the Act II Finale. We seek two volunteers to play these parts, which will involve minimal rehearsal time, though full commitment the week before production and through the nine performances.

JOSEPHINE (*the Captain's Daughter*) **(Soprano):** A beautiful and dutiful daughter who tries valiantly to ignore—even reject—Ralph despite her love for him until his near attempt at suicide leads her to defy her doting (and socially ambitious) father. She's a clever woman, who turns Sir Joseph's assertion that "love levels all ranks"[2] against him, noting that "He little realizes how eloquently he has pleaded his rival's cause!"[2]

HEBE (*Sir Joseph's First Cousin*) **(Mezzo):** Hebe appears at Sir Joseph's right hand and is ready to echo his sentiments, and perhaps even dominate him! Her loyalty pays off at the end when the First Lord realizes that he cannot marry a person of lowly rank and she steps forth and offers to marry him and "soothe and comfort [his] declining days."[2] He buys it— and the social order is maintained. (What marrying his first cousin does to the gene pool is something beyond the scope of comic opera—and perhaps propriety!) Hebe has only two short speeches in dialogue (before the Act II finale).

MRS. CRIPPS (LITTLE BUTTERCUP) (*a Portsmouth Bumboat Woman*) **(Contralto):** That is, she rows a small boat between the ships in the harbor, selling snacks, trinkets, and personal items to the sailors. A "plump and pleasing person,"[2] Little Buttercup has a long history with Ralph and Captain Corcoran, having nursed them "in childhood's happy hour."[2] In fact, she has a hopeless passion for the Captain. When she learns of Ralph's presence aboard the *Pinafore*, she sings, "Remorse! Remorse!"[2] At the end we find out why. She also sings one of the most well-known songs in all Gilbert & Sullivan—right after the opening chorus.

I've said perhaps too often that there's only one G&S activity more fun than seeing one of their operas—and that's actually *working* on one. If you need a little push to encourage you to audition, please consider this it. Jeffrey and I do all we can to make the auditions fun and relaxed.

Please encourage a friend or two to audition so that even *more* can share the delight of Gilbert & Sullivan. Our audiences have been growing, and I suspect we'll have even larger crowds in June than we had for *Princess Ida* last summer!

*References

[1]William Cox-Ife, *How to Sing Both Gilbert and Sullivan*. London: Chappell & Co., Ltd., 1961.

[2]W. S. Gilbert, *The Savoy Operas: I*. London: Oxford University Press, 1962.

[3]Peter Kline, *Gilbert & Sullivan Production*. The Theatre Student Series. New York: Richards Rosen Press, Inc., 1972.

*Pinafore*an Roots in *Bab*

In Act II of *The Yeomen of the Guard*, jester Jack Point tells the dour jailor Wilfred Shadbolt that he will not only teach him his original songs, riddles and paradoxes, but will go farther—and reveal his source! His source is a book, *The Merrie Jestes of Hugh Ambrose*.

This is why a writer decades ago in *The Gilbert & Sullivan Journal* referred to Gilbert's collection of light verse as the librettist's "*Hugh Ambrose*," for Savoyards have for over a century now taken delight in reading these early verses, most of them written in the 1860s, for ideas that W. S. Gilbert "self-plagiarized" into the Savoy operas.

Many of those poems reflect Gilbert's love for the sea (his financial success as a writer enabled him to purchase yachts), and he may have thought that the sea was in his blood, for he claimed (not too seriously) to be descended from Sir Humphrey Gilbert (1539-1583), the half-brother to Sir Walter Raleigh, and an explorer, adventurer, Member of Parliament, a soldier in Queen Elizabeth's army, and pioneer in the colonization of North America.

Whether William Gilbert was descended from Humphrey Gilbert has never been established, but the former Gilbert's relationship to Bab is beyond dispute, for Bab was Gilbert's childhood nickname (short for "babby"). When Gilbert started signing his illustrations for his anonymously published verses with "Bab," they quickly became known as the "Bab Ballads." Most of them were culled from the weekly *Fun*, a penny comic paper (a rival to the twice-as-expensive *Punch*) for publication in book form, first in 1869, then 1874; these two collections were then combined, and to them were added additional ballads along with lyrics from the Savoy operas ("The Songs of a Savoyard"), and since the late nineteenth century, *The Bab Ballads* has never been out of print. In fact any public or academic library worthy of the name has at least one edition—and so should *yours*.

The Bab Ballads were called "Gilbert's *Hugh Ambrose*," as suggested above, because many ideas were taken from them and incorporated into his libretti. And perhaps no libretto has more antecedents in *The Bab Ballads* than does *H.M.S. Pinafore*.

I'd like to refer to but four and suggest what Gilbert adapted from each. Under each title I'll add a link to the ballad online so you can read the entire text for yourself. (Sue would have to add a couple pages to this issue if I were allowed to quote as extensively as I'd like!)

"The Bumboat Woman's Story"
gsarchive.net/bab_ballads/html/bumboat_woman.html

If you are familiar with the music to *Pineapple Poll* (arranged from Sullivan's music by Charles Mackerras), you will know that this ballad formed the plotline for the ballet, originally choreographed by John Cranko for the Sadler's Wells Ballet in London. Read it! It's worth your time! You'll discover that Poll Pineapple, the bumboat woman of the ballad, loved the Captain of *The Hot Cross Bun*, who used to call her "Little Buttercup." (Need I mention that Little Buttercup, a bumboat woman in *H.M.S. Pinafore*, loves the Captain of that ship?)

"Joe Golightly; or, The First Lord's Daughter"
gsarchive.net/bab_ballads/html/joe_golightly.html

Pity poor wretched Joe Golightly! As the subtitle to the ballad suggests, he loves the First Lord of the Admiralty's daughter, who snubs him. He sings a "willow song" because of his unrequited love. Alas, there's no joy and rapture unforeseen at the end of this ballad as there is in *H.M.S. Pinafore*. (Need I mention that Gilbert adjusted the relationships in his opera, and had Joe's counterpart, Ralph Rackstraw, fall in love with the *Captain's* daughter instead of the First Lord's? *And* has the First Lord pick, in *H.M.S. Pinafore*, that same young lady as his matrimonial target?)

"Captain Reece"
gsarchive.net/bab_ballads/html/capt_reece.html

This ballad is perhaps the richest of the four in *Pinafore*an influences. Do read it for yourself—and you'll find a solicitous Captain (even more so than the *Pinafore*'s) who is overly concerned with the comfort and well-being of his crew who serve aboard *The Mantelpiece*—so much so that when Able Seaman William Lee suggests:

> "You have a daughter, CAPTAIN
>   REESE,
> Ten female cousins and a niece,
> A ma, if what I'm told is true,
> Six sisters, and an aunt or two.

> "Now, somehow, sir, it seems to me,
> More friendly-like we all should be
> If you united of 'em to
> Unmarried members of the crew.

> "If you'd ameliorate our life,
> Let each select from them a wife;
> And as for nervous me, old pal,
> Give me your own enchanting gal!"

All this is agreed to—and more. The Boatswain, grateful for the Captain's generosity, has an idea:

> The boatswain of *The Mantelpiece*,
> He blushed and spoke to CAPTAIN REESE:
> "I beg your honour's leave," he said,
> "If you would wish to go and wed,

> "I have a widowed mother who
> Would be the very thing for you—
> She long has loved you from afar,
> She washes for you, CAPTAIN R."

Well, of course the Captain couldn't be more delighted with the suggestion:

"Well, well, the chaplain I will seek,
We'll all be married this day week —
At yonder church upon the hill;
It is my duty, and I will!"

The sisters, cousins, aunts, and niece,
And widowed ma of CAPTAIN REECE,
Attended there as they were bid;
It was their duty, and they did.

(Need I mention that "sisters, cousins, aunts" is a recurring phrase in *H.M.S. Pinafore*—or that a lowly sailor aspires to marry the Captain's daughter—or that Captain Corcoran ends up with the bumboat woman Little Buttercup at the end of the opera?)

One of the delights of *H.M.S. Pinafore*, in addition to all of the pairings of soon-to-be-marrieds at the end, is Little Buttercup's revelation that she switched Corcoran and Ralph Rackstraw in childhood's happy hour when she was young and charming. Each man had been sent belowdecks in disgrace before she confesses, and when the revelation is made, Ralph returns miraculously dressed as the Captain, and the Captain returns dressed as a common sailor. Nobody questions Buttercup but accepts this *volte-face* readily—for it leads to the inevitable happy ending.

Gilbert's idea for this ending may have come from this Bab Ballad:

"General John"
gsarchive.net/bab_ballads/html/general_john.html

The title really *should* be "General John and Private James," for these are the two antagonists, as far apart on the military pecking order as are Captain Corcoran and Ralph Rackstraw.

One day Private James expresses his doubts as to their respective names:

> "A glimmering thought occurs to me
>   (Its source I can't unearth),
> But I've a kind of a notion we
>   Were cruelly changed at birth."

General John accuses Private James of making "a joke of doubtful taste," but then adds:

> "But, being a man of doubtless worth,
>   If you feel certain quite
> That we were probably changed at birth,
>   I'll venture to say you're right."

And Bab Balladeer Gilbert ties up the situation as quickly and as neatly as Librettist Gilbert does in *H.M.S. Pinafore*:

> So GENERAL JOHN as PRIVATE JAMES
>   Fell in, parade upon;
> And PRIVATE JAMES, by change of names,
>   Was MAJOR-GENERAL JOHN.

I do hope that I have whetted some appetites for Gilbert's *Bab Ballads*. There are delights to be found in *all* of them, and anyone who professes to be a Savoyard should give them the attention they deserve. (I often check abe.com, and there always seem to be many, many copies available for less than five dollars. Heartily recommended is my friend James Ellis's scholarly edition, published in paper and hardback by Belknap/Harvard University Press.)

"That Ole *Pinafore* Magic"

My title is in quotation marks because that's what my valued colleague and collaborator Jeffrey Jones-Ragona calls it: that mysterious something that comes over a bunch of people working on this most tuneful and merry of Victorian musicals—and then what happens when it is presented before an audience.

That magic has been much on my mind of late while sitting here in the Gilbert & Sullivan room in Bridgewater and hearing wonderful things from Jeffrey about the incredible sound our cast is making in music rehearsals, about the early record-setting box office advance sales from David Wieckowski, and responding to emails from Bill Hatcher as he attends to countless details while working toward our show in June.

As I write, there are still four days before I fly to Austin (on Sir Arthur Sullivan's birthday, in fact) to start staging rehearsals. I'm looking forward to seeing so many Austinite friends (and I anticipate making new ones) and jumping into the staging of *H.M.S. Pinafore*.

Now I think this will be my sixth—the third in Austin—and I've been asking myself why I'm so excited about another *H.M.S. Pinafore*. Well, working on *any* show in Austin is fun and gratifying. But this one is special.

What makes H.M.S. Pinafore *so special—and magical?*

It's brilliantly constructed. W. S. Gilbert was a master at plot construction, and the show proceeds as easily as a ship might glide through calm waters. A male chorus? Sailors, of course! But what a wonderful inspiration to make the female chorus "an admiring crowd of sisters, cousins, and aunts"! Gilbert unfolds his tale clearly, with musical numbers carrying the plot forward. Note that the motivations for exits and entrances are never forced, and surprises and plot-twists and turns are effectively distributed throughout the two acts.

It's so tuneful. Arthur Sullivan was at his most ebullient in writing the score for this show in 1878—even though (as he told an interviewer much later) he was laboring under excruciating pain during its composition. And he did something in *H.M.S. Pinafore* that he did nowhere else that I can think of: he used multiple reprises—*lots* of them—of catchy musical numbers. I can't imagine *anyone* leaving a performance without "I am the monarch of the sea," "What, never? Well, hardly ever," or "He is an Englishman!" ringing in ears for days after. (*H.M.S. Pinafore* also contains the only entr'acte in all of Gilbert & Sullivan; it features "I'm called Little Buttercup," another all-time catchy tune.)

It's so colorful. Gilbert often uses color subtly in his operas; *H.M.S. Pinafore* opens with the male chorus—all white and blue, spit and polish. Captain Corcoran arrives, resplendent in his uniform, but color doesn't arrive until the ladies do, and they're a feast of pattern and hue in their Victorian bustled smocks. Dazzling!

It's so clever. Those lyrics! The situations! The catchphrases! The climax and the dénouement! Even the title of the ship on which the action takes place!

It's compact. *H.M.S. Pinafore* is one of the earlier Gilbert & Sullivan works, and thus it's one of the shorter ones. And while we can regret that there's not more of it, we can also admire its "trim" nature. (That word is always a compliment when used in seafaring lingo.)

It's a classic. In 1981, when musical-theatre historian Gerald Bordman published a history called *American Operetta*, his subtitle was "From *H.M.S. Pinafore* to *Sweeney Todd.*" Pick up *any* history of *American* musical theatre and there's invariably a satisfying amount of paper and ink devoted to the veddy British Gilbert & Sullivan and *especially* to *H.M.S. Pinafore*; its original production in London and then in New York in 1878 set a new standard for good music, wholesome fun, and cleverness in thought, word, and deed. And like the other Gilbert & Sullivan works, *H.M.S. Pinafore* is as fresh and delightful as it was when presented over a century ago. The secret is to present it as its creators wished, and without updates "for modern tastes," changes for "contemporary sensibilities," or new and "clever" musical arrangements.

Sometimes I think of *H.M.S. Pinafore* rather like a favorite sweater: it's comfortable, familiar, and easy to take for granted. We Savoyards know it so well that many of us can probably recite it from "We sail the ocean blue" to that final grand "Hurray!"

Last summer after leaving Austin, Alice and I visited Wooster and the Ohio Light Opera. I'd purchased tickets well in advance for their final show of the season, *The Gondoliers*, but didn't bother to book the afternoon matinee of Gilbert & Sullivan's not-so-new "nautical comic opera," even though we had planned to arrive in Wooster the day before. The antique shops had more of a draw, I thought, than another *H.M.S. Pinafore*.

Until lunch on the day. I know it was weakness—but the weakness was so strong! The website told me that the matinee was sold out. So I called the box office: "Come to the lobby and get on a list for returns," I was told, and so I did. Five minutes before the show was to begin, I paid for my seat. It was in the very back row, and I think it was a house seat because the Artistic Director Steven Daigle sat next to me for part of the first act.

Then just last month, I saw another production, this one at James Madison University in Harrisonburg, Virginia. Each time—in Ohio and in Virginia—I watched as this venerable ship magically sailed the ocean blue one more time into the hearts of the theatre-goers of all ages who packed the houses. And I feel certain the same phenomenon is about to take place again here in Austin next month.

So call your sisters, cousins, and aunts (and also your brothers, parents, children and grandchildren—and wives and husbands, too!) and make your reservations while there are still tickets to be had. Next month the Worley-Barton Theatre at Brentwood Christian School will be a place of enchantment, filled to the rafters with that ole *Pinafore* magic!

This Saucy Ship's a (Topsy-Turvy) Beauty!

Mike Leigh's 1999 film *Topsy-Turvy* brought to international audiences a realistic, provocative, and justly acclaimed look at the creative process Gilbert & Sullivan used in writing *The Mikado*. At the end of the film, thoughtful cinemaddicts came to appreciate the title, for while Gilbert's sense of fun was often expressed in his works through "topsy-turvydom," ironic inversions were also at the heart of the G&S collaboration itself.

But first and foremost, "topsy-turvydom" was one of W. S. Gilbert's principal comic techniques, and nowhere did he use it more delightfully than in 1878 when he wrote *H.M.S. Pinafore; or, The Lass that Loved a Sailor*.

Gilbert (1836-1911) originally intended to call his ship *H.M.S. Semaphore* (to rhyme with "one cheer more"), but his composer and collaborator Arthur Sullivan (1842-1900) suggested christening the vessel

with the name of a Victorian children's smock. It was the perfect suggestion, showing that Sullivan, too, had a taste for the topsy-turvy. The composer's suggested title appropriately encapsulates Gilbert's tongue-in-cheek look at life aboard an English man-o'-war—so different from reality, song, or story—with a satiric nod at a recent political appointment that turned a businessman into "the First Sea Lord" or "the Ruler of the Queen's Navee."

On board *H.M.S. Pinafore* we find a captain who must accompany his military commands with an "if you please" and who is 180 compass degrees different from Captains Queeg,

Ahab, Bligh, and other seafaring martinets in being genuinely concerned about his crew's well-being. We find Captain Corcoran to be the very model of civility, scrupulously observing the social amenities with his men—to say nothing of checking his salty language in their presence. (Bad language or abuse on *this* ship? No, never!)

Aboard this peaceful man-o'-war we also find a First Lord of the Admiralty who pays official visits "accompanied by the admiring crowd of sisters, cousins, and aunts that attend him wherever he goes." And we learn that, before his appointment, this civilian official (roughly the equivalent to our Secretary of the Navy) had never been to sea—or even seen a ship! (Gilbert was poking fun at the Prime Minister Disraeli's appointment of London businessman W. H. Smith as first Lord of the Admiralty. But, as usual, Gilbert's satire transcends the topical, and we laugh today because political appointments—dare we say it?—are sometimes based on considerations *other* than merit, experience, or even competence.)

Aboard this topsy-turvy vessel we also find a hero in Ralph, a lowly and uneducated tar, talking as if he had studied the classics, and a villain in Dick Deadeye (in the best nautical melodramatic tradition)—but one who is the only character on board (listen to him carefully!) who speaks common sense.

H.M.S. Pinafore glides so effortlessly and tunefully in performance that it's easy to overlook her topsy-turvy subtleties. Only aboard *this* ship would ecstatic lovers, finally united, "murmur forth decorous joy in dreamy roundelays," would a First Lord of the Admiralty proclaim his incompetence to all who will listen in memorable (and amusing) song, and would a contrived dénouement leave a heroine with her true love—but a man who *must* be the same age as her father!

Topsy-turvy, too, was *H.M.S. Pinafore*'s initial reception, for this English masterpiece of nautical engineering proved eminently seaworthy in the United States before doing so at her home port. In her wake, she left a boatload of catchy phrases and tunes, and in America she was also pressed by Yankee entrepreneurs to advertise products ranging from hams to beer, shoes to corned beef, and "magnolia balm" to seeds.

Her international success was the true launching of the Gilbert-and-Sullivan partnership, an enterprise that would enrich the world with ten additional comic operas, lead to the construction of the Savoy Theatre, reform the musical stage, and delight for over a century countless thousands of audiences from church basements to opera houses on *both* sides of the Atlantic with freshness, compelling tunefulness, and innocent merriment.

Perhaps most topsy-turvy of all, shortly after *H.M.S. Pinafore* opened at the Opéra Comique in London in 1878, a reviewer from *The Daily Telegraph* characterized the show as a "frothy production destined soon to subside into nothingness." Well, as Little Buttercup sings, "Things are seldom what they seem"!

Thank you for coming aboard. It has been our mission to present *H.M.S. Pinafore* as Gilbert wanted it staged and as Sullivan wanted it sung and played, leaving in our wake still another series of performances that will affirm the G&S legacy of timeless delight. We also hope to provide happy memories of a pleasant cruise for you passengers who sail the ocean blue with us into that enchanted land Gilbert called "Topsyturvydom." Getting there, we hope, will be all the fun!

To learn more about Gilbert & Sullivan and *H.M.S. Pinafore*,
visit your local library or surf to The Gilbert & Sullivan Archive at:
gsarchive.net
To join SavoyNet, the International Gilbert & Sullivan Bulletin Board,
surf to: savoynet.oakapplepress.com

The Gilbert & Sullivan Society of Austin

The Zoo

Artistic & Stage Director: Ralph MacPhail, Jr. · Music Director: Jeffrey Jones-Ragona

Worley Barton Theater at Brentwood Christian School
Austin, Texas

February 15, 2015

The Zoo

The Story

We meet the chorus (**The British public here you see**) and Æsculapius Carboy, an apothecary who attempts suicide because his love's father doesn't approve of him (**I loved her fondly**). He'd been communicating with Lætitia through prescriptions; he also sent her peppermint, but the label got mixed up with that for her father's prescription (not to be taken internally). As Carboy returns to his noose (**And now let's go back**), Eliza Smith tries to stop his suicide (which wouldn't help her refreshment business). Thomas Brown enters, wooing Eliza. Lætitia then arrives, looking for Æsculapius (**I miss my Æsculapius**), and inquires after him (**Where is he?**). The four lovers then sing a quartet: Lætitia and Carboy express their love (**Once more the face I loved so well**) in counterpoint to Eliza and Thomas's list of the food he's been eating. **Help! Ah! Help!** sings Thomas, and in a splendid operatic parody, everyone sings about Thomas's need of medical aid but nobody moves! Thomas revives (**Ho— guards! Minions!**) and reveals his noble birth. He then attempts a speech (**Ladies and gentlemen!**) to proclaim his love for Eliza, which the crowd interprets (**We gather from what you have said**). Thomas, Lætitia, and Carboy exit, just as Lætitia's irate father, Grinder, appears, asking **Where is my daughter?** Meanwhile, Eliza is assured by everyone that Thomas will return, and all then leave her alone to sing about the innocent (?) little life she's led (**I'm a simple little child**). All reenter (**My father!**), and Grinder again expresses his antipathy toward Carboy, who attempts suicide again by climbing into the bear-pit. Suddenly Thomas Brown returns as his true self, the Duke of Islington (**What do I see in this disguise?**). Eliza, reluctant to leave her beloved zoo animals, is assured by the Duke that he's purchased them all for her. Everyone then realizes that Carboy is in the bear-pit being devoured. But he reappears! We learn that "in consequence of some repairs," "they've moved the bears"! The Duke makes a financial arrangement with Grinder leading the way to a happy ending for Æsculapius and Lætitia. So the chorus was right, earlier on, when they sang that "it will all end pleasantly."

The Story Behind the Story

This "musical folly," with words by "Bolton Rowe" (B. C. Stephenson) was originally staged at the St. James's Theatre, London, in 1875, shortly after the incredible success of Gilbert & Sullivan's *Trial by Jury*. *The Zoo* resembles *Trial by Jury* in several ways: it is through-composed (there is no dialogue), it lasts about 45 minutes—and it was composed by Arthur Sullivan.

It was not, however, produced by Richard D'Oyly Carte, and it closed after a five-week run in mid-1875. After two brief revivals later that year and in 1879, the score, never published, began to gather dust; the published but ephemeral libretto was a rarity; and *The Zoo* became but an interesting and tantalizing footnote to the composer's career—and to the history of "G&S.". . .

Until 1966, when Dr. Terence Rees purchased Sullivan's autograph score at auction, and commissioned a piano reduction. This led to a production in London by an amateur group in 1971.

The work was recorded in 1978 on LP by the D'Oyly Carte Opera Company (though they never presented it onstage), and since then it has entered into the standard "G&S repertory," frequently as a curtain-raiser for a shorter two-act work or combined with other one-acts for a full evening's entertainment. We believe this production to be an Austin première.

The Zoo is a high-spirited comic work with strong parody of melodramatic and grand operatic conventions—conventions that Gilbert & Sullivan were to exploit in several of their earliest works (notably *H.M.S. Pinafore* and *The Pirates of Penzance*).

I'm not the first to suspect that *The Zoo* was hastily written following the overwhelming success of *Trial by Jury* to "cash in on" the success of Sullivan's other "opera." However, while preparing for this production I was reminded of evidence that work had begun on a two-act version of what became *The Zoo* before *Trial by Jury* opened, and it's likely that following the success of *Trial by Jury*, the work was rewritten in the format we know it today—and rushed to the stage.

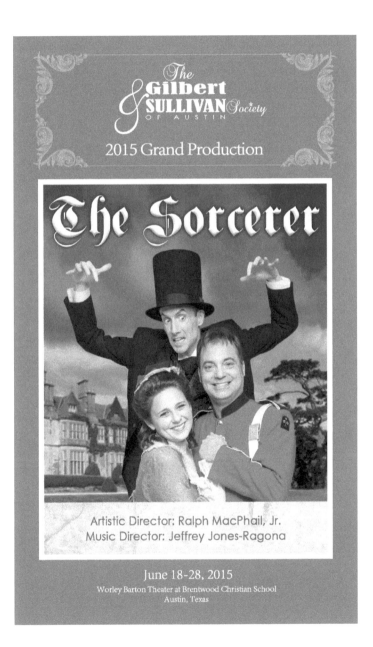

The
Gilbert
&SULLIVAN *Society*
OF AUSTIN

2015 Grand Production

The Sorcerer

Artistic Director: Ralph MacPhail, Jr.
Music Director: Jeffrey Jones-Ragona

June 18-28, 2015
Worley Barton Theater at Brentwood Christian School
Austin, Texas

Looking Ahead to *The Sorcerer*

My title expresses the purpose for this article, but it could also be phrased "Looking Ahead with *The Sorcerer*," for this early Gilbert & Sullivan collaboration might be considered what's sometimes called these days a "seminal" work: one that contains the seeds of something even more creative to come.

The Sorcerer was written for and produced by Richard D'Oyly Carte at the Opéra Comique in London in 1877. It was the third collaboration of William Schwenck Gilbert (who, of course, wrote the words) and Arthur Seymour Sullivan (who composed the music). And as suggested above, *The Sorcerer* was in many ways to provide the foundation on which the subsequent works would be built.

Gilbert & Sullivan first collaborated in December 1871 on what was assumed to be an ephemeral post-Christmas entertainment, the two-act *Thespis; or, The Gods Grown Old*. The man who brought the two together was John Hollingshead, the manager of the Gaiety Theatre, which he had opened almost exactly three years earlier with Gilbert's burlesque of Meyerbeer's opera *Robert le Diable*; Gilbert called it, *Robert the Devil; or The Nun, The Dun, and the Son of a Gun*. *Thespis* was not, as is so often stated, a failure; following a decent run, it closed with the rest of the post-Christmas "pantomime season," and all but forgotten; most of the score was subsequently lost. When Gilbert & Sullivan resumed collaboration, they wanted to do more than write burlesque or pantomime.

But *Thespis* was not forgotten by Richard D'Oyly Carte, who brought the two collaborators together again three and a quarter years later at the Royalty Theatre for *Trial by Jury*, that 40-minute "dramatic cantata" we presented last February. It was not a logical successor of *Thespis*: *Trial by Jury* was through-composed (truly an opera; there is no dialogue), presented in one act, and its comedy was several cuts above what passed for humor with the Gaiety audience.

But if *Trial by Jury* was not a logical outgrowth of *Thespis*, it solidified Richard D'Oyly Carte's determination to present "true English" light opera in London instead of the usual burlesque or extravaganza—or, worse, French operetta imports bowdlerized beyond intelligibility for prim and proper Victorian English audiences.

So Richard D'Oyly Carte raised some money and formed with other investors "The Comedy Opera Company." (Gilbert & Sullivan had insisted they be paid guarantees before starting to work.) The new company's first production was *The Sorcerer*.

In what ways does *The Sorcerer* anticipate subsequent early works? First, it was based on earlier work by Gilbert (in this case, a short-story called "An Elixir of Love" published the previous Christmas; Gilbert had earlier in his career—in 1866—also treated the ages-old "magic love potion" story in another operatic burlesque, *Dulcamara; or The Little Duck and the Great Quack*. This title will bring to opera lovers' minds Donizetti's *L'Elisir d'Amore*, a basis for Gilbert's burlesque).

Gilbert & Sullivan also structured their story around character types that would shortly become prototypes of their subsequent *dramatis personæ*: the soprano-tenor romantic couple (hardly revolutionary), the heavy and light baritones, the bass, the perky soubrette, the aging contralto.

They also engaged for *The Sorcerer*, instead of established opera singers with big names and bigger voices, relatively unknown actor-singers with projectable personalities who could be trained in the Gilbertian style of understated humor.

A glance at the original cast of *The Sorcerer* of 1877 reveals names that would before long become so closely associated with the characters they created that the parts are sometimes even today named after them: George Grossmith (the sorcerer John Wellington Wells), Rutland Barrington (the lovelorn Dr. Daly), and Richard Temple (the aristocratic Sir Marmaduke Pointdextre). (*H.M.S. Pinafore*, which followed *The Sorcerer*, further refined the "formula"—and its English-speaking-world-wide popularity made the collaborators' names household words.)

Sullivan provided a score that is almost universally praised by my music-knowledgeable Savoyard friends, and as I've started listening to the score with more attention in anticipation of next summer's show, I've come to understand why. If Gilbert was still feeling his way in terms of what he could provide his collaborator in terms of lyrics, Sullivan provided a *lovely* score. Following the première, both collaborators came in for their share of praise. Reginald Allen, in his *First Night Gilbert & Sullivan*, quotes a number of press reports reflecting the delight of the scribes and the anticipation that had greeted the opening:

> "Messrs. W. S. Gilbert and Arthur Sullivan have once again combined their efforts with happiest result," was the opinion of the *Times*. "*The Sorcerer*, produced at the Opéra Comique on Saturday night before an audience that crowded the theatre in every part, achieved a genuine success, and moreover, a success in every respect deserved." "The production of the new

opera," added the *Daily News*, "has been for some time looked forward to with much interest. . . . The new work . . . was brought out . . . with a result that fulfilled the most sanguine anticipations."

So we have a lot to look forward to. Yes, it's a "seminal" work, and while we'll be able to appreciate it for its music, humor, pageantry, and more, we'll also be able to appreciate it as the very model of the Gilbert & Sullivan operas to come.

The Source of *The Sorcerer*

E arlier columns have attempted to show Gilbert's indebtedness to Gilbert in writing his libretti, for one of the delights of studying Sir William is discovering his self-plagiarism (self-inspiration?). Even his early reviewers frequently noticed this, and Gilbert himself, late in life, expressed his "indebtedness to the author of the Bab Ballads . . . from whom I have unblushingly cribbed. I can only hope that, like Shakespeare, I may be held to have so far improved upon the original stories as to have justified the thefts that I committed."

The Sorcerer is unique among the Gilbert & Sullivan collaborations in that it was inspired by a Gilbert short story, not by his light verse or one of his earlier dramatic works. I added those "hises" for, of course, the use of "love potions" is centuries-old in stories, plays, and operas, some of which remain well-known today; Shakespeare's *A Midsummer Night's Dream* (1590-96?) and Donizetti's *An Elixir of Love* (1832) are two of the most famous. (As noted in the last issue, *Dulcamara* was a burlesque by Gilbert of *An Elixir of Love.* And Donizetti's opera, incidentally, was an Italian adaptation by Felice Romani of Frenchman Eugène Scribe's libretto, *Le philtre*, set to music in 1831 by Daniel Auber.)

But in 1877, when Gilbert was casting about for an idea for his first full-length collaboration with Arthur Sullivan to be produced by Richard D'Oyly Carte, he went to his own short story, "An Elixir of Love," which had been published in the Christmas issue of *The Graphic* the year before. It's worth your attention, and you can read it at The Internet Archive here: archive.org/details/foggertysfairyot00gilb (note: the 00 before "gilb" are zeroes; the o before the "t" is an oh. The story runs on pages 43-68 in Gilbert's collection, *Foggerty's Fairy and Other Tales*).

Gilbert's method of writing his libretti centered on developing his plots in short-story form, then revising, revising, and (after consultation with Sullivan as to musical situations) revising some more. While "An Elixir of Love" is very similar to *The Sorcerer*, many adjustments were made to convert it to a libretto. In it you will find that the romantic couple in *The Sorcerer* (Alexis Pointdextre and Aline Sangazure) have different names (The Rev. Stanley Gay and Jessie Lightly). J. W. Wells & Co., Family Sorcerers, located in St. Mary Axe in London are "Baylis & Culpepper, magicians, astrologers, and professors of the Black Art" located in St. Martin's Lane. And while romantic mix-ups are similar in both works, the Rev. Mr. Gay loses his love to his bishop, and his love's father, Sir Caractacus Lightly, baronet, ends up marrying the Rev. Gay's cook and housekeeper, Zorah.

It's a delightful read. If you'd like to compare it with *The Sorcerer*, and don't have a copy of the Savoy operas in your nightstand (which you should), surf over to: gsarchive.net/sorcerer/html/index.html.

At the risk of repeating myself, I'll conclude by saying that to *really* appreciate the Gilbert of Gilbert & Sullivan, it's necessary to become acquainted with his earlier works. It will be a delightful experience and will increase your appreciation for his libretti.

Audition Notes on *The Sorcerer*

*T*he Sorcerer (1877) is one of the early Gilbert & Sullivan operas; it was composed between the two shows GSSA produced last year, *Trial by Jury* (1875) and *H.M.S. Pinafore* (1878). It was the first feature-length G&S production of the ambitious impresario Richard D'Oyly Carte, and it proved to London audiences not only the promise of *Trial by Jury*, but also D'Oyly Carte's belief that comic opera written in England by Englishmen on an English subject could be as effective as a French import—if not more so.

As noted in an earlier column, this opera was built on *Trial by Jury*, adding character types that would become standard in subsequent works, and several members of the original cast went on to create roles in the operas that followed.

Set in the rural village of Ploverleigh, it's a charming tale of Sir Marmaduke Pointdextre's son Alexis' betrothal to Lady Sangazure's daughter Aline. Pretty conventional stuff—except that Alexis wants the rest of the world to be as happy as he is, so he engages a London tradesman, John Wellington Wells (of J. W. Wells & Co., Family Sorcerers) to provide a love philtre. This potion, administered in innocent-appearing cups of tea to all in the village, would make the villagers as deliriously happy as he is by falling in love with the first *unmarried* person of the opposite gender they meet. (Mr. Wells's potion is of course, a very *respectable* one.)

And this is where the fun begins: from this innocent (not to say naïve) notion, topsy-turvy reigns as the villagers, under the influence of Wells's elixir, fall in love—but with people out of their own social class. (Think of it as plot strands in *Downton Abbey* a century and a quarter before its time.) *The Sorcerer* is filled with Gilbert's wit, clever and romantic lyrics, and of course the wonderful and tuneful musical situations one expects to find in a Sullivan score.

My purpose below is to provide information for auditionees concerning the auditions and also concerning the characters in *The Sorcerer*. If you're planning to audition, please read this in its entirety. And even if you're *not*, please read it anyway: I hope you will find it interesting—and that it will give you a foretaste of the delights coming in June.

Auditions will be held on Saturday and Sunday, February 21 and 22, in room A-112 on the campus of Brentwood Christian School. Music Director and Conductor Jeffrey Jones-Ragona and I request that auditionees memorize a song from Gilbert & Sullivan or something similar that will show their voice and range to best advantage. *It is also mandatory to provide a copy of the music for the auditions accompanist. No a cappella auditions will be heard. An accompanist will be provided, but singers will be welcome to bring their own accompanist if they wish.*

If *The Sorcerer* is not in your library, you can download the libretto from the Gilbert & Sullivan Archive; call on gsarchive.net/sorcerer/html/index.html, where you will be able to read a plot synopsis, see vintage images, or download audio files. Go to GSOpera (gsopera.com/lexicon/operas) for other good information on the work.

The Sorcerer is filled with roles that are fun to play, and several of them have serious sides—and challenges—too; the work is not as familiar as the two we presented last year, and thus it is deserving (as is all of Gilbert & Sullivan) of careful characterization and effective singing and acting. Gilbert & Sullivan are both on record as saying that when they produced *The Sorcerer* they were looking for good actors who could sing well: Gilbert wanted his words heard and understood and Sullivan, of course, wanted them well sung.

THE CHORUS is composed of the men: **The Male Villagers of Ploverleigh** (14 gentlemen, of various ages, in rather rustic or "service" attire); and the women: **The Female Villagers of Ploverleigh** (14 females, idealized Victorian maidens of various ages, also in rather rustic or "service" attire).

THE PRINCIPALS: Here are brief character sketches, with nods of gratitude to the writings of Harry Benford, Peter Kline—and a certain W. S. Gilbert*:

Sir Marmaduke Pointdextre (*an Elderly Baronet*) (Bass-Baritone): "Pointdextre" is an heraldic term suggesting his "top-of-the-tree" status, as does his rank of Baronet.[1] Kline calls him a "paragon of dignity and ancestral snobbery" and notes that he "sets the tone of the whole opera."[3] He has been in love with Lady Sangazure for years, but has never declared it. Love finds its way, eventually, but not before the philtre makes him fall—for his housekeeper, Zorah Partlet! Gilbert paints him as a generous and hospitable lord of the local manor.

Alexis (*of the Grenadier Guards—his son*) (Tenor): His position in the Grenadier Guards is evidence of his aristocratic status, since such soldiers needed a private income.[1] Kline doesn't mince words: "This is in some respects the most difficult part in the opera. Vocally it is not terribly demanding, and a good strong A is the highest note needed. But the part requires an actor capable of giving charm to a basically unsympathetic character whose lines can be tedious if they are not well handled."[3] *I* see him as so blinded by his love for Aline that he's not aware of his own silliness.

Dr. Daly (*Vicar of Ploverleigh*) (Light Baritone): The clergyman of the local parish.[1] This loveable character has a couple charming songs to sing, and his nostalgic ruminations that his time for love has passed him by are invariably audience-pleasers. "The part requires a warm, light baritone voice with a strong high F-sharp. The most attractive music in the opera is his, and the quality of his singing will tend to set the musical tone of the whole production."[3] (No pressure!) The good doctor is probably slightly past his middle age.

Notary (Bass): As in this country, a Notary (Public) authorizes documents and records the fact that certain persons swear something to be true[1]; Benford also notes that his presence may be Gilbert's "take-off of similar scenes in grand opera, such as *The Barber of Seville* and *Lucia di Lammermoor*."[1] Peter Kline offers a succinct overview of this small but memorable role: "He must be capable of a low E-flat that can be clearly heard. . . . He has no spoken lines, and his part in the first act does little to develop his character, since he merely supervises the signing of the marriage contract." But this part, like Mr. Bunthorne's Solicitor, can be made a memorable part of the show through excellent characterization.

John Wellington Wells (*of J. W. Wells & Co., Family Sorcerers*) (Light Baritone): This "dealer in magic and spells"[2] needs a good singer-actor-comedian to portray him as a magician in the guise of a middle-class tradesman—and a Cockney to boot. George Grossmith created the role, and went on to create Wells's descendants: Sir Joseph Porter, Major-General Stanley, Bunthorne, etc. etc. etc. Our JWW won't perform "magic tricks"—he's not *that* sort of magician! But as the "title character," he carries a lot of weight under his top hat—and is willing to make the ultimate sacrifice to restore the status quo (or *is he???*).

Hercules (*Mr. Wells's Page*) (Male child of ten-ish; speaking role): "This character has three lines, two of which are 'Yes, sir.' If he is a cheerful young boy in a fancy costume who lisps, he should be able to get a laugh."[3]

Lady Sangazure (*a Lady of Ancient Lineage*) (Contralto): Her family name means, of course, "blue blood" (see *Iolanthe*), but her lineage may not be quite as lengthy as Pooh-Bah's (see *The Mikado*). (Her lineage only goes back to Helen of Troy—not a protoplasmal primordial atomic globule.) "This is the first of the aging contraltos that are so often objected to by critics of Gilbert's libretti. Lady Sangazure is a woman of dignity and passion. She has no spoken lines, two duets, and one recitative."[3] And that magic potion she imbibes makes her fall head over ears in love with J. W. Wells himself.

Aline (*her Daughter—betrothed to Alexis*) (Soprano): "Aline is perhaps the most sympathetic of all Gilbert's sopranos. She is, throughout, the victim of Alexis' narrow-mindedness, yet she never complains or wavers in her love for him, strong as her misgivings are."[3] She "has no opportunities for comedy," and "She is perhaps the only character in the opera who maintains the audience's unqualified sympathy throughout."[3] Of course she needs a glorious and clear soprano. (And you'll *never guess* whom she falls for while under the potion's spell!)

Mrs. Partlet (*a Pew Opener*) (Mezzo-Soprano): Her name, according to Benford (citing the *OED*) is "A word used as the proper name of any hen, often *Dame Partlet*; also applied like 'hen' to a woman."[1] (Benford also notes that "a pew-opener was an impoverished parishioner who was allowed to gather tips by escorting the well-heeled worshipers to their family pews and holding the pew doors open for their benefit."[1] "The role is confined to one scene in each act, but Mrs. Partlet is the focal point of interest much of the time she is onstage. . . . Like Lady Sangazure, she is an aging woman, but she should contrast with her as much as possible in style and manners. . . . She is warm and loving, and in her attempts to marry off her daughter she reminds one a little of one of Jane Austen's characters." She also appears in the finales, of course. It's a *wonderful* character role.

Constance (*her Daughter*) (Mezzo-Soprano): Constance "has some good comic business in the second act with the Notary. . . . She is young, pretty, and lovesick. Her melancholy shyness contrasts strongly with Mrs. Partlet's down-to-earth aggressiveness, and one feels that she is completely dependent on her mother."[3] *Actually*, she has some good comic business in the first act with Dr. Daly, too!

I've said perhaps too often that there's only one G&S activity more fun than seeing one of their operas—and that's actually *working* on one. Jeffrey and I do all we can to make the auditions fun and relaxed.

If you have questions, contact me at RafeMacPhail@ Yahoo.com.

*References

[1]Harry Benford, *The Gilbert and Sullivan Lexicon*, 3rd ed. (Houston: Queensbury, 1999) and online at www.GSOpera.com/lexicon.

[2]W. S. Gilbert, *The Savoy Operas: I* (London: Oxford University Press, 1962.

[3]Peter Kline, *Gilbert & Sullivan Production* (The Theatre Student Series) (New York: Richards Rosen Press, Inc., 1972).

*The "Two" Sorcerer*s

R eaders of this column, like all students of Gilbert & Sullivan, know that an interesting aspect of Savoy Opera scholarship is studying the changes made in the libretti before and after the opening nights. We treasure early material that didn't make it, for one reason or another, to the opening night version, and we delight in noting how the libretti were changed following their premières. We value Gilbert's various drafts and enjoy learning (or perhaps interpreting for ourselves) the reasons for the changes.

Readers of this column will also know that changes after opening usually entailed the deletion of songs (or parts of songs). Rarely were lyrics actually *changed*, for adjustments were usually made to condense the work. A notable exception is *Ruddigore* for which the ending dialogue and finale of Act II were changed, and years after the deaths of the collaborators, the D'Oyly Carte Opera Company deleted verses and entire numbers and condensed and further changed the finale.

But possibly none of the works was changed as radically by Gilbert & Sullivan themselves as was *The Sorcerer*. When the work opened at the Opéra Comique on November 17, 1877, the action, set in front of the *"Exterior of* SIR MARMADUKE'*s Elizabethan Mansion,"* proceeded as we know it today—until the very end of Act I, when almost everyone had sipped the love-philtre-spiked tea. But while they *"struggle[d] against its effects"* they did not *"fall insensible on the stage"* as the libretto now has it; they *"resume[d] the Brindisi with a violent effort"* and sang:

> Eat, drink, and be gay,
>> Banish all worry and sorrow—
> Laugh gaily to-day—
>> Weep, if you're sorry, to-morrow.
> Come, pass the cup round—
>> We will go bail for the liquor;
> It's strong, I'll be bound,
>> For it was brewed by the vicar!
> None so cunning as he
>> At brewing a jorum of tea.
>> Ha! ha!
>> At brewing a jorum of tea!

And the curtain descended on Act I.

Act II in the first version took place in the Market Place in the Village of Ploverleigh. The first stage direction is *"Enter* PEASANTS *dancing, coupled two and two, an old man with a young girl, then an old woman with a young man, then other ill-assorted couples."* This chorus then sang:

> Happy are we in our loving frivolity,
> Happy and jolly as people of quality;
> Love is the source of all joy to humanity,
> Money, position, and rank are a vanity.
> Year after year we've been waiting and tarrying,
> Without ever dreaming of loving and marrying.
> Though we've been hitherto deaf, dumb, and blind to it,
> It's pleasant enough when you've made up your mind to it.

The youthful Constance then entered with the ancient Notary, and she sang her "Dear friends, take pity on my lot" aria. She solicited pity because of her new elixir-induced mismatch, and the story unfolded as we know it.

Why the change seven years later? When *The Sorcerer* was revived in 1884, following the relative failure of *Princess Ida* and while Gilbert & Sullivan were at work on *The Mikado*, I think that both collaborators saw the weakness in the end of Act I of their early work and were determined to improve it.

And they did. The audience on October 11, 1884, were left at the end of Act I with the company (except for Alexis, Aline, and the Sorcerer, John Wellington Wells himself), insensible on the stage. Act II takes place exactly where Act I transpires: at the *"Exterior of* SIR MARMADUKE'S *Mansion"*—but in that most romantic of scenic effects, *"by moonlight."* Wells, Alexis, and Aline enter with lanterns, inspecting the sleeping chorus, but leave when the sorcerer sings:

> But soft—they waken one by one—
> The spell has worked—the deed is done!
> I would suggest that we retire
> While Love, the Housemaid, lights her kitchen fire!

They do, and she does—and the Villagers (they are not referred to as "Peasants" in the revised version) sing as they fall in love with one another and they dance; only after all that does Constance enter with the Notary, and all proceeds as it had seven years earlier.

Why is the 1884 version an improvement over the 1877 one? There are probably as many answers to that as there are people analyzing the question. Here are *mine*:

> The revised ending of Act I is more dramatic and builds more suspense with virtually everyone unconscious on the ground as a result of drinking the "spiked" tea instead of remaining on their feet and struggling against the drug's effects.
>
> There is more unity to the story with both acts taking place in front of Sir Marmaduke's Elizabethan mansion (and one set was more economical as well).
>
> The new beginning of Act II "by moonlight" is a very picturesque scene, and the entrance of Wells, Alexis, and Aline with lanterns builds suspense.
>
> The new Act II builds in comic intensity when the chorus awakens and find themselves ill-matched but proclaiming their love for one another (in an enthusiastic chorus sung in dialect), and then indulging in a vigorous "country dance," none of which happens in the earlier version.

All of this provides a fine prelude to the increasingly ludicrous mis-matches of the principals that follow, building to the final resolution.

The revision left some inconsistencies. How long does it take for the philtre to work? In 1877 it took a half-hour, and it didn't affect consciousness; but by 1884, this had been expanded to 12 hours, and of course the imbibers lose consciousness within minutes—by the end of the act. But why, in the revised version, doesn't Aline lose consciousness when she finally drinks the philtre toward the end of Act II? And why didn't Gilbert tidy up his details in the libretto?

There's an unbounded field of speculation on which I could discourse for hours!

Communicating through *The Sorcerer*

The Gilbert & Sullivan Society of Austin is in the business of entertaining audiences. This is perhaps a self-evident truth, along with another that says that entertainment may be but one of the goals of a theatrical production; others might include teaching, persuading, or even provoking an audience into action.

But rather than explore these various goals, it occurred to me that whatever is accomplished through theatrical performance can only happen through *communication*, and that virtually all of the decisions Jeffrey, Bill, and I and our friends and colleagues on the artistic staff have been and will be making in preparation for *The Sorcerer* relate to that "C word."

Gilbert's primary vehicle of communicating is of course the written word. Through his lyrics and dialogue, skillful actors, under reasonable direction, communicate much: emotions, thoughts and ideas, and relationships to name but several. In his libretto for *The Sorcerer,* diction (in terms of not only clarity but also effectiveness of the spoken word) tells us much about the characters, and allows us (for instance) to distinguish between the social levels of the lord of the manor Sir Marmaduke Pointdextre, the lowly Mrs. Partlet, and the tradesman-sorcerer John Wellington Wells. In Act II, Gilbert even writes a chorus lyric in dialect, a rarity in his libretti. Generational differences are amusingly sketched when Alexis and Aline's rapturous greeting of one another is contrasted with their parents' Victorian reserve.

In addition to dialogue and lyrics, Gilbert uses stage directions to communicate with those who would interpret his ideas. The fact is that there are remarkably *few* stage directions in the Savoy operas, which leaves many choices to those who would bring their stories to life. Some directors, myself included, like to recreate Gilbert's world of over a century ago, but with a contemporary sensibility for pacing, stage pictures and movement, and technology. (The miracle is, of course, that Gilbert's words need *not* be changed to communicate a highly entertaining show, and the operas can be presented as written and then sparkle and delight as they did over one hundred years ago. And I don't deny that imaginative directors have successfully adapted these classic works in "many various ways," such as gender-switched *Trials by Jury, Star Trek Pinafore*s, all-male *Iolanthe*s, and English-seaside-resort or corporate American *Mikado*s, often without changing words.)

The stage directions in *The Sorcerer* specify a "Country Dance" in Act II, which tells us something about the Villagers of Ploverleigh, their status, and their relationship to Sir Marmaduke who is hosting the wedding celebrations on his lawn for his son and soon-to-be daughter-in-law.

Gilbert's stage directions also are valuable to scenic, lighting, and costume designers, all of whom are also in the communication business. We have production meetings in order that we all understand just *what it is* that we seek to communicate through the production. (One of the delights of working with this group is the cooperative nature of the entire production staff in realizing shared visions for the final shows.) Gilbert specifies that Sir Marmaduke lives in an *Elizabethan* Mansion, that "Twelve hours are supposed to elapse between Acts I and II," and that Act II takes place at Midnight; these specifications are valued guidance for setting and lighting designers.

The plot itself is a primary inspiration for costumers, for Gilbert is remarkably silent regarding costumes; however, costumers are also researchers, and with the given that the action takes place at the time of the first performance (1877) in rural England, the plot makes clear the social differences of the various characters—from rustic villagers to a middle-class London tradesman to the quartet of aristocrats. These relationships, especially when the principals become "mixed-up" because of the love philtre in Act II, are most clearly communicated by costume (and reinforced, of course, by what is said and done by those wearing them).

Music is also a great communicator, of course, and can sometimes communicate more quickly than words or what is seen. Sullivan more than "knew his stuff" and was always looking for opportunities in the operas for music to step to the forefront in communicating to audiences. The composer was more than adept at using music to characterize: compare the "two sides" of the Marmaduke/Sangazure duet, for instance; and note the differences between the sorcerer's "spiel," the romantic soli of Alexis and Aline, and the chorus at the end of Act I as the love philtre starts to take effect and the denizens of Ploverleigh are about to fall senseless.

I reflect on all of this as I sit in my study in Bridgewater, staging notebook "completed," and anticipating returning to Austin to meet the cast, which will already "know the score" and are as anxious as I am to put the show on its feet. Putting it on its feet is good, but what we'll all be striving to do is to put it in the heads and hearts of our audiences.

And we'll all do it by communicating.

With Heart and with Voice Let Us Welcome this Mating!

T he words above are sung twice by choruses in Act I of *The Sorcerer*, first by the ladies and then by the gentlemen. These villagers are heralding the union of Alexis Pointdextre and Aline Sangazure, two young aristocrats in a little English village called Ploverleigh. *She* believes that "true love, faithfully given and faithfully returned" is "the source of every earthly joy," and *he* believes that "in marriage alone is to be found the panacea of every ill." This charming comic opera tells a romantic story based on these idealistic attitudes, tempered with a teapotful of magical elixir, a teaspoonful of irony, and more than a tea-chest full of musical delights.

But rather than discuss the plot, which will unfold in due course, let us focus on why we who love Gilbert & Sullivan are grateful for *The Sorcerer*. The main reason we are grateful is the "mating" it solidified, a mating that would lead to nearly a dozen additional works for the lyric stage, most of which attained and retain more popularity than *The Sorcerer* but none of which, perhaps, would have been possible without it.

Gilbert & Sullivan had collaborated on stage works twice before the 1877 première of *The Sorcerer*. *Thespis; or, The Gods Grown Old* was produced in 1871 by John Hollingshead as little more than a post-Christmas entertainment. It was Richard D'Oyly Carte who brought the two men together for *Trial by Jury* in 1875. This one-act "afterpiece" for

Offenbach's *La Périchole* quickly eclipsed the French import, and convinced D'Oyly Carte that his ambition of presenting *English* comic opera written and composed by *Englishmen* using *English* themes could succeed.

So he formed a partnership with several other investors and launched the Comedy Opera Company, paid librettist W. S. Gilbert and composer Arthur Sullivan the advance they demanded, and then gave these creative geniuses their lead, supporting them as their producer. *The Sorcerer* was the result.

Gilbert (as he often did, especially early in the collaboration) went back to an earlier work, in this case a longish short-story called "An Elixir of Love" which had been published in the Christmas number of the *Graphic* the year before. Sullivan provided his many felicities in word-setting, choral writing, and orchestration. And D'Oyly Carte provided money and artistic freedom. Paramount to this freedom (in addition to the librettist's and composer's freedom to create) was the casting of the production, most notably, perhaps, the casting of three men who would go on to create so many memorable characters in subsequent works that their roles are often, even today, designated with their names.

The first was George Grossmith, who portrayed the sorcerer himself, John Wellington Wells. His later roles included Sir Joseph Porter, Major-General Stanley, Reginald Bunthorne, The Lord Chancellor, King Gama, Ko-Ko, Robin Oakapple/Sir Ruthven Murgatroyd, and Jack Point.

The second was Rutland Barrington, who played Dr. Daly, the wistful Vicar of Ploverleigh. Subsequent "Barrington parts" include Captain Corcoran, the Sergeant of Police, Archibald Grosvenor, the Earl of Mountararat, King Hildebrand, Pooh-Bah, Sir Despard Murgatroyd, and Giuseppe Palmieri. (Gilbert must have relished devising roles contrasting the diminutive and agile Grossmith and the tall and lumbering Barrington.)

The third was Richard Temple, courtly Sir Marmaduke Pointdextre in *The Sorcerer*. His subsequent roles were Dick Deadeye, the Pirate King, Colonel Calverley, Arac, the Mikado of Japan, Sir Roderic Murgatroyd, and Sergeant Meryll.

Success begat success, and *The Sorcerer* was duly followed by *H.M.S. Pinafore*. The resulting and international "*Pinafore* mania" not only set the partnership on firm footing, but led, "by a set of curious chances," Richard D'Oyly Carte to take total control of the Comedy Opera Company, which came to bear his name, and with Gilbert and Sullivan to sire a string of theatrical blockbusters. The D'Oyly Carte Opera Company would long outlive the triumvirate, but will always be known as the remarkable theatrical enterprise it was, touring year after year (for 48 weeks each year), presenting Gilbert & Sullivan in the style its creators fostered. When it folded in 1982, due to the escalating costs of touring so many productions week in and week out, it left the works as the theatrical classics they had become, to be interpreted anew—sometimes wildly so—but still available to companies such as ours whose mission it is to present the Gilbert & Sullivan operas in the D'Oyly Carte tradition: combining sensitive interpretations of the original words and music in a context Gilbert called the "grave and quasi-respectful treatment of the ludicrous."

So let us, with heart and with voice, be grateful for the mating of Gilbert & Sullivan in 1877 and their creation of *The Sorcerer*. Like all dramatic works, this comic opera has a beginning, a middle, and an end; but one could also say that *The Sorcerer* was only a beginning.

To learn more about Gilbert & Sullivan and *The Sorcerer*, visit your local library or surf to **The Gilbert & Sullivan Archive** at:
gsarchive.net
To see the online edition of **Harry Benford's *Gilbert & Sullivan Lexicon*** and other material of interest, surf to:
GSOpera.com/lexicon
To join **SavoyNet**, the International Gilbert & Sullivan Bulletin Board, surf to
savoynet.oakapple.press.com

The Gilbert & Sullivan Society of Austin

presents

VERY TRULY YOURS,
Gilbert & Sullivan

Artistic & Stage Director: Ralph MacPhail, Jr.

Music Director: Jeffrey Jones-Ragona

First Presbyterian Church

Austin, Texas

February 21, 2016

A New Play on an Old Subject

*V*ery *Truly Yours, Gilbert & Sullivan* is the third in our series of "mid-season special productions"; it follows Gilbert & Sullivan's *Trial by Jury* (2014) and Sullivan & Rowe's *The Zoo* (2015). These "chamber" productions are a natural outgrowth of our long-standing custom of offering frequent "musicales" to the public, and they have multiple goals—sharing our love for Gilbert & Sullivan, learning more about their careers and collaboration, and providing our singer-actors additional opportunities to perform, thus offering their talents and delighting our members—all during the "down time" between our annual June "grand" productions.

Unlike our first two special productions, each of which was first produced in 1875, *Very Truly Yours* is a new play—but on an old subject. Like the other two, all of the music was composed by Arthur Sullivan. Like *Trial by Jury*, all of the lyrics were written by W. S. Gilbert. The play was written by Gayden Wren with a big assist from the surviving correspondence, diaries, reviews, reminiscences, and other verbal material for the spoken word, which he ingeniously combined with musical delights from the 14 collaborations of Gilbert & Sullivan (plus one of the several songs written by the team but not for the stage).

This "old subject" was needing this new play. Gayden Wren has written that too often the story of the Gilbert-Sullivan collaboration is defined in popular understanding by their quarrels; and while there is no denying their several quarrels had important influences on their joint work, there's also no denying that these two geniuses, working together more harmoniously than not over a span of a quarter-century, produced a body of work for the light lyrical stage that has never been equaled.

Many of the selections are among Gilbert & Sullivan's most popular, and we expect these will be so well-known by many that our audience will be singing along *in their minds*. We also hope that the lesser-known selections will prompt, for some, memories of our recent productions past. And we hope that there will be unfamiliar selections to remind many that there are still delights to be discovered in "G'n'S."

Finally, a word about the words between the musical selections: most of them are from Gilbert and Sullivan themselves, with others by their friends and associates—and their critics. It is through these words that many will probably meet a Gilbert and a Sullivan they've not known through performances of their works. You will meet them as businessmen, as artists, and as friends with mutual admiration and, yes, at times when they were not so friendly. We hope that you will learn to know them as you've never known them before.

Gilbert & Sullivan Austin

presents

COX and BOX

Artistic & Stage Director: Ralph MacPhail, Jr.

Music Director: Jeffrey Jones-Ragona

Worley Barton Theater at Brentwood Christian School

Austin, Texas

March 4 and 5, 2017

Cox and Box: Another Austin Première!

*C*ox and Box was Arthur Sullivan's first comic opera. It was also the first Sullivan comic opera I ever directed. And our production in March will, I believe, be the first production in Austin of this little musical, nonsensical gem.

Its history is more complex and interesting that those of Sullivan's other comic operas. It all began when Sullivan was five years old: in 1847, when John Maddison Morton's "screaming farce" (as Victorian critics called them) *Box and Cox* opened at the Lyceum Theatre in London. It was based, as were so many British farces, on a couple of French plays, but it was distinctly English in its tone and subject matter.

Set in a rented room in Mrs. Bouncer's house, the action centers around Mrs. B's wily renting of the same room to two men: Box, a printer who works all night "setting up long leaders for a daily paper" and Cox, a hatter who works, of course, during the day. By a sly switching around of each man's personal belongings as they travel to and fro' work, Mrs. Bouncer gets "double rent for [her] room, and neither of [her] lodgers is any the wiser for it."

We, of course, meet this trio just before a moment of crisis. Cox prepares and goes to work, Box comes home to cook his breakfast and retire, and just after he does so—Cox reappears, having been given the day off!

This leads to chaos, recriminations, accusations—and revelations. The two learn that both had been engaged to one Penelope Ann Wiggins, and each had broken off his engagement and fled. One had even faked suicide to escape! Each man tries to foist Penelope Ann on the other, and their arguments lead to the threat of a duel. Mrs. Bouncer can't find her pistols, but she finds that she has a letter she forgot to deliver the day before.

This letter brings the news that Penelope Ann perished in a boating accident and left her estate "to her intended husband." *Well*, as you might expect, both Cox and Box mourn the loss of their "intended" as they claim the right to her fortune—until a second letter arrives explaining that the lady was rescued and would be coming that morning to claim her intended husband. More panic, especially when we hear her arrive downstairs.

But she doesn't appear; only Mrs. Bouncer does, with still another letter explaining that Penelope Ann intends to marry—Mr. Knox!

Rejoicing from both Box and Cox—and then a startling discovery: they are long-lost brothers! And they determine to remain in their snug little room for as long as Mrs. Bouncer welcomes them.

"Nonsense, perhaps" (as Lady Jane says), "but oh, what precious nonsense!" And the play literally became one of the most frequently-produced farces of the Victorian era—and beyond. The venerable dramatic publishers Samuel French in New York keep it in print to this day.

But how did *Box and Cox* become *Cox and Box*? It happened in 1866 and "The Moray Minstrels" were responsible. This was a group of artistic and literary men—bohemians who met regularly and entertained one another with recitations, songs, and other performances. They met at Moray Lodge in Kensington, the home of one of the members. Frank C. Burnand, who would later become a long-time editor of the English humor magazine *Punch*, came up with the idea of adapting the play into a libretto for a one-act comic opera, reversed the names in the title, and enlisted his friend Arthur Sullivan to write the music and accompany the performance.

Since the Moray Minstrels was an all-male club, Burnand changed Mrs. Bouncer into Sergeant Bouncer, and gave him a stirring martial lyric which included the refrain "Rataplan" so beloved by opera composers. (The word is onomatopoetic for the sound of a snare drum.) Sullivan ran with this (it recurs throughout the piece) and also composed solos, duets, and trios to Burnand's libretto—the most amusing, perhaps, being the lullaby that Box sings to his bacon as it fries on the grid in his fireplace!

It was a hit—and soon it was revived at a charity matinee, for which Sullivan composed an overture—and an orchestration for the entire work. (He had accompanied the original production at Moray Lodge on a harmonium.)

Two years later, *Cox and Box* had a long professional run at the Royal Gallery of Illustration, and it was in this theatre one fateful day that

Arthur Sullivan first met W. S. Gilbert.

Countless performances of both the play and comic opera were given in the years that followed, and the 65-minute work was cut down to serve as a curtain raiser for a production of one of Sullivan's non-Gilbert comic operas at the Savoy in the 1890s: *The Chieftain*, with a libretto by F. C. Burnand.

Then in the 1920s, another abbreviation was made, the "Savoy Edition," for the D'Oyly Carte Opera Company to serve as a curtain raiser for one of the shorter Gilbert & Sullivan works, the only other one in their repertory being the sturdy *Trial by Jury*.

The "Savoy Edition," which runs about 35 minutes, eliminates the middle letter from Penelope Ann, a duet for Cox and Box, a verse here, and makes other nips and tucks there, and it toured with the D'Oyly Carte until the 1960s or so when economics forced its removal from the repertoire. (The company recorded the work twice.)

For me, working on *Cox and Box* in Austin completes a circle. I directed the full-length version in 1972 as a part of my Master of Fine Arts thesis production (along with Gilbert's Shakespearean burlesque *Rosencrantz and Guildenstern*). I directed it again during my early years at Bridgewater College. And I'm really looking forward to our production of the full work in March. Jeffrey Jones-Ragona will be music director, Jeanne Sasaki will accompany, Bill Hatcher will produce, and Ann Marie Gordon will provide the set.

I think just listing the cast gives some idea of the fun we're going to have on March 4th and March 5th:

Cox...............………......Julius Young
Box......................….…Andy Fleming
Bouncer.......….......…..David Fontenot

So put Saturday evening, March 4th, and Sunday afternoon, March 5th, on your calendar and join us for this tuneful, colorful, and highly entertaining work. Rataplan!

Must Have a Beginning, You Know!

*C*ox and Box* was written within a decade of Sullivan's return as a young man from musical studies in Germany and several years before he met W. S. Gilbert. It's only one act long (lasting a little over an hour), but it is filled with the sorts of delights he would bring to his collaboration with Gilbert: a rousing march, mock-operatic pyrotechnics, and super-silliness all the more amusing when sung with a straight face.

Perhaps its most important influence was on the composer himself. During his decades-long career, he aspired to write in higher spheres, notably oratorio and grand opera. Posterity has, however, affirmed his true calling, which was evident in 1866 when he composed his first comic opera, *Cox and Box*.

At the end of his career, after the artistic success but limited run of his grand opera *Ivanhoe* and the waning popularity of a handful of oratorios that he hoped would be his enduring contributions to English music, he sighed, "A cobbler should stick to his last."

I've always found this a profoundly sad statement, for "cobbler" today suggests something "thrown together," and his light-operatic scores are anything but. Musical historians have affirmed that Sullivan lavished all of his considerable talent on his lighter works, and contemporary musical scholarship is beginning to give him his due.

A few words about Sullivan's two collaborators on *Cox and Box*: The basis for the work was John Maddison Morton's 1847 farce called *Box and Cox: A Romance of Real Life*. Morton was famous for his farces (he was probably Victorian England's most successful farceur), and this one was his greatest hit.

In 1866, Francis C. Burnand had the happy idea of turning *Box and Cox* into a one-act comic-opera, and his young composer friend Sullivan was enthusiastic. The original production was a "one-off" performance in a private home, Moray Lodge, by and for a club of bohemians. Burnand reversed the title and gave his adaptation a new subtitle which gave away the ending, and, since the Moray Minstrels was an all-male club, he changed Morton's landlady, Mrs. Bouncer, into Sergeant Bouncer. Burnand wrote lyrics for the work, but most of the dialogue and overall structure of the piece remained Morton's.

Posterity has not been as kind to Morton and Burnand as it's been to Sullivan. *Box and Cox* is still in print, but none of his other plays are. Burnand wrote a large number of burlesques, extravaganzas, and adaptations for the stage, published books of humor and reminiscence, and even served for years as the editor of *Punch*, the famous English humor magazine. But his dramatic and literary output is all but unknown today. *Cox and Box*, Sullivan's first comic opera, is Morton's and Burnand's sole enduring theatrical legacy.

Gilbert & Sullivan Austin is pleased to be presenting this early gem, another example of a nineteenth-century theatrical work appearing fresh as a proverbial daisy with the ebullient and engaging music of Sir Arthur Sullivan.

❖

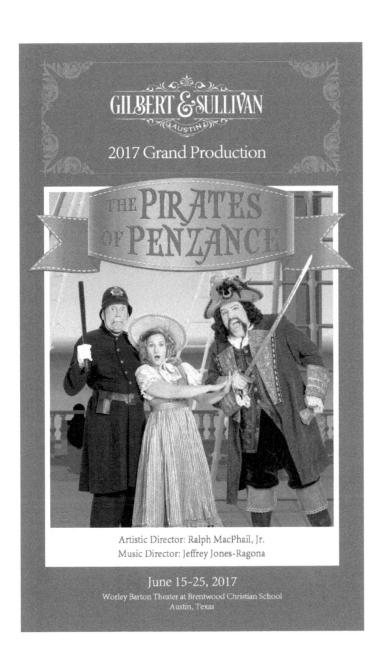

GILBERT & SULLIVAN

AUSTIN

2017 Grand Production

THE PIRATES OF PENZANCE

Artistic Director: Ralph MacPhail, Jr.
Music Director: Jeffrey Jones-Ragona

June 15–25, 2017

Worley Barton Theater at Brentwood Christian School
Austin, Texas

Why I Love *The Pirates of Penzance*: It's *Personal!*

I'm often asked, "Which is your favorite Gilbert & Sullivan opera?" I sometimes paraphrase the great Savoyard Martyn Green and say, "The one I'm working on now—unless it's the one I'll be working on next."

But truth-to-tell, when I started directing in Austin in 1998, I had four favorites, and even though I'd spent a lot of time researching *The Mikado*, if anyone really pinned me down, I'd have admitted that *The Pirates of Penzance* was at (or near!) the top of my list.

Since then, I've had the opportunities to direct, in Austin, quite a few of the other operas for the first time, and now the question becomes even harder to answer truthfully.

But equally truthfully, I think that *The Pirates of Penzance* is still at (or near!) the top of my list. Here's why:

The first music I ever heard from Gilbert & Sullivan was, as I recall, "A policeman's lot is not a happy one," sung by my father. As a young émigré from Glasgow, he sang in *The Pirates of Penzance* at Flint (Michigan) High School. (He was also booted out of a production of *Ruddigore* for giggling in his Act II picture frame, but that's another story.)

In 1966, the D'Oyly Carte Opera Company came to the National Theatre in Washington, D.C., and that week I saw three of the five operas they were touring. (Alice and I subsequently saw the other two in New York.) The very first was *The Pirates of Penzance* on the Monday night of the week's run, and I bought my dad a ticket and thus have the happy memory of sharing this life-changing experience with him. (And it was life-changing. That week was to set the direction for a significant part of my life.)

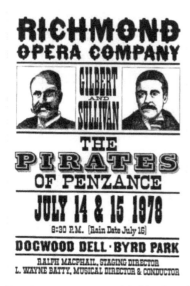

The Pirates of Penzance was the first Savoy opera I directed with professional singers—for the Richmond (Virginia) Opera Company in 1978. In preparing for this production I discovered that there are only seven dialogue sequences in this show—and one of those is very short. And the music! Much as I loved its predecessor, *H.M.S. Pinafore*, I discovered what Sullivan meant when he wrote to his mother from New York in 1879, ". . . it is exquisitely funny, and the music is strikingly tuneful and catching. It's more humorous and operatic, too." Elsewhere the composer noted that the musical situations were more highly developed than in *H.M.S. Pinafore*.

Subsequently, I've directed seven additional productions of the opera—more than any other—and have never tired of it. And I've often pictured my father seated in a celestial loge seat taking them all in, Tarantara-ing away.

My son Alexander appeared as Major-General Stanley at Bridgewater College (wearing his new optician-ground-to-his-prescription monocle!), and one of my happiest Gilbert and Sullivan memories is of the dress-rehearsal when he appeared on the rocks in Act I, resplendent in his red tunic and plumed headgear,

snapped off a salute, and sang, "Yes, yes, I am a Major-General!"

Back in 2004 Alice and I stopped by New York City on the way to Ivoryton, Connecticut, to teach an elderhostel course on *The Pirates of*

Penzance. "This is a perfect time to cross something off my bucket-list," thought I. So we hopped in a cab and headed to East 20th Street, very near Teddy Roosevelt's birthplace. It didn't take us long to find the plaque on a building that reads, "On this site, Sir Arthur Sullivan composed 'The Pirates of

Penzance' during 1879." (More about the circumstances of writing the show in The Big Apple in a future column.)

Just two days before I'm writing this, I was invited to Eastern Mennonite (High) School in Harrisonburg, Virginia, to talk with the participants in a production of *The Pirates of Penzance* to be presented in October. The Mennonites have a reputation for strong choral singing, and I can't wait to see (and hear) their show.

And finally, and on a very personal note, my father died just days after Alice and I moved to Bridgewater in 1972 so that I could begin teaching and directing at our alma mater. Subsequently, while going through my father's papers, I found two small photographs: one of a skirted pirate and another of an English Bobby. They're clearly of my father, and were probably taken in his school-yard about 1930.

They are now on the first page of the first volume of my Gilbert & Sullivan scrapbooks.

Audition Notes on *The Pirates of Penzance*

*T*he Pirates of Penzance* (1879) is one of the early Gilbert & Sullivan operas and one of their most consistently popular works; it
was composed following the international success of *H.M.S. Pinafore* in 1878. Produced in the United States and in England by the collaborators' impresario Richard D'Oyly Carte, with Gilbert providing stage
direction and Sullivan the musical direction, it proved to audiences on both
sides of the pond that the popular successes of *Trial by Jury*, *The Sorcerer*,
and *H.M.S. Pinafore* were not flukes. It was also further confirmation of
D'Oyly Carte's belief that comic opera written in England by Englishmen
on an English subject could be as effective as a French import—if not more
so.

The Pirates of Penzance* also solidified the team's evolution of the
various character types and topsy-turvy plotting that would continue to be
more-or-less standard (with clever variations) in subsequent works. Set on
the coast of Cornwall and at the ruins of a nearby chapel, it's a hilarious
tale of tender-hearted pirates, timorous policemen, and a bevy of beautiful
Victorian maidens and their father, "the very model of a modern Major-
General."

"Tender-hearted" pirates and "timorous" policemen suggests
Gilbert's sense of topsy-turvydom, and this notably Gilbertian point-of-
view is carried further into his main theme, which is suggested by the
subtitle for the piece, "The Slave of Duty." Only in Gilbert would we meet
a conscientious pirate apprentice (*pirates* taking *apprentices*?) who puts
duty above all, even if it means he must exterminate his tutors once
released from his indentures on his twenty-first birthday.

No need to go into detail here, perhaps, for most Savoyards are
familiar with where this premise leads. But if you're not, I promise that
the richly deserved popularity of the work is based on an incredibly
wonderful score supporting Gilbert's witty, romantic, and at times
dazzling lyrics; hilarious situations, colorful sets and costumes, and a
timelessly amusing story told by memorable characters.

My purpose below is to provide information for performers
concerning the auditions and also concerning the characters in *The Pirates
of Penzance*. If you're planning to audition, please read this in its entirety.
And even if you're *not*, please read it anyway: I hope you will find it
interesting—and that it will give you a foretaste of the delights coming in
June.

Auditions will be held on Saturday and Sunday, February 25 and
26. The Gilbert & Sullivan Archive has additional material at
gsarchive.net, where you may read a plot synopsis, see vintage images, or

download audio files. Go to GSOpera (gsopera.com/opera/62/ lexicon) for other good information on the work.

    The Pirates of Penzance is filled with roles that are fun to play and sing, and several of them have serious sides—and challenges—too; much of the delight of the work is in its frequent send-ups of "grand" operatics. In addition, the lower voices in the male chorus have the additional fun of being Pirates in Act I and Policemen in Act II.

    THE CHORUS is composed of the men collectively known as **The Pirates of Penzance** (14 gentlemen, of various ages, dressed as their calling suggests). At the end we learn they are of noble birth, which may explain why they prefer sherry to rum in the opening chorus and have such tender hearts toward orphans; in Act II, those with lower voices don British policeman's uniforms to become rather reluctant "**Bobbies**" whose lot is not a happy one—especially at the end, when they become the only males onstage (except for the Major-General) to end up without a lady. The ladies of the chorus are **The Daughters of Major-General Stanley** (14 females, idealized Victorian maidens in lovely hooped skirts, augmented with shawls in Act II and changing into dressing-gowns at the end). They know how to enjoy themselves on an outing, are sympathetic to Mabel and her new love, are loyal to their father—and end up happily ever after, for they're about to be "parsonified," a Gilbertian term for "conjugally matrimonified"!

    THE PRINCIPALS: Here are brief character sketches, with a nod of gratitude to the writings of William Cox-Ife, W. S. Gilbert, and Peter Kline*:

    Major-General Stanley (Light Baritone): Traditionally a short, wiry military man, with a military precision in a number of challenging "patter" lyrics, including one of G&S's signature songs. He has a chance for more lyricism in "Sighing softly to the river" at the end of Act II (and to perform some mock-ballet steps). He can tell a "terrible story" to save his life (and his daughters from a fate worse than death), but experience remorse. Like Sir Joseph Porter in *H.M.S. Pinafore*, the Major-General is a character who seems for many to personify Gilbert & Sullivan Opera. He is "somewhat a phenomenon as a family man, with his large brood of daughters, all more or less of the same age."[1]

    The Pirate King (Heavy Baritone): This larger-than-life buccaneer seems to have stepped directly from a Victorian "penny-plain/tuppenny-colored" toy theatre. A bloodthirsty pirate and an orphan, he is a tough character to deal with, until he comes face-to-face with another orphan, and his contrast with Major-General Stanley couldn't be stronger. As with a number of Gilbert's "villains," he's topsy-turvily likeable, one reason being, perhaps, that he is of noble birth, something we don't learn until the end.

Samuel, *his Lieutenant* (Baritone) is the Pirate King's right-hand man whose success onstage is dependent on creating a memorable personality, one infused with good-will. He occasionally leads the chorus with solos, has some early dialogue, gets to distribute burglarious tools while singing about them in Act II, and often has his own vocal line in ensembles.

Frederic, *the Pirate Apprentice* (Tenor): One of the most challenging and gratifying tenor roles in G&S, Frederic is on stage a huge percentage of the time with many singing and acting opportunities ranging from mock-operatic to tender-romantic. He is "the slave of duty" of the subtitle of the piece, and is buffeted between loyalty to the pirates and his abhorrence to their calling. Reared by the middle-aged Ruth among the pirates, he feels an affectionate loyalty toward her until he encounters "a bevy of beautiful maidens," and suddenly learns the truth of the expression that "a lad of twenty-one usually looks for a wife of seventeen."[2]

Sergeant of Police (Bass): As Peter Kline notes, "Although he is onstage for only seventeen minutes, the Sergeant is truly unforgettable."[3] He is the center of two highlights in the second act: the memorable "When the foeman bares his steel" (with encores!) and his famous big solo lamenting that "a policeman's lot is not a happy one." Perhaps his appeal is universal, for he understands that "work must be done" and acknowledges that loyalty to the hierarchy transcends workplace malaise. He puts on a brave front: "Though in body and in mind, we are timidly inclined. . . . Yet when the danger's near, we manage to appear as insensible to fear as anybody here."[2]

Mabel, *General Stanley's Daughter* (Coloratura Soprano): Again from Peter Kline: "Mabel has little chance to establish her character in the spoken dialogue, and consequently must do most of it in the singing. Here she has an excellent opportunity, provided she has a voice that combines coloratura agility with dramatic bravado."[3] Her signature aria is, of course, "Poor wandering one," but there are also opportunities for romantic duets with Frederic (to whom she is attracted at least as much as he is to her) and various other mock-operatic solos.

Edith, *General Stanley's Daughter* (Soprano): "Down-to-earth and somewhat hedonistic,"[3] Edith has important solos in the opening number for the girls and in "When the foeman bares his steel." As for her "hedonism," she suggests that she and her sisters "Make the most of fleeting leisure" and then offers the shocking suggestion that they all "take off [their] shoes and stockings and paddle!"[2] (This is before the men show up, of *course*.)

Kate, *General Stanley's Daughter* (Mezzo-Soprano): "Kate is more the romantic. She admires the countryside and idealizes it. She has only one short solo"[3] (it's in the girls' opening chorus). If the solos are short, she has dominant positions in the traditional staging and frequently has her own vocal line in ensembles.

Isabel, *General Stanley's Daughter*: Isabel has no solo singing and two lines of dialogue. The traditional staging gives her more prominence than the solo opportunities of the part suggest, so she must be a good actress. Her lines suggest that she is empathetic and has a good imagination.

Ruth, *a Piratical Maid of all Work* (Contralto): Ruth is 47 years of age, ancient compared to the other women in the cast. She loves her "pirate apprentice," but realizes, as soon Frederic catches sight of the Major-General's daughters, that all is "Lost! lost! lost!"[2] Her Act I duet with Frederic has real tragic proportions, and her appeal to him at the end of the act is unacknowledged. By Act II, she has reestablished her status with the pirates, proves to be "a good sport," and even helps the pirates in their attempt to bring Frederic back to the band and subsequently attack the castle. And while there is no place in the libretto or score to indicate it, she ends up with a husband after all. (He is *not* the Major-General!)

I've said perhaps too often in these pages that there's only one G&S activity more fun than seeing one of their operas—and that's actually *working* on one. If you need a little push to encourage you to audition, please consider this it. Jeffrey and I do all we can to make the auditions fun and relaxed.

Please sign up for an audition slot today, and then please encourage a friend or two to audition so that even more can share the delight of Gilbert & Sullivan. Our audiences have continued to grow in recent years, and *The Pirates of Penzance* always draws record or near-record houses. Do plan to be a part of the fun.

*References

[1] William Cox-Ife, *How to Sing Both Gilbert and Sullivan* (London: Chappell & Co. Ltd., 1961).

[2] W. S. Gilbert, *The Savoy Operas: I* (London: Oxford University Press, 1962).

[3] Peter Kline, *Gilbert & Sullivan Production* (The Theatre Student Series) (New York: Richards Rosen Press, Inc., 1972).

Fighting Piracy with *The Pirates*

*T*he Pirates of Penzance premièred at the Fifth Avenue Theatre in
New York on New Year's Eve 1879. It was directed by Gilbert and
Sullivan themselves—but the London première would not come
until April of the following year.

The reasons for this unique première are two: the lack of an
international copyright agreement at the time and the phenomenal success
of *H.M.S. Pinafore* in America in 1878-79. This combination led to
literally hundreds (if not *thousands*) of productions of *H.M.S. Pinafore*
presented in this country in venues ranging from church basements to
opera houses—all without a dollar being returned to the Englishmen
across the pond. "It's not that I miss the money," Gilbert snorted. "It upsets
my digestion."

Gilbert, Sullivan, D'Oyly Carte, music director Alfred Cellier, and
valued members of their *Pinafore* company in London sailed to New York
in early November of 1879. The given reason was that they wanted
Americans to know what the authentic *H.M.S. Pinafore* was like—with
Gilbert's stage direction and Sullivan's orchestration. If there was an
ocean between London and the United States, there was an ocean of
differences between the original production running merrily in London at
the Opéra Comique and the countless pirated productions in the U.S.,
cobbled together from libretti and vocal scores imported and then
published without authorization (but quite legally).

Anyone who's performed in a Gilbert & Sullivan production
knows that Gilbert's published libretti are rather threadbare regarding
stage directions, and yet the fun of traditional production is knowing the
"whys and wherefores" that the author/stage director originally provided.
(Former GSA Executive Director Robert Mellin calls this "knowing where
the diamonds are buried.") So while anybody could present an *H.M.S.
Pinafore*, virtually nobody in this country knew the little bits of staging,
the quirky dances, the interpolations to the published "script," and perhaps
most important, the Gilbert dictum that "All humour, so-called, is based
upon a grave and quasi-respectful treatment of the ludicrous." And of
course when one of these productions used an orchestra, their arrangement
was that of pirate orchestrator, *not* that of Arthur Sullivan.

So in many of the productions that proliferated here in the late
1870s there were "improvements" that would have turned Gilbert's and
Sullivan's (and D'Oyly Carte's) hair grey—songs were interpolated, and
men played Little Buttercup to name but two. *H.M.S. Pinafore* was
translated into Pennsylvania "Dutch." It was, legally, in the public domain,
so anybody could twist and adapt the original and present it with impunity.

If Gilbert called the work "only burlesque of the lowest possible kind," he was being ironic. *H.M.S. Pinafore* is certainly in many ways burlesque, but not of the lowest possible kind. In fact, Gilbert's stagecraft, revolutionary for its time, is what insured the success of his work with Sullivan, who of course brought his own considerable talents to the collaboration with his lyric-setting and masterful orchestrating.

But the Triumvirate had another and secret mission to accomplish when they came to America in 1879: to present the first performances of their new work, and thus to secure the American copyright. (A "scratch" and imperfect performance was given in Paignton, Devon, several days earlier by actors from one of D'Oyly Carte's touring *Pinafore* companies to secure the English copyright. The lore tells us that the chorus men wore their *Pinafore* costumes with bandanas tied around their heads to suggest pirates! And of course they were using early materials left behind by the creators, who continued writing and refining their work in New York.)

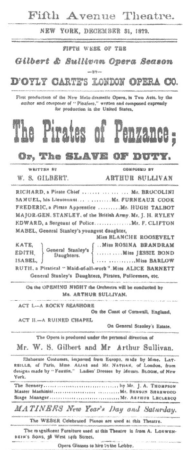

So as the "authorized" *H.M.S. Pinafore* ran at night (it opened on December 1), Gilbert & Sullivan were completing the creation of and rehearsing their new opera, which came to be known as *The Pirates of Penzance; or, Love and Duty*. It was, of course, a success, and if it did not become the rage on the magnitude of *H.M.S. Pinafore*, this was probably because the vocal score was not published until the London première in April in order to protect it from the American pirates.

Gilbert & Sullivan pulled off another remarkable coup during their busy stay: they rehearsed and sent out on tour *four complete companies* of *The Pirates of Penzance* in an attempt to reap their rewards before their work could be pirated; these companies covered the nation literally from coast to coast, performing the work "more than 550 times in more than 100 cities within the first seven months of 1880," according to Reginald Allen (in *Gilbert & Sullivan in America*).

There are some interesting things to be learned by studying the version of the show first presented in New York and on tour (and the program reproduced on the previous page). For instance, the original subtitle for the show, *Love and Duty*, was changed to *The Slave of Duty* by the time it opened in New York. Two characters had forenames that disappeared by the time of the London première. "Richard, The Pirate Chief," became "The Pirate King," his name having vanished. (Maybe this was because the part was originally played in London by Richard Temple?) And the timid Sergeant of Police whose "lot is not a happy one" was known as "Edward" in the playbills in New York and on tour, but his name was missing in London—and has been ever since.

There were differences in the libretto as well, one of the most interesting being the reprise of the Major-General's famous patter-song in the Act II finale. (To learn more, find a copy of Reginald Allen's wonderful *First Night Gilbert and Sullivan*.)

Gilbert & Sullivan did not again take America by storm until 1885 when *The Mikado* became a success from sea to shining sea. This work even led a few steps further toward the achievement of an international copyright agreement (D'Oyly Carte's name is found frequently in court records), but not in time to protect the majority of Gilbert & Sullivan's works in this country from falling into the public domain.

If *The Pirates of Penzance* did not duplicate the overwhelming success of *H.M.S. Pinafore*, it has certainly found its way to the top or near the top of most fans' lists of favorites. The D'Oyly Carte Opera Company as well as Gilbert & Sullivan Austin and countless other production groups have certainly found that "piracy pays"!

A Pass Examination on
The Pirates of Penzance

This exam (unlike those I had the great pleasure of administering when I was teaching at Bridgewater College) is designed to be fun to take. It will never be turned in or graded. It's actually designed to impart knowledge, rather than test it. (I'm anxious to acknowledge my debt to Ken Levine's "Put Yourself to the Test" test, which appeared in the June '87 issue of *Reader's Digest*. Mr. Levine's test has nothing to do with Gilbert & Sullivan, but its format has been adapted to what follows.)

1 In the Gilbert & Sullivan collaboration, which came first?
        Words   Go to 12
        Music   Go to 6

2 Although Sullivan often made *suggestions* for the plotting of the operas, the plots invariably *originated* with Gilbert. Skip to Question 8 for another question.

3 No, "Talk Like a Pirate Day" came along decades after Frederic turned 21 (in 1940). Please go back to Question 8 to continue with this arduous examination.

4 No, Bridget (later Dame Bridget) D'Oyly Carte was the granddaughter of the original producer. Slip back down to Question 10 and make another selection. (HINT: He was Bridget's grandfather, and his name starts with an R.)

5 With whom did the plots originate?
        Sullivan   Go to 2
        Gilbert   Go to 9

6 This is not the answer you should have picked because, well, er, um, it's, well, incorrect. Slip back to Question 1 (it'll be our secret), and start over again.

7 That's correct: Richard D'Oyly Carte united Gilbert & Sullivan for *Trial by Jury* in 1875, and over the next twenty-one years, the duo wrote twelve additional comic operas, most of which continue to be performed frequently today. These three men are frequently referred to as The Triumvirate. Go to Question 19 for a question about the one G&S opera that Richard D'Oyly Carte did not produce.

8 In *The Pirates of Penzance*, Frederic was born on:
        February 29th   Go to 11
        Talk Like a Pirate Day   Go to 3

9 Kee-rekt. Although Sullivan offered *suggestions*, the plots always *originated* with Gilbert, who often adapted ideas from his Bab Ballads, short stories, or plays. Now go back to Question 8 for a choice two-choice question.

10 The Gilbert & Sullivan Operas were produced for over one hundred years by the D'Oyly Carte Opera Company. Which D'Oyly Carte was the original producer?

Bridget	Go to 4
Richard	Go to 7
Rupert	Go to 14

11 Right! The fact that Frederic only has a "real" birthday every four years is a major plot development in Act II. Continue now with Question 10, another question about names.

12 What a wonderful way to begin this test. You're right: with the exception of a frustrating bit of early work on the Finale to *Utopia Limited*, the words always came before the music in the Gilbert & Sullivan collaboration. Now head to Question 5 for another question about the working habits of the collaborators.

13 *Thespis* was produced by John Hollingshead at the Gaiety Theatre in London on December 26, 1871. *Trial by Jury* was originally presented at the Royalty Theatre (1875), and *The Sorcerer* (1877), *H.M.S. Pinafore* (1878), *The Pirates of Penzance* (1880), and *Patience* (1881) all had their London premières at the Opéra Comique. But we've yet to mention the most important theatre of all. See Question sweet 16.

14 No, Rupert D'Oyly Carte was the son of the original producer. Go back to Question 10 to decide whether his parent was Bridget or Richard.

15 No, actually *Love and Duty* was "working subtitle," but it was changed before the New York première. That leaves just one answer—the other one you'll find at Question 18.

16 In 1881, Richard D'Oyly Carte moved *Patience* to a new theatre he built exclusively for the production of Gilbert & Sullivan operas. He called it

The Sorcerer	Go to 21
The Savvy	Go to 26
The Savoy	Go to 29

17 Well, *The Gods Grown Old* is actually the subtitle. But you're close, so go ahead to question 16. (Or you can go to Question 13 for more fascinating information on *Thespis* and other theatres where early Gilbert & Sullivan productions were originally performed.)

18 The sub-title of *The Pirates of Penzance* is:
      The Slave of Duty.   Go to 20
      Love and Duty.   Go to 15

19 What is the name of the Gilbert & Sullivan opera that was not produced by Richard D'Oyly Carte?
      The Gods Grown Old   Go to 17
      Thespis   Go to 13

20 Absolutely! And if Frederic, the slave of duty himself, were writing this exam, I am sure he would suggest that you trudge along to Question 30.

21 Oops! Actually, *The Sorcerer* is the name of the first full-length comic opera by G&S produced by Richard D'Oyly Carte. Go back to Question 16 and guess again at the name of the theatre that D'Oyly Carte built. (Hint: the first three letters are "Sav.")

22 No, it is Sir Joseph Porter in *H.M.S. Pinafore* who does this. Now that we have that important point straightened out, please go back to Question 30.

23 Right! He knows a lot of other arcane stuff, too—but little about tactics, gunnery, and other military matters. Now that we've clarified that important point, please head for Question 31.

24 Well, Ruth's not too happy in Act I after being spurned by Frederic, but this famous phrase is not associated with her. It's the Sergeant of Police who makes this lament. Are you ready to finish? Whether your answer is Yes or No, please go to Question 27.

25 The best Gilbert & Sullivan Opera? Why the one you think is best, of course! But in June in Austin, there'll be no question: it will be *The Pirates of Penzance*! See you at the Worley Barton Theatre! With best wishes,

26 Ah! You fell for my trick question (or didn't read the question carefully). Richard D'Oyly Carte had a lot of savvy to get G&S together—and keep them together—but that was not the name of the theatre he built for production of their works. It's close. Go back to Question 16 and try, try again.

27 Congratulations at arriving a Good Old Question 27. Whether your route to this point was short or a little longer, I hope that you found taking this "exam" was fun and that in enlarged your knowledge of Gilbert & Sullivan and of our grand production. Here is just one more question—an age-old one that Savoyards have been wrestling it for years: Which is the *best* Gilbert & Sullivan opera? You'll find the answer at Number 25.

28 You're right! The lament of the Sergeant of Police is one of the most frequently quoted expressions in all of Gilbert & Sullivan. Have you had enough? Whether your answer is Yes of No, kindly go to Question 27.

29 You're right as right can be. In fact, all of the Gilbert & Sullivan works are frequently called the Savoy operas, and the people who act in them are called Savoyards, a designation often adopted by enthusiasts like us. The Savoy Theatre is recognized in theatrical annals as the first theatre in the world to be lighted entirely by electricity. D'Oyly Carte also made innovations designed to make attendance more pleasant; for instance, he abolished gratuities to ushers and instituted a queue system for those interested in unreserved seating. Now go to Question 18. You're getting close to the end!

30 In *The Pirates of Penzance*, does Major-General Stanley sing that he:
        "polished up the handle of the big front door"?
        Go to 22
        "knows the scientific names of beings animalculous"?
        Go to 23

31 Whose lot, in *The Pirates of Penzance*, "is not a happy one"?
        The Sergeant of Police's   Go to 28
        Ruth, a Piratical Maid of all Work's   Go to 24

Gilbert and Sullivan: The Very Model of a Merry Musical Partnership

*T*he *Pirates of Penzance* premièred at the Fifth Avenue Theatre in New York on December 31, 1879. Producer Richard D'Oyly Carte planned an American première to outwit the theatrical "pirates" who had produced *H.M.S. Pinafore* without paying royalties to the creators. In an attempt to keep the rights to *The Pirates of Penzance*, W. S. Gilbert, Arthur Sullivan, and D'Oyly Carte sailed to New York to complete and then stage the work; they kept the music unpublished, and then launched four touring companies, rehearsed by librettist Gilbert and composer Sullivan. The London production did not open until April 1880.

Following the New York opening, the critic from *The Sun* reflected on whether the new work was successful—and if it was as good as *H.M.S. Pinafore*:

> Both of these inquires we should be inclined to answer affirmatively. Its success with the audience was instantaneous.
>
> The performance was constantly stopped by the laughter and applause. . . . As for a comparison with "that infernal nonsense *Pinafore*," . . . Gilbert's share of the present work is even brighter than in the former opera. . . . As for Mr. Sullivan, he has evidently spared no pains to prevent himself from falling behind his previous reputation, and has given to *The Pirates of Penzance* a more elaborate and carefully written score, and a broader and more scholarly treatment, than he brought to the composition of the *Pinafore*.

The Pirates of Penzance has established itself as one of the favorites of Gilbert & Sullivan's comic operas, and also as one of the favorite works on the English lyric stage. In July 1980 Joseph Papp presented Wilfred Leach's "Broadway musical" version in the Delacorte Theater in Central Park, then transferred it to two Broadway theatres and sent it out on tours. With pop stars in the leads, synthesizers replacing violins, and a high-energy chorus, it was a radical departure from "traditional G&S," but it did not replace one hundred years of performance tradition. Gilbert, who staged his own works, enhanced them with by-play, interpolations, and stage business that are irresistible—and which enhance the dramatic situations and underscore their humor. It has been our goal to stage this work as Gilbert intended and to sing and play the score as Sullivan wanted it performed.

What's made it possible for pirate apprentice Frederic to spend over a century celebrating his birthday before delighted audiences in countless productions? The answer, I believe, lies in two words: *Gilbert* and *Sullivan*.

Although William S. Gilbert took great delight in poking fun at Victorian pretense and humbug, his shafts are as familiar in the twenty-first century as they were in the late-nineteenth. To cite just two examples, consider a major-general who knows everything about "matters vegetable, animal, and mineral"—but nothing whatever about tactics, gunnery or strategy. He's living proof of the "Peter Principle," having reached his level of incompetence. Then there are Mabel and Frederic who vow to be faithful to their pledge of love 'til they are wed—and (shocking for Victorians to mention it) *even* (not *ever*) after.

Many expressions that are parts of our language came from Gilbert's pen: "The flowers that bloom in the spring," "To let the punishment fit the crime," "I've got a little list" (all from *The Mikado*) and "What, never? No, never! What, never? Well, hardly ever!" (from *H.M.S. Pinafore*) are familiar to us all. *The Pirates of Penzance* gave us an expression that has been used countless times: "A policeman's lot is not a happy one." And since the show's opening, people from all walks of life have been characterized as "the very model of" their professions—words borrowed from the Major-General's patter-song in Act I.

If we enjoy recognizing such expressions in their original contexts, we also enjoy hearing familiar musical themes. American audiences almost invariably chuckle soon after the orchestra begins the overture to *The Pirates of Penzance*: during the first run in 1880, the Act II Pirates' Chorus—the tune of which is used early in the overture—was appropriated by American college students and given new lyrics. We're all familiar with "Hail, Hail! The gang's all here!" (That Sullivan may have been mocking the "Anvil" chorus from Verdi's *Il Trovatore* is an added bonus for music lovers.)

Gilbert's libretto contains only seven dialogue sequences; this gave Sullivan scope to burlesque grand opera—and he did, with choruses, melodramatic recitatives, separation duets, ensembles, and arias that give singers chances for "operantics"—and the jokes are not lost on audiences.

Contemporary critics often say that Sullivan's music neutralizes the acid of Gilbert's satire and makes it more palatable. After all, if we read the libretto of *The Pirates of Penzance*, we find the writer mocking Victorian melodrama and respectability by purchase, calling policemen cowards and military officers dishonest and otherwise unfit to hold their commissions, and (oh, horror!) implying that married people do not always remain faithful. Add Sullivan's music to Gilbert's words, and the songs turn into good-natured fun.

Or consider the irony near the end of Act I. No doubt Gilbert had his tongue stuck firmly in his mutton-chopped cheek when he had the pirates ("rough men who lead rough lives") seize General Stanley's daughters and announce they'll "quickly be parsonified, conjugally matrimonified, by a doctor of divinity, who resides in this vicinity." No "fate worse than death" for *these* young ladies!

Perhaps, then, the enduring and endearing appeal of *The Pirates of Penzance* is to be found in *three* words: the name of the librettist, the name of the composer, and the conjunction that united them and made them Gilbert *and* Sullivan.

Gilbert & Sullivan Austin

presents

Trial By Jury

Artistic & Stage Director: Ralph MacPhail, Jr.

Music Director: Jeffrey Jones-Ragona

Worley Barton Theater at Brentwood Christian School

Austin, Texas

March 3 and 4, 2018

Richard D'Oyly Carte:
He Had a Dream

S everal weeks ago, I visited my favorite thrift store. It's run by Mennonites in Harrisonburg, Virginia, it's lovely to visit, and when I shop there I usually add a CD or two to my audio opera library for a dollar or two.

During that recent visit, I found some real treasures (to me): five CD reissues of original cast recordings of "Golden Age" American musicals (from the '40s and '50s), including a couple by Rodgers and Hammerstein.

I have never been a great fan of these shows, preferring the brittle irony and wit of Gilbert and those I think of as his sophisticated successors (Gershwin, Hart, Porter) to the sometimes (to me) soggy sentimentality of R&H.

Years ago I read or heard an interview with either Richard Rodgers or Oscar Hammerstein II; he admitted that he and his partner had been accused of excessive sentimentality, but he noted that they worked in the formula they knew best and found most congenial. What he didn't say (nor did he have to!) is just how successful that formula had been.

So in my old age, I've come to acknowledge the great and deserved success and stage worthiness of these shows, and the delight they've brought countless people over generations (though I'm still waiting to hear of my first R&H society).

Listening to my new if used CD of *South Pacific* reminded me of another strength of these musicals: they usually contain a rather hard-hitting, philosophical lyric quite different from the others. *South Pacific* has a biting song against racism ("You've Got to Be Carefully Taught"), but the lyric that captured my attention is sung by "Bloody Mary," originally conceived as a Tonkinese (Vietnamese) woman, though in performance she often comes across as a Pacific Islander.

The Bloody Mary lyric that caught my attention was "Happy Talk," which includes this:

> "You've got to have a dream—
> If you don't have a dream—
> How you gonna have a dream come true?"

. . . and I was reminded of two things: in February of 2013, Bill and Nan Hatcher and I attended the Georgetown Palace production of *South Pacific* where we saw award-winning GSA soprano and director Michelle Haché in her wonderful characterization of Bloody Mary.

Second, it gave me the genesis for this article about our mid-season show, *Trial by Jury.* You see, that ground-breaking dramatic work grew out of a young man's dream.

His name was Richard D'Oyly Carte, and in the early 1870s, he was a concert manager and operatic impresario. He produced Offenbach's operetta, *La Périchole,* translated into English of course, and he needed a short work to round out the evening's entertainment.

D'Oyly Carte's dream was to continue producing operettas, but rather than bowdlerized versions of imports from scandalous France, he wanted to produce new works by English librettists and English composers based on English subjects that were appropriate for his audience.

A happy circumstance brought him into contact with William S. Gilbert, a young dramatic author who'd also made a name for himself as a writer of light verse. Several years before, he had expanded a one-page contribution to the humor weekly *Fun* called "Trial by Jury" into a libretto for a one-one act opera, but the project, due to the death of the leading soprano, was pigeonholed. Gilbert suggested this to Carte, who loved the idea and sent Gilbert to see Arthur Sullivan.

The name was more than a familiar one to Gilbert, who had reviewed the composer's first comic opera, *Cox and Box,* in 1867, and even collaborated with him four years later—on *Thespis; or, The Gods Grown Old.* Designed as a short-running, post-

Christmas entertainment during the pantomime season, *Thespis* had a decent run, but it was under-rehearsed. Also mitigating against the future,

Gilbert had to tailor his plot and characters to the abilities and "shticks" of the resident company at John Hollingshead's Gaiety Theatre, and Sullivan had to tailor his score to the, um, limited vocal resources of this band of audience-favorites.

So *Thespis* didn't lead to future collaboration, and Gilbert and Sullivan went their separate ways . . . until Richard D'Oyly Carte's dream brought them together again. Clearly the collaborators shared their producer's dream. Gilbert's libretto for *Trial by Jury* was as English as it could be. The plot centers on a "breach of promise" trial in those days when a man extricating himself from a promise of marriage could be sued by the jilted lady. It's set in an English court of law. It concerns English people. And Sullivan seldom if ever wrote anything but the most English-sounding music.

Gilbert's dream was to be a successful dramatist, to rise above his journeyman days of setting lyrics to pre-existing tunes in his operatic burlesques; to be able to stage his own works, select his own players, imbuing them with his theory of comic acting, and setting those works and costuming them in ways that reinforced his creative vision.

Sullivan had a dream, too. The historians and biographers tell us that he wanted to make a living as a composer, and while he set his sights higher than comic opera (on oratorio, on opera), he came to realize that his strength lay in the works with Gilbert—works that came to support his rather lavish life style.

So three dreams came together for the March 25, 1875 première of *Trial by Jury* at the Royalty Theatre in London. The one-act "dramatic cantata" (as the creators styled it, for it is "through-composed"—an opera, in fact) came to eclipse *La Périchole*, and then enter the standard repertory of the English lyric theatre where it has remained to the present day. (I often recall with pleasure the enthusiasm with which our two performances were received by Austin audiences three years ago—and how much fun we had working on it.)

Perhaps, most important, that first production of *Trial by Jury* was the first step toward making Richard D'Oyly Carte's dream come true. It also reinforced Gilbert's dream of putting his theories of comedy and stage production to work. Since it led to an even dozen further works, all produced by Richard D'Oyly Carte and most of them profitable hits, Sullivan's financial dream was also to come true, a delightful result shared by all three collaborators.

So maybe Oscar Hammerstein's lyric is more than just "happy talk": if you don't have a dream, how are you going to make that dream come true?

❖

Trial by Jury

*T**rial by Jury** premièred on March 25, 1875, at the Royalty Theatre
in London. It was the first Gilbert & Sullivan opera produced by
Richard D'Oyly Carte and is the only one-act work the duo wrote,
although they had written others with other collaborators. It is also their
only through-composed work—a true opera (without dialogue)—although
they called it a "dramatic cantata."

SCENE FROM "TRIAL BY JURY," AT THE ROYALTY THEATRE.

It is a cliché but no exaggeration to say that *Trial by Jury* took
London by storm, affirming D'Oyly Carte's feeling that English comic
opera could be more successful than the usual musical theatre of the age
which was frequently composed of adaptations of French works (with all
of the French sexiness excised). (*Trial by Jury* was, in fact, originally presented as an afterpiece for a production of Offenbach's *La Périchole*.)

In 1877, D'Oyly Carte launched his own company devoted to
English comic opera, and over the next two decades produced another
dozen works from Gilbert & Sullivan, all of which continue to hold the
stage with countless productions each year by groups such as ours. Pay
careful attention to *Trial by Jury*, and you will discover the seeds for the
distinctive style and characteristics of their later works.

We hope you will enjoy this "chamber" production—fully staged and sung, with grand piano accompaniment, costumes, props, and the suggestion of a set—as we sing so merrily, "Trial-la-law"!

The Story

*H**ark, the hour of ten is sounding*** we hear as the Usher tries to bring order from the Great British Public to the courtroom, and separates the spectators from jurors in preparation for a trial for breach of promise of marriage. He encourages the Jury to adopt his own bias (***Now, Jurymen, hear my advice***) just before the arrival of the Defendant, Edwin (***Is this the Court of the Exchequer?***), who explains his roving eye with the ladies (***When first my old, old love I knew***). The Jury agrees that they were cut from the same cloth (***Oh, I was like that when a lad!***) but assert they have become respectable. All welcome the Judge, who explains how he came to his exalted position. He had a roving eye, too, and it helped! (***When I, good friends, was called to the bar***) The Jury take their oath (***Oh, will you swear***) before the entrance of the Bridesmaids (***Comes the broken flower***) and the Plaintiff, Angelina (***O'er the season vernal***). She quite captivates the Jury *and* the Judge. The Plaintiff's Counsel then presents her case (***With a sense of deep emotion***) which is supported by Angelina's tears (***That she is reeling***). All threaten the Defendant, leading Edwin to present his defense (***Oh, gentlemen, listen, I pray***), suggesting he would thrash and kick his wife, since he is "such a very bad lot," especially when drinking. After objections, the entire ensemble considers this ***A nice dilemma***. The Plaintiff declares her love for this rake, asking the jury to consider her distress when assessing "the damages Edwin must pay," which leads the Judge to consider making Edwin tipsy as a way to determine the truthfulness of his defense. All but the Defendant object, leading the Judge to solve the impasse in an unexpected but delightfully humorous way, and all sing of ***joy unbounded***.

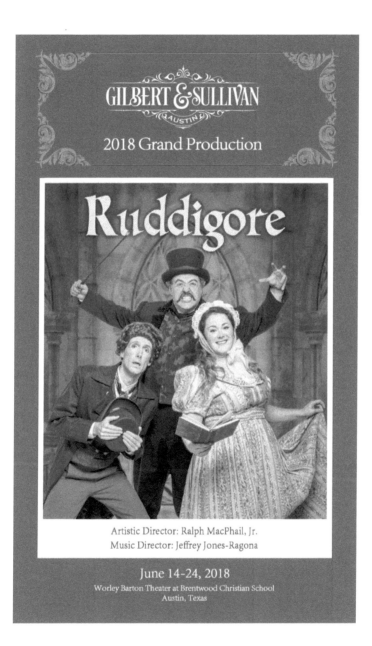

GILBERT & SULLIVAN
AUSTIN

2018 Grand Production

Ruddigore

Artistic Director: Ralph MacPhail, Jr.
Music Director: Jeffrey Jones-Ragona

June 14-24, 2018
Worley Barton Theater at Brentwood Christian School
Austin, Texas

SFX in G&S

W hat kind of title is that for an article? (Please note that the second letter in the title is an F, not an E.)

As you may suppose, "G&S" stands for "Gilbert & Sullivan," but unless you're a film or theatre techie, you might not realize that "SFX" in these professionals' argots stands for "special effects."

G&S is remarkably free of demands for SFX, but I'm expecting that more than a few of my readers are recalling a highlight in our production of *The Sorcerer* several years ago in which a table glided to center stage under the magical direction of Arthur DiBianca's masterful characterization of Family Sorcerer John Wellington Wells. That worthy also conjured up some eerie flashes of light from a teapot that had been shown empty only a few moments earlier. (He also managed to magically fill his teapot with enough of the brew to serve to the entire company on stage.)

Even though I've been a practicing magician most of my years, I *still* have not been able to figure out how he did these things, but Dame Rumour whispers that GSA member Andy Heilveil might just hold the key to JWW's secrets, so ask him if you're interested. (Being familiar with the Magician's Code, however, I'm inclined to believe Andy will keep mum —mum, mum.)

Ruddigore; or, The Witch's Curse, our Grand Production for 2018, is the only other Savoy opera calling for supernatural happenings, and they're doozies! In the middle of Act II, the entire male chorus and one principal character, represented onstage by portraits in a gothic Victorian picture gallery, become animated and step from their frames onto the stage to threaten Sir Ruthven Murgatroyd, the protagonist, with terrible agonies unless he commits the daily crime he must—the result of a family curse.

The scene always presents challenges, but theatrical challenges are worth meeting. And while I'm not about to reveal how we're going to meet them, I will mention a couple of secrets about the history of *Ruddigore* that, unless you're a student of G&S, you may not know.

Number One! (as John Wellington Wells might say): *Ruddigore* was not Gilbert's first use of the portraits-coming-to-life motif; he'd used it decades earlier in his long one-act comic opera *Ages Ago* (which was composed by Sullivan's friend Frederic Clay). It was at a rehearsal for a revival of *Ages Ago* at the Gallery of Illustration in London, in fact, where G first met S; FC introduced the two gentlemen about two years before the first G&S Collaboration in 1871.

I've not the space to give *Ages Ago* the attention it deserves, but I highly recommend reading the libretto; you will find it available at this address: www.gsarchive.net/gilbert/plays/ages_ago/ages_ago_home.html along with the play's history and other delights. (It would make a wonderful mid-season production.)

Number Two! Gilbert wasn't the first to use the name "Ruthven" on the operatic stage. That honor may go to Wilhelm August Wohlbrück, whose opera *Der Vampyr* was composed by Heinrich Marschner and premiered in 1828. (The opera was based on a play which in turn was based on a short story—see *Wikipedia* for details.) The eponymous vampire is named Lord Ruthven in the libretto, a name Gilbert (as noted above) used for his protagonist in *Ruddigore*.

Number Threeeeeeee! "The Electricity," which Richard D'Oyly Carte had installed in the new Savoy Theatre six years before *Ruddigore*, must have made the darkening of the stage necessary for the portraits' transformations easier than it would have been with the old gas lighting. And it also had its influence on the musical side of the production, for on the opening night Sullivan conducted the "ghost music" as the lights dimmed to dark with a special baton graced with a glowing filament so that his orchestra could follow his direction.

*Sir Arthur Sullivan as a conductor,
sketch by Charles Lyall, c.1879*

My valued collaborator Jeffrey Jones-Ragona won't need a glowing baton next June, but many will be working in advance and during performances to make Sir Ruthven Murgatroyd's ancestors come to life in a suitably ghostly and memorable fashion.

Audition Notes on *Ruddigore*

*R*uddigore; or, The Witch's Curse (1887) is one of the mature Gilbert & Sullivan operas and one of their most popular works with Savoyards who love them all; its première followed the international success of *The Mikado* in 1885. Something of the "black sheep" of the Savoy opera family, it makes fun of a Victorian melodrama, a form that was passé by the time *Ruddigore* was written, something of which contemporary critics and audiences knew, but that doesn't affect its stage worthiness today. Theatre has been making fun of melodrama for over a century.

Ruddigore was written for the actor-singers at the Savoy, most of whom had created roles in earlier Gilbert & Sullivan productions. So there are roles for tenor and soprano, mezzo and baritone, heavy baritone and contralto. But Gilbert, as usual, brought new wrinkles to character types, as I hope will be seen below.

Set on the coast of Cornwall in the village of Rederring (Act I) and in the picture-gallery of Ruddigore Castle (Act II), the story moves from a sunny exterior to a spooky interior, telling the tale of a family curse placed on an ancestor in the Murgatroyd family:

> Each lord of Ruddigore,
>   Despite his best endeavour,
> Shall do one crime, or more,
>   Once, every day, forever![2]

In Act I, Dame Hannah relates the story of this curse to a chorus of professional bridesmaids. We meet her foundling charge, Rose Maybud, who must marry before the other girls in the village do; her shy suitor Robin Oakapple (really the elder, titled Murgatroyd in disguise); his foster-brother Dick Dauntless, able seaman; Mad Margaret, the village lunatic; and finally, in this act, Sir Despard Murgatroyd, Baronet of Ruddigore, current victim of the curse because his elder brother is hiding to escape his title and its curse.

Complications are many and humorous, and Gilbert turns his topsy-turvy lens on each melodramatic character, exposing a heroine who is self-centered, a true villain who is meek and cowardly, a madwoman who is not so mad, a jolly jack-tar who is really a rogue, and a fake villain who is aspires to goodness.

And of course there are the magnificent choruses, beautiful solos, lovely duets and trios, and funny ensembles with sometimes quirky little dances that are hallmarks of Gilbert & Sullivan productions. The "madrigal" in the Act I finale is worth the price of admission.

And there are more musical and comic delights in Act II *plus* a supernatural ghost scene in which the Murgatroyd ancestors come to life to threaten agony to the "real" Baronet of Ruddigore, who's so meek he can't bring himself to commit his daily crime—all supported by Sullivan's marvelous score.

My purpose below is to provide information for performers concerning the auditions and the characters in *Ruddigore*. If you're planning to audition, please read this in its entirety. And even if you're *not*, please read it anyway: I hope you will find it interesting—and that it will give you a foretaste of the delights coming in June!

If *Ruddigore* is not in your library, you can read or download the libretto from at the Gilbert & Sullivan Archive; call on gsarchive.net, where you will also be able to read a plot synopsis, see vintage images, and download audio files. Go to GSOpera (gsopera.com/opera/57/lexicon) for other good information on the work.

Ruddigore is filled with roles that are fun to play and sing; much of the delight of the work is in its frequent send-up of melodramatic posturing and declamation. In addition, the male chorus of city playboys in Act I change costumes to become ghosts-come-to-life in Act II—and then revert to city gentlemen for the Finale.

THE CHORUS is composed of the men collectively known as <u>Bucks and Blades</u> or "dandies" (10 gentlemen, of various ages, dressed fashionably; they are gentlemen of the town visiting the country to flirt with the pretty girls). As noted above, in Act II, those same choristers become ghosts who step from their picture frames to threaten dire consequences on Sir Ruthven Murgatroyd unless he commits his daily crime. Seven of these choristers have "names" in the program and a number have a few speaking lines.

The ladies of the chorus are **Professional Bridesmaids** (10 females, idealized Victorian maidens in lovely bridal attire). They cannot marry until Rose Maybud does because "every young man in the village is in love with"[2] Rose. One of the recurring jokes is a chorus which bursts forth from them whenever it is suggested that a wedding is imminent.

THE PRINCIPALS: Here are brief character sketches, with a nod of gratitude to the writings of William Cox-Ife, W. S. Gilbert, and Peter Kline*:

Sir Roderic Murgatroyd (Bass): "*the twenty-first Baronet.*" Sir Roderic appears only in Act II, after the ghostly chorus "Painted emblems of a race," and launches into a magnificent solo, "When the night wind howls." He is intimidating and powerful, threatening Sir Ruthven with agonies unless he "commit his daily crime," but wilts into a loving swain toward the end of the act when he meets his old flame Dame Hannah and with her sings a lovely duet. "He should have a bass voice of almost operatic quality, and the charisma of his acting should transcend the irritability of his character."[3]

Sir Ruthven Murgatroyd (Light Baritone): "*dressed as Robin Oakapple—a Young Farmer.*" Robin in Act I is an innocent and shy farmer, hiding his true identity and enlisting his foster-brother Dick Dauntless to woo Rose Maybud on his behalf. Not a good idea: not only does Dick fall in love with Rose himself, but he betrays Robin's true identity to Sir Despard, Robin's younger brother who had assumed the family baronetcy and curse, thinking Ruthven dead. So by the end of Act I, mild and meek Robin must become the wicked and threatening Ruthven. Much of Act II is concerned with this uneasy transformation—but all ends happily. This is a challenging role—a "red-meat" opportunity for the actor-singer.

Richard Dauntless (Tenor): *"his [Ruthven's] Foster-Brother—a Man-o'-War's Man"* (a sailor). Handsome, virile, possessing a good sense of humor, and a good dancer (his hornpipe is a highlight of Act I), his sunny disposition masks his self-interested guile. He's a loveable rogue, with a twinkle in his eye, and his "hornpipe is the talk of the fleet."[2] "He is light-footed, light-headed, and lighthearted."[3]

Sir Despard Murgatroyd of Ruddigore (Baritone) *"a Wicked Baronet."* Sir Despard is an ancestor of Snidely Whiplash of "Bullwinkle" fame—and the very model of the Victorian villain, however reluctantly. He has assumed his baronetcy and the family curse thinking that his elder brother is dead. In Act II, when released from his position (and curse), he becomes mild-mannered, conservative (and hilarious) "district visitor"—"a sanctimonious 'do-gooder'"[1] in partnership with his old love Margaret. "Ferocity is the keynote in the first act, and the same ferocity is enlisted in the cause of virtue in the second act."[3]

Old Adam Goodheart (Bass-Baritone): *"Robin's Faithful Servant."* Clearly an ancestor of many an Igor in horror flicks, Old Adam serves Sir Ruthven when he's disguised as Robin Oakapple in Act I and becomes his henchman when Robin reverts to the baronetcy in Act II, going so far as to carry off a maiden—any maiden—at his now-evil master's behest. "He is old and decrepit, but not exaggeratedly so."[3]

Rose Maybud (Lyric Soprano): *"a Village Maiden."* Rose lets it be known that she is "sweet Rose Maybud"[2] though some of her charitable actions show either cruelty or cluelessness (take your pick). She's the romantic interest, in love with Robin, then Dick, then—well, back and forth through most of the rest of the opera. "A simple village maiden, until it comes to choosing the man with the most money."[1] "Vocally this role lies a little lower than most [G&S] leading soprano roles."[3]

Mad Margaret (Mezzo-Soprano): This village maiden has been jilted by Sir Despard Murgatroyd after he inherited the title and curse, and her grief has led her to madness (another typical character-type in Victorian melodrama). In her madness, she sings one of the most beautiful songs Gilbert & Sullivan ever wrote. In Act II her love, Despard, is restored to her (having relinquished the curse to his elder brother), and her insanity is on the wane. She fights mad impulses while trying to be good, but it is a constant challenge to Despard to keep her "in line." "A part calling for an exceptionally good actress as well as a good singer."[1]

Dame Hannah (Mezzo-Soprano/Contralto): *Rose's Aunt.* This is one of Gilbert's mysteries—or slips: Rose describes herself as a foundling. If this is true, Dame Hannah is more a guardian than aunt. No matter—Hannah is one of the librettist's more dignified elder women. She mourns the death of her old flame, Sir Roderic Murgatroyd, and stays true to her love. She is rewarded by a reunion with him toward the end of Act II after her abduction by Old Adam at Sir Ruthven's behest. As for how this can be—Dame Hannah is alive and Sir Roderic is dead—it's best not to ask! And let's not worry about it, for they sing a lovely duet!

Zorah and Ruth: *Professional Bridesmaids*. **Zorah** (Soprano/Mezzo) has a lovely solo in the opening chorus; **Ruth** has no solo singing. Each of these two supporting principals has several speaking lines of dialogue and always sings ensemble with the female chorus.

I've said perhaps too often that there's only one G&S activity more fun than seeing one of their operas—and that's actually working on one. If you need a little push to encourage you to audition, please consider this it. Jeffrey and I do all we can to make the auditions fun and relaxed.

Please sign up for an audition slot today, and then please encourage a friend or two to audition so that even more can share the delight of Gilbert & Sullivan. While *Ruddigore* is not as well-known as several of the others, it's been one of my favorites for decades, so I eagerly anticipate working on it and hope you will want to be a part of the fun.

*References

[1] William Cox-Ife, *How to Sing Both Gilbert and Sullivan* (London: Chappell & Co. Ltd., 1961).

[2] W. S. Gilbert, *The Savoy Operas: II* (London: Oxford University Press, 1963).

[3] Peter Kline, *Gilbert & Sullivan Production* (The Theatre Student Series) (New York: Richards Rosen Press, Inc., 1972).

A Unique Gilbert Lyric

In my "Audition Notes on *Ruddigore*" (above) I noted that in the opera Mad Margaret sings one of the most beautiful songs Gilbert & Sullivan ever wrote.

The lyric for this song is, I think, unique in Savoy opera history. We know of course that W. S. Gilbert recycled ideas from his early published verse in constructing a number of his plots for the Savoy operas. But Mad Margaret's song is unusual in that Gilbert published the entire lyric about five years before he constructed his libretto in 1887. It appeared in the December 10, 1881, issue of *The Illustrated Sporting and Dramatic News*:

"ONLY ROSES"
by W. S. Gilbert

In a garden full of posies
  Cometh one to gather flowers—
  And he wandered through its bowers
Toying with the wanton roses,
  Who, uprising from their beds,
  Held on high their shameless heads.
  With their pretty lips a-pouting,
  Never doubting–never doubting
That, for Cytherean posies
He would gather aught but roses.

In a nest of weeds and nettles
  Lay a violet, half hidden—
  Hoping that his glance, unbidden,
Yet might fall upon her petals.
  Though she lived alone, apart,
  Hope lay nestling at her heart:
  But, alas! the cruel awaking
  Set that little heart a-breaking,
For he gathered for his posies
Only roses–only roses!

Alert Savoyards will note that Gilbert only changed four words when adding the lyric to his *Ruddigore* libretto (the initial "In" became "To"; "wandered" became "wanders"; "Held" became "Hold," and "Set that" became "Set her"); he also altered several punctuation marks and adjusted his always-interesting scheme of indentations (from the earlier, published version).

Clearly Gilbert liked this most "un-Gilbertian" of lyrics, and of course it reached its maximum potential when Sullivan recognized its merit and embraced it with his lovely and sympathetic music.

A Genealogical Fantasy

P ity the poor Artistic Director who must come up with an idea for a column but whose well is dry! Then he remembered an article he wrote for *The Savoyard*, the magazine published in London for Associate Members of The D'Oyly Carte Opera Trust—'way back in 1970.

He hopes that his readers will understand the necessity for this bit of literary recycling—and perhaps even enjoy the result. He begs to remind them that *Ruddigore* takes place in the fishing village of Rederring, Cornwall, and he invites them to think back on our recent productions of *Trial by Jury* and *H.M.S. Pinafore* as he weaves again, over half a century later, the yarn he called

TRIAL BY JURY—*A Sequel to H.M.S. Pinafore*

Over the years, *Trial by Jury* has been frequently played as a curtain-raiser to *H.M.S. Pinafore*—a decided mistake, for evidence is great proving the Dramatic Cantata is clearly a brief but important *sequel* to the romance of Josephine and the lowly tar turned Captain from the Original Nautical Comic Opera. An examination of the two libretti makes this clear.

Mrs. Cripps ("Little Buttercup") reveals in her song concerning her early experiences as a baby farmer that she mixed the captain and the tar in infancy, making Rackstraw Edward Corcoran (later to become Captain Sir Edward Corcoran, K.C.B.—see *Utopia Ltd.*) and Corcoran Ralph Rackstraw.*

Throughout *H.M.S. Pinafore* there are hints that Josephine is not Edward's (Ralph's) first love: "Unlearned he in aught save that which love has taught (for love had been his tutor)," "A British tar is a soaring soul, as free as a mountain bird," and so forth. It is therefore not surprising to find that Angelina, a lovely fishing village girl and one of Edward's many girls in many ports, has been jilted for the *Pinafore* Captain's daughter. (This knowledge of Edward's Rederring fiancée gives new insight to Edward's "I am but a living ganglion of irreconcilable antagonisms" speech.) Josephine, who loves Edward well, has probably heard the scuttlebutt of his Rederring lover—possibly from Mrs. Cripps—and seizes upon this knowledge when she tries to conceal her affection by bursting

---

* *Josephine, ironically, already possesses her future married name, and on becoming conjugally matrimonified, would obtain her maiden name. This is Topsy-Turvydom if there ever was such.*

forth, "Go, sir, and learn to cast your eyes on some village maiden in your own poor rank!"

Of course, the difficulties of unequal rank are solved by Buttercup, and Edward Corcoran's marriage to Josephine Rackstraw is considered imminent at the end of the opera, probably to be solemnized by a Doctor of Divinity who resides in the vicinity of Portsmouth.

But just as Mrs. Cripps heard in Portsmouth the gossip of Ralph's—that is Edward's—promise of matrimony to Angelina in Rederring, the news of the impending marriage between Edward and Josephine in Portsmouth was conveyed to Angelina and the "corps of professional bridesmaids" in Rederring, possibly by man-o'-war's man Richard Dauntless, who undoubtedly heard naval gossip of the Rackstraw/Josephine/Porter triangle aboard the "Pinafore." Angelina, having already bought her trousseau, decides to bring immediate suit against Edward—formerly Ralph. (Unfortunately the Court records in Rederring are no longer extant, but it is a fair assumption that Angelina misunderstood the true name of her former fiancé, and mistakenly filed suit against "Edwin" Corcoran.) Edward is subpoenaed to Court in Rederring by Angelina's solicitor as the final plans are being made for his marriage to Josephine.

The statement and resolution of Edward's dilemma may be examined in the transcription of the trial. Edward informally states his case before the Usher calls for order: "Joy incessant palls the sense; and love, unchanged, will cloy. . . ." When court convenes, Counsel for the Plaintiff enumerates the mental anguish Edward caused Angelina: "Picture him excuses framing—going from her far away." (Surely she knows that Edward, an "honest brown right hand" at sea, must of necessity cast off for extended periods of time.) Edward, on rebuttal, candidly states that his "heart has been ranging," that nature's laws he obeys, "for nature is constantly changing. . . . Consider the moral, I pray, nor bring a young fellow to sorrow, who loves this young lady today, and loves that young lady tomorrow." In a desperate last attempt to show incompatibility, Edward admits the seafaring traits he has developed: smoking, drinking, and bullying; and ironically states, "I'll marry this lady today, and I'll marry the other tomorrow."

The Judge solves the problem, of course, by marrying Angelina in Rederring, leaving Edward and Josephine free to plight their troth in Portsmouth.

But His Honour the Judge—could he be the same Justice who later was to hand down "judgements in F sharp minor, given andante in six-eight time," as this breach of promise trial would suggest? The same Justice who watched his "professional advancement with considerable interest"—from the "incubus" to Angelina to Iolanthe? The same susceptible Justice who perpetually seems "quite prepared to marry again"?

"There's an unbounded field of speculation on which one could discourse for hours!"

The following issue of *The Savoyard* ran a rebuttal from my friend Diana Burleigh in Australia called "But who was Frederic's Father?" in which she "proves" that "*Trial* does not follow *Pinafore*; it precedes *The Pirates of Penzance*," along with another article by one Gerald Benson that asks "Who was Josephine's mother?"

That was followed by a note from the editor: "Readers may now take a rest from these genealogical fantasies"!

Setting Contrasts

Ann Marie Gordon's wonderful set designs for *Ruddigore* arrived in Bridgewater two weeks ago, and I was filled with delight—not only with the designs themselves and the suggestions they convey for what we'll all be seeing onstage in June, but also because they suggested the idea for this column.

As a dramatist, W. S. Gilbert was well aware of the value of contrast as a dramatic device and the many ways contrast can be used to add variety, make points, provide humor, and—well, the list could be as long as Ko-Ko's!

Ann Marie's renderings started me thinking about the string of Savoy operas, focusing on how Gilbert used contrast in his settings. In *Thespis* (1871), the "Ruined Temple on the Summit of Mount Olympus" for Act I is the same for Act II, but with the "Ruins Restored." Skipping over the one-act *Trial by Jury* (1875), it is interesting to point out that the original version of *The Sorcerer* (1877) moved from the "Grounds of Sir Marmaduke's Mansion" to the "Market-Place of Ploverleigh"; however, when Gilbert & Sullivan revised the show in 1884, both acts took place at the "Exterior of Sir Marmaduke's Mansion," Act I at Midday and Act II at Midnight.

Perhaps one reason for this change was that in the two works that followed *The Sorcerer* (*H.M.S. Pinafore* in 1878, and *The Pirates of Penzance* in 1879), Gilbert contrasted the times of day in the two acts to provide very atmospheric second acts as he would do in the revised version of *The Sorcerer*: moving the action from "Noon" to "Night" (aboard the ship) and from "half-past-eleven-ish" at the sea-shore in the morning to "A Ruined Chapel by Moonlight" in the piratical work. *Patience* (1881) shifts locations near Castle Bunthorne, but both acts take place during the day. *Iolanthe* (1882) moves from "An Arcadian Landscape" by day to "Palace Yard, Winchester" by moonlight. All three acts in *Princess Ida* (1884) take place outside and during the day, though the location shifts from King Hildebrand's Castle to Castle Adamant. The action of *The Mikado* (1885) takes place in Titipu in the Courtyard of Ko-Ko's palace and in his garden, each in daytime.

Next in the series is *Ruddigore* (1887), and what makes it unique is that for the first time Gilbert moves his action from *outdoors* to *indoors*, providing a shift of setting that is not only very dramatic but also sets the stage for one of the most memorable scenes in all of Savoy opera: the Baronets of Ruddigore Past animate, step from their frames, and threaten the current holder of the title with unspeakable agonies.

If *Ruddigore* was the first of the operas to shift from outdoors to indoors, we should note that the following one (*The Yeomen of the Guard*, 1888) does not. *The Gondoliers* (1889) *does*—sort of—for Act II is set in a pavilion (like Act I of *Princess Ida*), which according to my online Merriam-Webster is typically "a large often sumptuous tent."

Gilbert moved his plot from outdoors to indoors in his penultimate work with Sullivan, *Utopia Limited* (1893), with the action moving from "A Utopian Palm Grove" to the "Throne Room in King Paramount's

Palace," and the time from clearly daytime to "Night." *The Grand Duke* (1896) moves from a daytime celebration in a Market-Place to a Throne room "the next morning."

I would argue that *Ruddigore* stands alone in terms of the contrast between the act settings in Gilbert & Sullivan.

But Gilbert set contrasts in other ways as well. The operas from *The Sorcerer* through *Ruddigore* consistently contrasted the tall, fleshy, lumbering, stolid Rutland Barrington with the short, thin, agile, witty George Grossmith (best examples: Captain Corcoran and Sir Joseph Porter, the Sergeant of Police and Major-General Stanley, Grosvenor and Bunthorne, King Hildebrand and King Gama, Pooh-Bah and Ko-Ko, and, finally, Sir Despard and Sir Ruthven (Robin) in *Ruddigore*). Note, too, how Gilbert often contrasts the silliness of his characters with the impeccable correctness of their dress and demeanor, especially those wearing uniforms.

I leave this theme to interested readers to pursue further on their own (and suggest that Sullivan often used contrast between his music and Gilbert's lyrics to humorous effect), but first suggest that Gilbert's main approach to comedy, often described with the term "topsy-turvy," is essentially based on contrast. As the Master himself said, "All humour so-called is based upon a grave and quasi-respectful treatment of the ludicrous," a concept Sullivan often embraced.

Libby and I have both written elsewhere that part of the delight of seeing *Ruddigore* is discovering the differences between who the characters *profess to be* and the sorts of people they *actually are*. *Ruddigore* is based upon the "stock, two-dimensional characters" of melodrama (virtuous heroes and heroines and evil villains, for instance), but we learn when we get to know them that none are as they seem to be at first, for Gilbert has worked his topsy-turvy magic.

Yes, *Ruddigore* is full of contrasts, set by both Gilbert and Sullivan. Discovering them is a lot of fun and one of the many sources of delight in this funny, delightful, and tuneful comic opera.

❖

"Curtain Up" on *Ruddygore*

Composer Frederick Clay introduced William S. Gilbert to Arthur Sullivan at the Gallery of Illustration, a small theatre in Regent Street, London, in 1870. Gilbert was collaborating with Clay on a revival of a short musical entertainment called *Ages Ago*, which they had written, composed, and originally staged the year before. The play featured five painted portraits that come to life in the middle of the show.

Seventeen years later, *Ruddygore; or, The Witch's Curse* opened at the Savoy Theatre. By this time the Gilbert & Sullivan partnership, united by producer Richard D'Oyly Carte, was firmly established as the leading purveyor of musical theatrical entertainment in London and had an equally strong reputation throughout the English-speaking world. In fact, what would become regarded as the G&S masterpiece, *The Mikado*, was withdrawn from the Savoy stage while still playing to full houses to make way for the "Entirely New and Original Super-Natural Opera."

Following such a tremendous hit as *The Mikado* was curse enough for the new work. But there were other problems. The title itself, in its original spelling, was not comfortable for Victorian lips, for "ruddy" sounded a lot like "bloody" (a corruption of "by Our Lady"), a word that was Just Not Used in polite society. The première performance ran long, some of the portraits stuck in their frames in Act Two, and the audience, while wildly appreciative of Act One and of the scene in which the ghosts of the dead Baronets of *Ruddygore* came to life, thought that bringing them back to life for the Act Two finale strained credulity.

The partners were dissatisfied too—with each other. Sullivan, who was hankering to compose grand opera—and light operas with "real human interest and probability"—complained privately that Gilbert's plot was too artificial, and Gilbert wrote to a friend that Sullivan's music for the ghost scene in Act Two was too grand-operatic and serious, "as though one inserted fifty lines of *Paradise Lost* into a farcical comedy."

The tepid press reaction and that of the opening-night audience led the two men to sit down for some post-première alterations. They cut, re-wrote, and revised, but changing the title's spelling to *Ruddigore* was one of the first steps. When someone asked Gilbert, "How is *Bloodygore* going?" the librettist replied, "It's not *Bloodygore*—it's *Ruddigore*!" When told, "Well, it's the same thing," Gilbert retorted, "It is certainly not! If I told you that I like your ruddy countenance, which I do, it is not the same as saying I like your bloody cheek, which I don't!" (According to the lore, Gilbert also used two G-rated retorts concerning the offending title, threatening to rename the new show *Kensington Gore; or, Not So Good as "The Mikado"* or *Kensington Gore; or, Robin and Richard were Two Pretty Men*!)

One of the ironies of *Ruddigore* is that, despite its initial reception, the comic opera is usually ranked as a favorite by Savoyards who know all 14 of the Gilbert & Sullivan works. The reasons are probably the same ones that the partners gave for the "modified rapture" they had for their collaborator's contributions to the work: Gilbert's plot and Sullivan's music.

Ruddigore was something of a change of pace for Gilbert. While the early collaborations with Sullivan made broader fun of "grand opera" than later ones, such spoofs (always brilliantly reinforced by Sullivan) were secondary to the topsy-turvy plots satirizing persons, institutions, and fads, the eye-pleasing sets and costumes, and of course the invariably compelling lyrics and music. But in *Ruddigore*, Gilbert, a man of the theatre, structured his libretto as a parody of the dominant form of dramaturgy of the first half of the nineteenth century in England: melodrama.

Melodrama (or "music-drama") was already rather passé at the time *Ruddigore* was written. Melodramas were always plot-driven, with picturesque changes of scenery, coincidence, supernatural happenings, poetic justice, incidental music used throughout to enhance the emotional impact of scenes, and a gallery of stock characters used and reused with expected regularity and limitless creative variations. Its appeals to working-class theatregoers in London were simple: the plots were exciting, and the playgoers always knew where they stood in terms of sympathy with the characters—or lack thereof. There were the brave, manly heroes, the pure-as-the-driven-snow heroines, the dastardly villains (usually aristocrats), the wronged maidens, the honest "jolly jack tar" sailors with nautical diction, the village outcasts. We're familiar with most of these conventions today: we've all seen silent movies and staged "meller-drammers" such as *Curse You, Jack Dalton!* and *Only an Orphan Girl.* In fact, a good argument can be made that melodrama forms the foundation for much of what passes for "serious drama" on TV and in the movies today—to say nothing of paperback "romantic fiction."

Trust Gilbert to topsy-turvify the form, however: Rose Maybud, the "virtuous heroine" of the piece, is determined to get what she wants, and is willing to settle for "the only one that's left" for a lover after losing

two other candidates. The virtuous hero, passing as a timid farmer, is actually a bad baronet in disguise. The villain commits his daily crime but then does a good deed that more than atones for it. The honest sailor listens to his heart's dictates, especially when it dictates self-interest over promises to others. "But behold!" as Rose Maybud says, "I have said enough" about this gallery of characters—and discovering these delicious incongruities is part of the delight of *Ruddigore.*

Other delights include Gilbert's catchy and at times moving lyrics (including one of his fastest), and Sullivan's music, whether "grand-operatic," romantic, or just plain high-spirited. The "madrigal" in the Act One finale is arguably one of the finest fruits of the entire collaboration, musically and lyrically. *Ruddigore* contains more dance than most of the earlier Savoy operas, more theatrical send-up, and perhaps the most spectacular single scene of all when those bad baronets come alive and step forth from their frames.

Ruddigore ran at the Savoy for 288 performances. When we see the show today, it's hard to believe it was initially considered a failure. After another of Gilbert's acquaintances called *Ruddigore* just that, the librettist replied, "Well, it put 7,000 pounds into my pocket, and I could do with a few other such failures."

Gilbert & Sullivan Austin

presents

H.M.S. Pinafore

or, The Lass that Loved a Sailor

Artistic Director: Ralph MacPhail, Jr.

Music Director: Jeffrey Jones-Ragona

Worley Barton Theater at Brentwood Christian School

Austin, Texas

March 2 and 3, 2019

Welcome Aboard!

If you enjoy an occasional cruise—on Lady Bird Lake or on the vast "ocean blue"—you know that when you set sail you're in for a good time. Like a good cruise, revisiting *H.M.S. Pinafore* never palls.

Gilbert intended to call his ship *H.M.S. Semaphore*, but his composer-colleague Arthur Sullivan suggested christening the vessel with the name of a child's smock. This topsy-turvy suggestion encapsulated Gilbert's tongue-in-cheek look at life aboard an English man-o'-war "in many various ways."

On board *H.M.S. Pinafore* we find a captain who must accompany his military commands with an "if you please" and whose behavior is the opposite of other seafaring martinets in song and story. We find Captain Corcoran to be the model of civility, observing the social amenities with his men—and even checking his salty language in their presence.

Aboard this peaceful man-o'-war we also find a First Lord of the Admiralty, a civilian official who before his appointment had never been to sea—or even seen a ship!

Also aboard this topsy-turvy vessel we find a hero in Ralph, a lowly and uneducated tar, speaking as if he had studied the classics, and a villain in Dick Deadeye who is the only character on board who speaks common sense.

H.M.S. Pinafore glides so effortlessly in performance that it's easy to overlook her topsy-turvy subtleties. Only aboard this ship would ecstatic lovers "murmur forth decorous joy in dreamy roundelays," would a First Lord of the Admiralty proclaim his incompetence in an amusing song, and would a contrived dénouement leave a heroine with her true love—a man who *must* be the same age as her father!

Topsy-turvy, too, was *H.M.S. Pinafore*'s initial reception, for the work proved eminently seaworthy in the United States before doing so at her home port.

Perhaps most topsy-turvy of all, shortly after *H.M.S. Pinafore* opened in London in 1878, a reviewer characterized the show as a "frothy production destined soon to subside into nothingness." Well, as Little Buttercup sings, "Things are seldom what they seem"!

Thank you for coming aboard. We hope that this "concert production" will affirm the G&S legacy of tuneful, timeless delight. We also hope it will provide happy memories of a pleasant cruise for you passengers who sail the ocean blue with us into that enchanted land Gilbert called "Topsyturvydom." Getting there, we hope, will be all the fun!

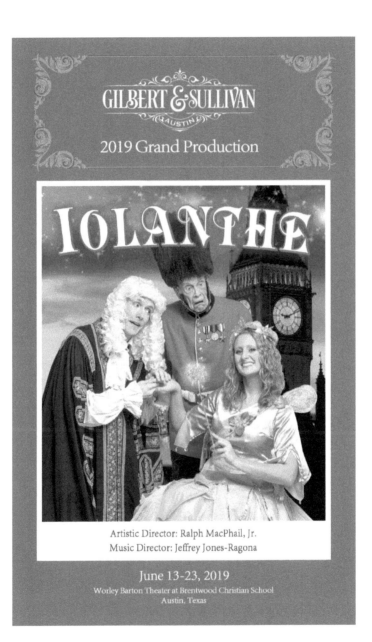

GILBERT & SULLIVAN

AUSTIN

2019 Grand Production

IOLANTHE

Artistic Director: Ralph MacPhail, Jr.
Music Director: Jeffrey Jones-Ragona

June 13-23, 2019
Worley Barton Theater at Brentwood Christian School
Austin, Texas

*Iolanthe*an Babs

Readers of this column will know that Gilbert often sought inspiration for plots and characters for his operas with Sullivan from his earlier works. For instance, *The Sorcerer* was based on a short story; *Princess Ida* was based on an early burlesque; the most memorable scene in *Ruddigore* was suggested by an earlier opera.

The most fertile source for Gilbertian self-plagiarism were his "Bab" Ballads, verses originally written for publication in the weekly humor paper *Fun*, later collected in various editions—and (most of them) still in print to this day. *H.M.S. Pinafore*, as we've seen, is based on a remarkable number of them.

For *Iolanthe* (1882), slated for production in Austin next summer, Gilbert used his verses as a source for the overall arc of his plot, for its amusing love-triangle, and also as prototypes for what was to become the longest, most challenging, and most complex patter song in the Savoy operas.

Grab your copy of *The Bab Ballads*, or go to the Gilbert & Sullivan Archive, or Google "Gilbert, 'The Fairy Curate,'" and you will be able to read the embryo of what became the plot of *Iolanthe*. In this

"The Fairy Curate"

amusing verse you will meet Georgie, the son of a fairy and a dull solicitor; these three eventually became Strephon, the son of Iolanthe (a fairy) and the Lord Chancellor of England (who "went to the bar as a very young man").

Gilbert's *Iolanthe* plot line went through a number of changes. From the start, the ladies' chorus was always composed of fairies, but the men were barristers on the Northern Circuit, then members of the House of Commons. Finally he settled on the House of Peers—and Georgie's father, a solicitor, became The Prime Minister, The Home Secretary, and finally The Lord Chancellor himself. (And of course, as suggested above, Georgie became Strephon, an Arcadian shepherd.)

A highlight of Act II is the wooing of Phyllis by two older Lords, Mountararat and Tolloller. Go to Gilbert's "Old Paul and Old Tim" and "The Periwinkle Girl," and you can read the seeds of this love triangle.

"Old Paul and Old Tim"   **"The Periwinkle Girl"**

Iolanthe contains the longest and most difficult of Gilbert's patter-songs. Go to the G&S Archive for "A Bad Night of It" under Bab Ballads and you'll discover its prototype. "Boulogne" is there, too; it's a Victorian travel commercial in verse in which Gilbert experimented with the metrical form of "The Nightmare Song," replete with intricate internal as well as end rhymes.

"Boulogne"

There's a mystery in Gilbert's *Songs of a Savoyard*, a large number of Savoy opera lyrics he published separately and then included with his collected Bab Ballads.

"Sleep On!" is the mysterious verse. Gilbert listed it under "*Iolanthe*" in his table of contents, but I don't remember reading anywhere that it was ever given to Sullivan to set. If you know *Iolanthe*, you will realize that if it was written for that opera, it was probably an early lyric for what became Private Willis's "When All Night Long" ("The Contemplative Sentry") which opens Act II. Instead of musing on the fact "That every boy and every gal/ That's born into the world alive/ Is either a little Liberal/ Or else a little Conservative!" however, this lyric reflects on the sentry's awesome responsibility:

Sleep On!

Fear no unlicensed entry,
　Heed no bombastic talk,
While guards the British Sentry
　Pall Mall and Birdcage Walk.
Let European thunders
　Occasion no alarms,
Though diplomatic blunders
　May cause a cry "To arms!"
　　　Sleep on, ye pale civilians;
　　　　All thunder-clouds defy:
　　　On Europe's countless millions
　　　　The Sentry keeps his eye!

Should foreign-born rapscallions
　In London dare to show
Their overgrown battalions,
　Be sure I'll let you know.
Should Russians or Norwegians
　Pollute our favoured clime
With rough barbaric legions,
　I'll mention it in time.
　　　So sleep in peace, civilians,
　　　　The Continent defy;
　　　While on its countless millions
　　　　The Sentry keeps his eye!

Another "Lost Lyric" from *Iolanthe*

L ast issue's column closed with the "lost lyric," which was probably for Private Willis in an early draft of Act II of *Iolanthe*. I write "probably" because, other than Gilbert's attribution of the song as being "From Iolanthe" in his collection of lyrics, *Songs of a Savoyard*, there seems to be no corroborative detail proving that it was ever sent to Sullivan for setting to music.

There is another "lost lyric" from Gilbert's "Fairy Opera," but its history is better known—including the fact that it was actually performed on stage.

In both the London and New York premières of *Iolanthe* in 1882, and following the show-stopping trio "If you go in," Strephon had a solo that was quickly cut and is little-known today. We will recall that Strephon has been, in Act II, sent to Parliament by the Fairy Queen after being insulted by the Lord Chancellor at the end of the previous act. Strephon, a lowly shepherd in Act I, is now member of the House of Lords—a Peer of the Realm!—and enters and sings the following lyric:

RECITATIVE

My bill has now been read a second time:
   His ready vote no Member now refuses;
In verity I wield a power sublime,
   And one that I can turn to mighty uses!
What joy to carry, in the very teeth
   Of Ministry, Cross-Bench, and Opposition,
Some rather urgent measures—quite beneath
   The ken of patriot and politician!

SONG

Fold your flapping wings,
   Soaring Legislature!
Stoop to little things—
   Stoop to Human Nature!
Never need to roam,
   Members patriotic,
Let's begin at home—
   Crime is no exotic!
Bitter is your bane—

Terrible your trials—
Dingy Drury Lane!
Soapless Seven Dials!

Take a tipsy lout
   Gathered from the gutter—
Hustle him about—
   Strap him to a shutter:
What am I but he,
   Washed at hours stated—
Fed on filigree—
   Clothed and educated?
He's a mark of scorn—
   I might be another,
If I had been born
   Of a tipsy mother!

Take a wretched thief
   Through the city sneaking,
Pocket handkerchief
   Ever, ever seeking:
What is he but I
   Robbed of all my chances—
Picking pockets by
   Force of circumstances?
I might be as bad—
   As unlucky, rather—
If I'd only had
   Fagin for a father!

Dickens was one of Gilbert's favorite authors; in fact, the librettist once admitted that he never traveled without a volume of Dickens in his luggage. Gilbert probably took great delight in his reference to *Oliver Twist*—and equal delight in referring to the irony of station in life being a product of birth and "force of circumstances" (a theme he had also treated in *H.M.S. Pinafore*—and elsewhere—but not as trenchantly as here).

Alas, some critics thought that the song was too serious for a light opera—it certainly was a change-of-pace from the ebullient trio that preceded it. But the argument that may have won Gilbert over was that it didn't further the plot, and delayed the very moving emotional climax of his story.

And while the song has been restored occasionally in more recent productions, it remains relatively unknown. (We will not perform it in our production this coming summer.)

Audition Notes on *Iolanthe*

*I*olanthe; or, The Peer and the Peri* (1882) is almost universally regarded as the most beautiful and fanciful of the Gilbert & Sullivan operas, and one of their most popular works with Savoyards who love them all; its première followed the "three P's"—a string of hits that included *H.M.S. Pinafore, The Pirates of Penzance*, and *Patience*. Sullivan's score is sometimes compared with Mendelssohn, and Gilbert's libretto is filled with political satire, for which he was becoming famous, and irresistible comedy—especially when the fairy world comes into conflict with the mortal one.

Iolanthe was written for the actor-singers at the Savoy (it was the first Gilbert & Sullivan work to première there), most of whom had created roles in earlier Gilbert & Sullivan productions. So there are roles for tenor and soprano, mezzo and baritone, heavy baritone and contralto. But Gilbert, as usual, brought new wrinkles to character types, as I hope will be seen below.

Set in an Arcadian Landscape (Act I) and in Palace Yard, Westminster, outside the Houses of Parliament with Big Ben's St. Stephen's Tower prominent (Act II), the story moves from a sunny, rural fairyland to a romantic and iconic urban setting by moonlight as the mortal world and fairy world "mix it up" with irresistibly comic results.

In Act I, we meet the fairies

> Tripping hither, tripping thither,
> Nobody knows why or whither.

The formidable Fairy Queen appears, and her band request that she pardon their sister-fairy Iolanthe, who had been banished 25 years earlier for the crime of marrying a mortal! The Fairy Queen relents, and Iolanthe appears rising from the bottom of a stream where she has lived (ugh!) among the frogs since her banishment. In short order, Iolanthe is reunited with her son Strephon, an Arcadian shepherd who (because of his parentage) is half-fairy and half-mortal. Strephon, we learn, is in love with a fully-mortal shepherdess named Phyllis, but the smitten Lord Chancellor of England is against the union, for he has eyes for Phyllis himself.

The fairies leave, assuring Strephon of their help if needed with his amour, just as Phyllis appears. Strephon learns that the entire House of Lords is in love with Phyllis, but Phyllis assures Strephon that "None shall part us from each other" in a lovely duet.

Enter the entire House of Peers ("Loudly let the trumpet bray! Tantantara!") in their ceremonial finery, and finally the Lord Chancellor with his train-bearer. The entrance of mortals into fairyland leads to complications many and humorous, culminating in Act I with the Fairy Queen declaring vengeance on the Lord Chancellor who insultingly "took her for the proprietor of a Ladies' Seminary"!

In Act II, Strephon has been sent to Parliament by the Fairy Queen. We meet Private Willis, a contemplative sentry, outside the Houses of Parliament. And we learn that Iolanthe's husband was the Lord Chancellor, and so Strephon is his son! Iolanthe begs his mercy, and the Fairy Queen is astounded to learn that her fairies have fallen in love with the Peers. She threatens death to them all, which is in accordance with Fairy Law, but the Lord Chancellor suggests that a slight alteration in the wording of the law would solve the problem—and it does!

This bare-bones synopsis doesn't even address the comic wooing of Phyllis by Lords Mountararat and Tolloller, the Lord Chancellor's famous patter-song, Private Willis's musings on life's ironies, and so many other delights such as the magnificent choruses, beautiful solos, lovely duets and trios, and funny ensembles with sometimes quirky little dances that are hallmarks of Gilbert & Sullivan productions. The Act I finale is regarded by many—myself included—as the best of these extended musical delights in the series.

My purpose below is to provide information for performers concerning the auditions and the characters in *Iolanthe*. If you're planning to audition, please read this in its entirety. And even if you're *not*, please read it anyway: I hope you will find it interesting—and that it will give you a foretaste of the delights coming in June.

For auditions Music Director and Conductor Jeffrey Jones-Ragona and I request that auditionees memorize a song from Gilbert & Sullivan or something similar that will show their voice and range to best advantage. It is also mandatory to provide a copy of the music for the auditions accompanist. No *a cappella* auditions will be heard and the song must be in English. An accompanist will be provided, but singers will be welcome to bring their own accompanist if they wish.

If *Iolanthe* is not in your library, you can read or download the libretto from the Gilbert & Sullivan Archive at gsarchive.net, where you will also be able to read a plot synopsis, see vintage images, or download audio files. Go to GSOpera (www.gsopera.com/lexicon) for other good information on the work.

Iolanthe is filled with roles that are fun to play and sing; much of the delight of the work is in the basic conflict of the fairy world meeting mortals—in this case, members of the House of Lords. Confusion results from the fact that fairies "never age" (lucky them!). In addition, the male chorus of Peers has one of the most famous and memorable of all entrances, and the female chorus gets to flit about with their fairy wings and wands, ultimately setting the House of Lords on its ear.

The Chorus of *Iolanthe* is composed of the **Chorus of Peers** (the gentlemen) and the **Chorus of Fairies** (the ladies). **The Men** can be of assorted ages and body-types and must be able to march; however **the women** should be—well, they describe themselves as "dainty little fairies"—and should be able to move balletically.

Iolanthe **offers ten principal singing/speaking roles and one female chorus role with a short speaking part. The chorus will be composed of 12 men and 12 women.**

About thirty years ago, my friend Jim Ellis (the editor of the definitive edition of Gilbert's *Bab Ballads*) put together some helpful, if general, "character sketches" for the Valley Light Opera (of Amherst, Massachusetts) *Newsletter*, and he and the editor Bill Venman have given me permission to reproduce it. Jim notes that none of these descriptions are absolute prerequisites (and I agree, of course). He had recently seen, for instance, a Pooh-Bah who was tall, limp, fey, who was "exceedingly good."

> **Iolanthe** (mezzo-soprano)—a figure of pathos or tragedy who has wandered into a G&S opera; elegant of movement; capable of sustained emotional highs and lows; poses like the figures on a Greek grave stele.
> **Phyllis** (soprano)—clear, flute-like voice; picturesque; Dresden china doll; naturally temperamental (like spring days of sun and showers); perfectly matched with Strephon; delicately determined.
> **Fairy Queen** (contralto)—commanding presence; powerful voice and gestures; fearful yet lovable; a cross between Margaret Dumont and Brünnhilde, but far more attractive and amorous.
> **Celia** (soprano)—perhaps small and quick; airy and flitty; delicate gestures; staccato (but not shrill) in voice and manner.

Fleta ([chorister with a] speaking part)—should be fleeter, no doubt, than her fellow fairies; all three of the principal fairies should be good dancers.

Strephon (high baritone)—resonant, clear voice; broadly graceful; "inclined to be stout"; confident; unabashed; your all-round Arcadian shepherd, good on the pipes.

Lord Chancellor (baritone)—flawless, effortless diction; stamina; perfect timing; "a clean old [gentle]man"; gouty but agile; deliberate yet ebullient; irascible yet benign.

Lord Mountararat (baritone)—rich, full voice; perhaps a bit of the walrus or Colonel Blimp about him; slightly ponderous; possibly drawly; discreetly arrogant.

Lord Tolloller (tenor)—aristocratic to the point of effeteness; supercilious; possibly stiff-necked and myopic; one of these two lords should, ideally, have the classic equine physiognomy (horse face) of the English aristocracy.

Private Willis (bass)—not like the Lords; low-born, possibly cockney; imperturbable; matter-of-fact; perhaps lacking a marble or two; good, but stiff, bearing; not necessarily tall.

Now you can see why I remembered this after all these years. And you can also now realize why I'm looking forward to auditions and the rehearsal cycle and performances with such keen anticipation.

Oh! We will also be casting **the Lord Chancellor's Train Bearer** (a non-speaking/singing role). A male (but could be female) child, 9-10 years of age, who appears once in the middle of Act I and once at the end of Act II. Follows the Lord Chancellor, holding his train, and performs a little dance with him.

Please sign up for an audition slot, and please do it today. Then please encourage a friend or two to audition so that even *more* can share the delight of Gilbert & Sullivan. *Iolanthe* is truly a musical, visual, and comedic delight, and I eagerly anticipate working on the show in this new year.

❖

A Ten-Question Quiz on *Iolanthe*

I'm sitting in the Gilbert & Sullivan room here in Bridgewater, keenly anticipating a return to Austin to stage *Iolanthe*. As I reflect on this beautiful and funny show, I also think of its history, some aspects of which make it unique in the G&S canon and some of which tie it to other works.

And I thought it might be fun to offer a little quiz. *Now don't panic!* I recall from my teaching career that quizzes are good not only for assessment of new learning but also as aids to learning new material. I am, therefore, appending the answers, and offer this dispensation for peeking.

1. What does the name *Perola* have to do with the history of *Iolanthe*?

2. Gilbert & Sullivan second acts usually begin with a chorus; however, several of the operas start with solos. Lady Jane opens Act II of *Patience* (though an off-stage chorus precedes a bit of dialogue before her famous solo with cello accompaniment). The second act of *Ruddigore* begins with a duet. Two of the operas begin second acts with male solos. *Iolanthe* is one. What are the first words of this solo? Who sings it?

3. Which *other* opera begins Act II with a male solo? Who sings it? What is the lyric's first line?

4. *Iolanthe* has at least two nods to Richard Wagner: one in costuming (in the original production, anyway) and the other in music. What are they?

5. *Iolanthe* contains at least one sung stage direction. What is it?

6. An ebullient trio in *Iolanthe* reads as if Gilbert plundered *Brewer's Dictionary of Phrase and Fable*, for in his lyric, he strings together a number of well-known expressions. List at least three of these expressions, worded as you've heard them stated.

7. Gilbert did the same in a duet from another opera. What are the first words of the lyric? In which opera does it appear? Who sings it? List at least five of the expressions from this duet, worded as you've heard them stated.

8. In the Lord Chancellor's famous "nightmare song" we learn details of the singer's stockings (at least those he was wearing in his dream). Of what material are they made and how are they decorated?

9. Although many actual persons are referred to in passing in the libretti for the Savoy operas, one real person is actually apostrophized at some length in *Iolanthe*. Who is this person? What was his profession? And where was he, usually, on the nights of Gilbert & Sullivan premières?

10. In the Act I finale of *Iolanthe* the Fairy Queen threatens the Peers with "dire revenge." How does she threaten to reform the hereditary Peerage?

EXTRA CREDIT. The doyenne of Gilbert studies, the late Jane W. Stedman, wrote about what she called Gilbert's "invasion plot," where a realistic setting is established, only to have it "invaded" by personages one would hardly expect to find present in such a setting (bridesmaids in a court of law; ladies aboard a man-of-war; a London sorcerer at a village betrothal, etc.). Discuss at length (or at least ruminate on!) how *Iolanthe* might be regarded as a more-than-usually skillful use of this motif—different in each act. Corroborative detail welcome!

Answers to
The Ten-Question Quiz on *Iolanthe*

1. Gilbert called the opera *Perola* in rehearsal, ostensibly to fool the theatrical pirates hoping to steal the work, but probably because another play with the title *Iolanthe* had been on the London stage several years earlier, and WSG wasn't on good terms with the manager who produced it. (It is sometimes thought that Perola was superstitiously used for the successor to *Pinafore*, *Pirates*, and *Patience*, which *Perola*—*Iolanthe*—followed.)

2. They are, of course, "When all night long a chap remains," sung by Private Willis to banish the monotony of sentry-go (and to delight us).

3. Aboard *H.M.S. Pinafore*, her commander, Captain Corcoran, sings "Fair moon, to thee I sing."

4. The Fairy Queen was dressed in garb reminiscent of Brünnhilde, and the Lord Chancellor is introduced musically several times by an orchestral *leitmotif*.

5. "Enter all the little fairies/ To their usual tripping measure" (in the Act I Finale). (Is there another?)

6. "Faint heart never won fair lady," "Every journey has an end," "Make hay while the sun shines," "None but the brave deserve the fair," "Nothing ventured, nothing gained," "Blood is thicker than water," "Love makes the world go 'round" (and others).

7. "Things are seldom what they seem" is sung aboard *H.M.S. Pinafore* by Mrs. Cripps (better known as "Little Buttercup"): "Black sheep dwell in every fold," "All that glitters isn't gold," "Only the brave

deserve the fair," "Spoil the rod and spoil the child," "Don't count your chickens before they're hatched," "Men are just big babies" (and others).

8. They're made of black silk and are decorated with gold clocks (and this information may be the most tongue-twisting phrase to articulate in the devilishly difficult "Nightmare Song").

9. Captain Eyre Massey Shaw was the leader of London's Fire Brigade, and a regular first-nighter at Gilbert & Sullivan premières. Recent research has suggested that the Fairy Queen's reference to Shaw as a "type of true love kept under" may have been Gilbert's sly dig at a rumor that Captain Shaw . . . well, this is a family newsletter, and I'd better let it drop (but see Ian Bradley's *Annotated Gilbert & Sullivan* for the juicy details).

10. By throwing it open to—gasp!—competitive examination!

EXTRA CREDIT. Peers of the Realm in Court regalia visit "an Arcadian landscape" and supernatural fairies visit Westminster in Central London. (Brevity is the soul of wit!)

What's So Great about *Iolanthe*?

It's become something of a cliché to say that for many, *Iolanthe* is the loveliest or most beautiful of the Gilbert & Sullivan operas. And that *The Yeomen of the Guard* is the closest the team ever came to grand opera. And that The *Gondoliers* represents the high water mark in high spirits. And that—well, completing this little list is a task I'd rather leave to *you*.

But it can't be denied: for many of us Savoyards, *Iolanthe* ranks high or highest on our list of favorites—when we're forced to pick favorites.

In 1882, when *Iolanthe* was written, Gilbert and Sullivan were at the height of their powers. After a rather shaky start in 1871, Richard D'Oyly Carte united the librettist and composer for their first great hit, *Trial by Jury*. Its success led to the formation of a company expressly for production of English light opera, and ultimately the comic operas of Gilbert & Sullivan. *The Sorcerer* was their next collaboration—and what a string of hits it heralded!

The Sorcerer led to *H.M.S. Pinafore* and international fame. *The Pirates of Penzance* followed, and then came *Patience*. During the original run of this "Aesthetic Opera," D'Oyly Carte completed the Savoy Theatre, and it was there that *Iolanthe* opened, making it, literally, the first "Savoy opera."

The Savoy, as has often been noted, was the first public building in *history* to be lit throughout by "the new electric light." Enterprising producer D'Oyly Carte even gave his fairies in *Iolanthe* headdresses that lit up thanks to batteries the ladies wore in the smalls of their backs.

It's hard to fault either librettist or composer for any shortcomings when thinking of *Iolanthe*. Gilbert's metrical challenges for Sullivan's settings were becoming more complex, and the composer invariably met them. But G also provided S with the musical opportunities he craved: compare "dainty little fairy" music (which is often compared with Mendelssohn's) with that rousing March of the Peers—or the high spirits of so much of the score with the moving appeal by Iolanthe to The Lord Chancellor at the end. The Act I finale is arguably the best in the entire series, and Sullivan even arranged the overture himself, something he usually delegated to an associate.

One of the great appeals of Gilbert & Sullivan for me is its very "Englishness," and *Iolanthe* is as English as Savoy opera gets. And, as usual with G&S, the humor still works beautifully across the pond and across the years.

Our last production of this endearing and enduring work was exactly ten years ago. Some veterans of that production will be back in their former roles: nimble-articulator Arthur DiBianca as The Lord Chancellor, rubber-faced Russell Gregory as Private Willis. Jay Young will again march with the Peers, Angela Irving will trade in chorister fairy wings for the mortality of Phyllis, and Andy Fleming, Earl Tolloller a decade ago, will be an unnamed Peer in the chorus while also serving as our Chorus Master and Assistant Conductor.

But one of the strengths of our band of enthusiastic Savoyards is that it is always changing and expanding, and you will also see (and hear) with delight others that have joined us since that last production—and there will be newcomers to this particular production, too.

As I write, I have just finished the first day of staging rehearsals in Austin. The cast has been prepared beautifully by Jeffrey Jones-Ragona, and I am confident I can promise an exceptionally fine production.

But the proof will be in the pudding. Join us at Brentwood Christian School in June to see and hear for yourself. Tickets are now on sale. I predict audiences will be leaving the theatre echoing a lyric from early in Act I: "Welcome to our hearts again, Iolanthe"!

So what's so great about *Iolanthe*? The answer, in a word, is, of course: *everything!*

A Postscript Concerning the Quiz in the Last Newsletter

Sometimes I wonder whether anyone really reads my deathless prose. But I learned recently that at least one person does when I received a text from an alert Savoyard who had read my *Iolanthe* quiz in the April-May issue. I had noted that "Two of the operas begin second acts with male solos. *Iolanthe* is one." I then asked, "Which other opera begins Act II with a male solo?"

The answer I gave was *H.M.S. Pinafore.*

My reader noted, "The question is misleading. There are three Act II openings that begin with a male solo!!!"

He was right, and the first person who sends email to RafeMacPhail@Yahoo.com with the name of that third Gilbert & Sullivan opera with an Act II that begins with a male solo will receive from this careless test maker a Gilbert & Sullivan gift.

By the way, my alert correspondent was Alexander MacPhail, who is at least as ardent a Savoyard as is his father.

Welcome to Our Hearts Again, Iolanthe

Though we Savoyards love our frequent visits to Titipu, Cornwall, and aboard H.M.S. Pinafore, we eagerly anticipate our rarer opportunities to take paths less traveled. Our journey to Fairyland this spring and summer has been a delightful adventure.

Iolanthe was written in 1882, when Gilbert and Sullivan were approaching the height of their dynamic creativity. The comic opera followed the successes of *H.M.S. Pinafore*, *The Pirates of Penzance*, and *Patience*, at a time when each new G&S première was eagerly anticipated by theatrical London. For *Iolanthe*, celebrities packed the stalls in Richard D'Oyly Carte's new theatre, the Savoy—the first public  building in the world lit with something new: "the electricity."

Each partner brought the best of his talent to *Iolanthe*, and this happy state of things led to a remarkable achievement. Arthur Sullivan's score is all but universally regarded as one of his two most beautiful (*The Yeomen of the Guard* is the other), and the composer even orchestrated the delightful overture himself, a task he usually left to an assistant.

W. S. Gilbert combined a couple of ideas from his "Bab" Ballads, mixed in a dose of English pantomime, stirred with his topsy-turvy swizzle stick, and an effervescent libretto emerged as light as a Fairy but with the political irony he was famous for as a garnish.

Pleasures come in endless series . . .

Gilbert gave Sullivan a remarkable variety of lyrics to set: love songs, comic turns, elfin and martial choruses, duets and trios (including one trio that surprisingly turns into a quartet), and an Act I finale (always a highlight of a Savoy opera) that is arguably the best in the series. Gilbert and Sullivan are of course well known for their "patter songs," and the longest and most challenging one is found in Act II of Iolanthe: the Lord Chancellor's famous musical description of his nightmare. Gilbert's complex and very regular metrical and rhyme schemes are given variety and color by Sullivan's masterful orchestration. Listen for them!

Gilbert was also a master of contrasts, and his two settings ("An Arcadian Landscape" by day and "Palace Yard, Westminster" in central London by night) reinforce the librettist's penchant for topsy-turvydom, especially when the first is invaded by the House of Peers (in full Court regalia!), and the second is invaded by the supernatural fairies, one of whom actually takes over Parliament.

Gilbert also gave Sullivan something else the composer craved: opportunities for music to enhance situations of "real human interest and probability." The most moving one comes toward the end of Act II. Listen for that, too!

Here's a pretty kettle of fish!

While the Savoy operas were very much "of their time," they have also transcended the late nineteenth century in the most delightful ways, for they have proved to be enduring as well as endearing works for over a century without changing a word or a note. The librettos continue to stand on their own in performance, and don't need "updating" (ugh!) or dozens of footnotes to be enjoyable to audiences a century later. However, *Iolanthe* differs from the other works in the series in that there remains in the conventional libretto an extended apostrophe by the Fairy Queen to a mysterious

> . . . Captain Shaw!
> Type of true love kept
>   under!
> Could thy Brigade
> With cold cascade
> Quench my great love, I
>   wonder!

   Captain Eyre Massey Shaw was Chief of London's Metropolitan Fire Brigade from 1861 to 1891, and was a regular attendee of opening nights at the Savoy. When the Fairy Queen addressed him in song on November 25, 1882, she brought down the house—and ensured that his name would not be forgotten for as long as *Iolanthe* continues to delight audiences.

   Some groups like to update the song. One of our auditionees for the role of the Fairy Queen used this version of the second verse, evidently found on YouTube, written by Holly Hindle and used by the Gilbert & Sullivan Very Light Opera Company of Minneapolis in 1992 and 2004:

> This fire that glows with lambent flame
> I now expose to scorn and shame
> And out it goes in duty's name.
> Our fairy law must be our guide;
> We're like a straw upon its tide;
> Its power raw a river wide.
>   Oh river wide! Oh Colorado mighty!
>   Not wet enough to fully snuff
>   The flame of Aphrodite.

   Long live *Iolanthe* as Gilbert wrote it, and thank you for joining us on our journey to Fairyland.

Artistic & Stage Director: Ralph MacPhail, Jr.

Music Director: Jeffrey Jones-Ragona

Worley Barton Theater at Brentwood Christian School

Austin, Texas

March 7 and 8, 2020

Mr. Jericho: A "Curtain-Raiser"

A "curtain-raiser" sounds like a stagehand who operates the grand drape in a theatre, and that's exactly what it is.

Or can be. But the term can also denote a short dramatic work that precedes the main work of a theatrical entertainment.

When our Victorian forebears went to the theatre, they might have gone for a full evening's entertainment roughly analogous to screenings in cinemas that those of us of a certain age may remember (previews, newsreel, cartoon, feature). The bill might have included a short dramatic work not related to the featured piece (a curtain-raiser), the main attraction, and an "after-piece" or another short dramatic work to conclude the performance. Newspaper advertisements often carried start times for the featured work so that playgoers could decide which piece(s) they wished to see, and in long runs, the curtain-raisers and after-pieces might (and frequently did) change.

And sometimes these shorter "ephemeral" works outlived the featured attractions they accompanied.

In recent years, Gilbert & Sullivan Austin has presented three short works by Gilbert and/or Sullivan which have served as curtain-raisers and after-pieces. *Trial by Jury* began its long life in 1875 as an after-piece but has spent more than a century as a curtain-raiser for shorter Gilbert & Sullivan operas. The slightly longer *Cox and Box*, originally written for private performance, was shortened twice for use as a curtain raiser and, like *Trial by Jury*, toured for years by the original D'Oyly Carte Opera Company. And *The Zoo*, rescued from obscurity and published for the first time several decades ago, started life as a part of a longer bill and is frequently used today by companies devoted to Gilbert & Sullivan as a curtain-raiser.

Which brings us to *Mr. Jericho*, a very funny one-act operetta which was not written or composed by Gilbert or Sullivan, but which was written in 1893 by Harry Greenbank and composed by Ernest Ford for the Savoy Theatre's production of Sullivan and Sydney Grundy's *Haddon Hall*. It was published at the time, but fell into obscurity until published in a new scholarly edition in England only last year.

Gilbert & Sullivan Austin will present it in March as the feature of a production we're calling *A Day at the Savoy Theatre*. This will include some favorite and familiar musical numbers from Gilbert & Sullivan operas that premiered at the Savoy; the five Austin Savoyards presenting these numbers will then present the fully staged and costumed Texas premiere of *Mr. Jericho.*

More about these performers, their selections, and the history of *Mr. Jericho* will follow in the next issue of *The Austin Savoyard.* In the meantime, please mark March 7th and 8th on your calendars and plan to be present for a performance. We promise you a rollicking good time!

A Day at the Savoy Theatre; or, Who is Mr. Jericho?

Mark your calendars: Gilbert & Sullivan Austin's mid-season show, *A Day at the Savoy Theatre*, combines history and enter-tainment in the best Victorian fashion and will be presented at Brentwood Christian School on March 7th and 8th. Our Chief Financial Officer, Dave Wieckowski, has written a wonderful narrative telling the tale of the first theatre in the world to be lit entirely by electricity. It was the Savoy in London, and it was built by impresario Richard D'Oyly Carte expressly to present the original runs of the Gilbert & Sullivan operas, now known collectively as the Savoy operas (even though several earlier works by G&S premièred before the Savoy was built).

The name of the theatre is also found in the word "Savoyard," which has traditionally been applied to people who perform Gilbert & Sullivan and to admirers of the Victorian duo's works (like us). And of course, Gilbert & Sullivan Austin has used the term in the new name for its venerable newsletter, now known as *The Austin Savoyard.*

Working with Dave was Janette Jones, who accepted the pleasant task of selecting musical numbers from the Savoy operas that opened at this theatre between 1881 and 1889. As she wrote, "I selected the songs for the beauty and fun. My intention was always to show off the talents of the wonderful performers singing in *Mr. Jericho.*" (Mr. Jericho? Who is Mr. Jericho? Read on!) Those wonderful performers are Patricia Combs, Reagan Murdock, Taylor Rawley, Amy Selby, and Julius Young, who will be accompanied by Jeanne Sasaki. Jeffrey Jones-Ragona will serve as Music Director. The numbers Janette selected run the Gilbert & Sullivan gambit, as some of my students used to say, from the patter of "When I first put this uniform on" from *Patience*; the ebullient trio from *Iolanthe*, "If you go in"; through Nanki-Poo's famous self-introduction, "A wandering minstrel, I" from *The Mikado*; Sir Roderick's ghostly "When the night wind howls" from *Ruddigore*; to poignant numbers from *Iolanthe*, *Princess Ida*, *The Yeomen of the Guard*, and *The Gondoliers*. And it will be my great pleasure to share Dave's research with you as master of ceremonies, along with the dozens of images Dave collected to enhance his narrative.

But that's just Act One! The second part of the program will be a performance of *Mr. Jericho*, written by Harry Greenbank and composed by Ernest Ford. It was first presented at the Savoy as a curtain-raiser (see last month's column) for Sullivan's *Haddon Hall* (libretto by Sydney Grundy) and later at the Savoy for an ill-fated work by Sherlock Holmes's creator Arthur Conan Doyle and Peter Pan's creator J. M. Barrie called *Jane Annie*. (And the less you know about that, the better.) *Mr. Jericho* was briefly in print, but for decades languished in obscurity until a recent republication in a scholarly edition (including the orchestration) spread the word of this delightful work. We believe our production will be its Texas première, and may be among the first half-dozen ever presented in this country.

So the real question is not *who* is Mr. Jericho, but *what* is *Mr. Jericho*? The answer is that it's a charming work filled with pleasant musical numbers and funny characters and dialogue poking fun (as Gilbert & Sullivan often did) at class distinctions and their impediments to "true love." It will be colorfully costumed and fully staged with the suggestion of a set, and will be performed with grand-piano accompaniment by Jeanne Sasaki. And to finally answer my question, the eponymous Mr. Jericho is actually the manufacturer of "Jericho's Jams," a popular breakfast staple, and we guarantee you'll be singing his advertising jingle long after the curtain rings down!

A Day at the Savoy Theatre will offer familiar Gilbert & Sullivan numbers as well as some new (to us) music and theatrical delight from two of Gilbert & Sullivan's dramatic and musical friends. Join us at Brentwood for the fun!

Mr. Jericho!

One of the delightful aspects of spending the last half-century devoted to Gilbert & Sullivan has been following the scholarship devoted to this remarkable collaboration.

I have seen Sullivan's full orchestral scores come out of London bank-vaults and made available to all. I have seen books strip away the mythology that has surrounded the storied collaboration of W. S. Gilbert and Arthur Sullivan (and Richard D'Oyly Carte). I have seen and heard performances of Sullivan's non-Gilbert works (including his oratorios) as well as Gilbert's non-Sullivan dramatic works. I have witnessed the lesser-known Savoy operas receiving more and more performances. I have been delighted to note that interest in Gilbert & Sullivan is now a part of the grist for scholarly journals and the repertoires of "grand" opera houses.

Today's presentation of *Mr. Jericho* represents another way in which scholarship into the history of the Savoy operas has deepened and broadened, for just five years ago, *Mr. Jericho* (words by Harry Greenbank; music by Ernest Ford) was an obscure footnote in the "post-carpet-quarrel" career of Gilbert & Sullivan. It was written in 1893 as a curtain-raiser for *Haddon Hall*, which was produced at the Savoy and composed by Sullivan, but written by Sydney Grundy. After a century of obscurity, *Mr. Jericho* was rescued from its fate by musicologist Christopher O'Brien and published in England.

I ordered a copy as soon as it became available, and found it a laugh-out-loud delight. The music sounds a lot like Sullivan's (Ernest Ford was Sullivan's pupil at the Royal Academy of Music), and Harry Greenbank was well on his way toward writing the tremendous successes of "the new musical comedy" at Daly's Theatre—works that for a while seemed to supersede comic opera in the public's estimation in the 1890s. Greenbank was surely familiar with his Gilbert & Sullivan, and in *Mr. Jericho* you may hear echoes of *The Sorcerer*, *The Pirates of Penzance*, *Iolanthe*, and—well, discovering Greenbank's possible antecedents is a delight I'd rather leave to *you*.

Our aim has been to offer an appealing array of familiar musical numbers that were first presented at the Savoy Theatre, and then give the same five singers a chance to present the Texas première of *Mr. Jericho*. GSA's CFO Dave Wieckowski wrote the historical narrative tying the first part together, thus with the singers setting the musical and historical stage for this little gem of an operetta.

❖

Appendix

Two Productions for
The Gilbert & Sullivan Society
of North Louisiana

Ducring the years of directing for Gilbert & Sullivan Austin, I had two opportunities to direct two short Gilbert plays in Shreveport for the G&S Society there. I hope I will be pardoned for adding them to this book of idle chatter "from Gilbert & Sullivan Austin."

The invitations for these memorable experiences came from Dr. John Goddard, President of the Society, who had the happy idea in 2007 of presenting Gilbert's Shakespearean burlesque *Rosencrantz and Guildenstern* (1874) as a curtain-raiser for Carl Rosa Opera Company's touring production *The Pirates of Penzance* at the Strand Theatre in downtown Shreveport. (How he got the Carl Rosa group to agree to this has always been a mystery to me, but I'm pleased that it worked out.)

Rosencrantz and Guildenstern was pre-cast by Dr. Goddard, and Alice and I flew in to Shreveport for a week of rehearsals before the show's one and only performance at the Strand on April 16th.

It was something of a nostalgia trip for me, for I'd directed *Rosencantz and Guildenstern* in 1972 as a part of my Master of Fine Arts thesis project and had been looking for an opportunity to work on it again for *years*. I'd also had an opportunity to present a paper on the history of the play at the W. S. Gilbert Sesquicentennial Conference at M.I.T. in 1986.

Alice and I enjoyed getting to know John and the participating actors, but on our return to Virginia (John drove us to Richmond, where we were reunited with our own car for the return to Bridgewater), we didn't anticipate a "return engagement."

John Goddard, however, had other ideas, and two years later I was back in Shreveport to direct Gilbert's charming two-act play, *Sweethearts* (also an 1874 product of WSG's pre-Savoy opera pen).

Though familiar with the play I'd never directed it, but thoroughly enjoyed this opportunity to work on a play showcasing Gilbert's "softer side."

I flew to Shreveport from Austin, where I'd been for casting a production of *Iolanthe* (and to perform in an *Iolanthe*-themed musicale dubbed a "Magicale").

Sweethearts ran for four performances in March 2009 at the Black Box Theatre at LSU-Shreveport; it attracted some positive press, and once again I left Shreveport with feelings of pleasure, being driven back to Austin by the ever-hospitable Russell and Kay Gregory who'd made the trip to Shreveport to see the production.

So I turned my attention to the summer's *Iolanthe* and then to the following summer's production of *The Yeomen of the Guard*.

John Goddard, however, had the wonderful idea of reviving *Sweethearts* and trucking the entire production to the Gilbert & Sullivan Festival scheduled for Gettysburg, Pennsylvania, in June of 2010.

Somehow I returned to Shreveport to whip up the revival, then return to Austin for duties associated with *The Yeomen of the Guard* as *Sweethearts* ran for two performances in Shreveport at the Anderson Auditorium, Centenary College.

After *The Yeomen of the Guard* closed in Austin, I returned to Bridgewater while the ever-energetic John Goddard then packed up the "impedimenta of illusion" and everything else associated with *Sweethearts*, and with the cast and crew traveled from Shreveport to the Festival, where I joined the company for the single performance there at Gettysburg College's Kline Theatre.

I'll always be grateful to John Goddard for these opportunities, which he initiated and then supported "in many various ways." Though I'm not used to working with casts selected by another, I have only happy memories of my "work" with those "friends of John," the Shreveport Savoyards who brought their considerable talents to both *Rosencrantz and Guildenstern* and *Sweethearts*.

They also showed, I believe, that these two short plays have been unjustly neglected.

❖

A Classic Night of Savoy Theatre

The Gilbert & Sullivan Society of North Louisiana
presents

Rosencrantz and Guildenstern

– and –

THE CARL ROSA OPERA'S
PRODUCTION OF

The Pirates of Penzance

G&S
of NLa

4.16.07 @ 7:30 PM
THE STRAND THEATRE

Bab and the Bard

A Short History of *Rosencrantz and Guildenstern*

O n October 31, 1874, English actor Henry Irving scored an incredible critical success with his revival of *Hamlet* at the Lyceum Theatre in London.

Irving was a wildly popular but idiosyncratic actor, with an unusual gait and equally unusual vocal delivery, honed for years while acting everything from melodrama to Shakespeare.

W. S. Gilbert found the positive press for Irving's adaptation, which ended with the death of the Prince (Irving was, after all, the star), another example of the undeserved adulation the English traditionally gave to dead dramatists in general and Shakespeare in particular—especially adulation for acting editions which were corruptions of the originals.

Irving's production inspired Gilbert's "Rosencrantz and Guildenstern, An Original Tragedy in Three Acts. Founded on an Old Danish Legend" which ran in *Fun* Magazine on December 12, 19, and 26, 1874. (It was Gilbert's final contribution to *Fun,* which had published most his "Bab Ballads" in the 1860s.)

Gilbert's burlesque was different from other burlesques of the day: it was written in blank verse instead of pun-filled rhymed couplets. And his satire was directed toward the variety of interpretations of the moody Dane, not just Irving's. Until the end, that is, when Hamlet is saved from execution for performing Claudius's banned play and is instead banished:

> *Ophelia.* Apollo's son, Lycaeus, built a fane,
> At Athens, where philosophers dispute.
> 'Tis known as the "Lyceum." Send him there,
> He will find such a hearty welcome, sir,
> That he will stay there, goodness knows how long!
> *Claudius.* Well, be it so--and, Hamlet, get you gone!
> [*He goes to the Lyceum, where he is much esteemed.*

"Rosencrantz and Guildenstern" lay buried in the brittle pages of *Fun* until 1890, when Gilbert added it to a volume of his short stories called *Foggerty's Fairy and Other Tales*. The playlet caught the eye of a young woman organizing a charity matinee, and Gilbert granted her performing rights.

The next year, a professional run of *Rosencrantz and Guildenstern* took place at the Court Theatre, where it ran as a part of a longer bill from April to July. For this production, Gilbert wrote a new and more generalized ending (the one we will be using in Shreveport):

> *Ophelia.* (*suddenly*).   A thought!
>   There is a certain isle beyond the sea
>   Where dwell a cultured race—compared with whom
>   We are but poor brain-blind barbarians;
>   'Tis known as Engle-land. Oh, send him there!
>   If but the half I've heard of them be true
>   They will enshrine him on their great good hearts,
>   And men will rise or sink in good esteem
>   According as they worship him, or slight him!
> *Claudius.*   Well, we're dull dogs in Denmark. It may be
>   That we've misjudged him. If such race there be—
>   (There may be—I am not a well-read man)
>   They're welcome to his philosophic brain—
>   So, Hamlet, get thee gone—and don't come back again!
>   . . . HAMLET, *who is delighted at the*
>   *suggestion, . . . strikes an attitude,*
>   *exclaiming,* "To Engle-land!" . . . *Picture.*

The play was presented at four additional charity matinees during Gilbert's lifetime (in 1902, '04, '06, and '08), with Gilbert usually staging the piece and invariably playing King Claudius himself.

Rosencrantz and Guildenstern was revived a handful of times during the later twentieth century, usually before Gilbert & Sullivan enthusiasts. It deserves to be better and more widely known.

A G&S Fringe Production
in association with
LSU-S Theater Department

GS

Sweethearts

by

W. S. Gilbert

with a
special soundtrack of music by
A.S. Sullivan

Directed by
Ralph MacPhail, Jr.

featuring

Anna Maria Sparke Keele
John Bogan
John Chambers
Michelle Loridans

LSU-S Black Box Theatre

19-22 March 2009

The Acclaimed *Sweethearts* Festival Production Sponsor

Your First Class
Ticket to Great
Entertainment!

Sweethearts

by

W.S. Gilbert

*An International Gilbert & Sullivan
Festival Select Production at the
Gettysburg Arts Festival*

directed by
Ralph MacPhail, Jr.

featuring
Anna Maria Sparke Keele
John Bogan
John Chambers
Chelsea David

Anderson Auditorium
Centenary College
18-19 June 2010

Kline Theatre
Gettysburg College
26 June 2010

W. S. Gilbert's *Sweethearts*

This charming play shows a softer side of the man who wrote the wittily brittle libretti for the Savoy operas. *Sweethearts* is set in a realistic garden and concerns two characters of some depth whom we meet in early adulthood and then thirty years later. Gilbert was paying homage to his theatrical mentor Tom Robertson and his "cup and saucer dramas" (so called because of the realistic stage "business" and small-talk which informs the unspoken "subtext" in dialogue).

But Gilbert can't resist giving Spreadbrow a quibble of time on Saturn (had he lived there, he tells Jane he would be a child of two, reminding us of Frederic's leap-year natal day in *The Pirates of Penzance*, making him, "legally," a little boy of five!). During rehearsals, we've enjoyed getting to know these characters—and discovering Gilbert's penchant for topsy-turvy humor that is imbedded in *Sweethearts*. The task of finding them in performance we'd rather leave to *you*.

Sweethearts, written in 1874, was one of Gilbert's most popular non-musical plays. Following its successful production, the dramatist reduced the plot to a song-lyric of three verses and a refrain and asked a friend to set it to music. That friend was Arthur Sullivan, and the song "Sweethearts" was composed in 1875, the year Richard D'Oyly Carte united Gilbert and Sullivan for the first of their thirteen collaborations under his ægis, *Trial by Jury*. A lovely new recording of this song, made expressly for this production, will be played after the lights dim for Act II.

Notes

The history of the Gilbert & Sullivan collaboration has been told and retold in what seem like countless books and articles, so much so that for students of Savoy opera, details have become "common knowledge."

I relied on this "common knowledge" in writing most of the articles in this book (and note below where I have found my memory faulty) but occasionally checked "the standard references" to confirm details, including the remarkable Gilbert & Sullivan Archive.

I also relied on two works, especially when writing about early or revised versions of the libretti; these two books were towering accomplishments at their time of publication and remain so to this day. They are Reginald Allen's *The First Night Gilbert & Sullivan* and Ian Bradley's *The Complete Annotated Gilbert & Sullivan*. Reginald Allen's book, originally published in 1958 (and slightly revised in 1975), gathered important textual matter regarding the libretti and presented it in an appealing if under-documented way; Ian Bradley started annotating Gilbert & Sullivan in 1982 and published an "even more complete" volume in 2016, after most of the texts in this book appeared. I frequently referred to the 2001 edition (a revision of the 1996 one), which (like the original paperback editions of 1982 and '84) shook loose an incredible trove of hitherto unpublished Gilbertian dialogue and lyrics, along with wide-ranging and always interesting annotations to the libretti.

The notes below do not attempt to document every fact in this book with corroborative detail; however, I have felt the need to help readers locate a number of sources of quotations and other information that in my judgement has not fallen into the category of "common knowledge." I have attempted to do this by, either in the text itself or in the notes below, giving enough information to send interested readers to the list of references that follows these notes where they should find sufficient details for further exploration.

Again I wish to thank Arthur Robinson for his valued contributions to these notes.

Most of the illustrations in this book were added to the texts by newsletter editor Sue Ricket Caldwell; the majority of them came from the Gilbert & Sullivan Archive, except for "head-shots" of Gilbert & Sullivan

Austin personnel, which came from her handy library of such "stock im-ages." Sue also occasionally used photographs from the Austin production being discussed.

In the few instances where illustrations from other sources were used (usually material from my own archive), I've offered detail in the following notes.

The following notes begin by giving information on where the foregoing texts originally appeared, and in some cases details of earlier versions on which they were based.

These are then followed by boldfaced quotations from the text and details concerning the quotations, including informal citations and often suggestions for further reading. Since the texts in the body of this book are rather short, I have not encumbered them with distracting signals to the notes following.

Finally, I'd like to note that Gilbert & Sullivan Austin maintains a wonderful website. In addition to giving information on current and fu-ture activities and productions, it also contains a complete run of its news-letter and details of its past productions, including the programs in full text, press releases, photographs, videos, and more, all at an easily memo-rized URL: gilbertsullivan.org.

The Yeomen of the Guard (2010)

Introducing *The Yeomen of the Guard* (p. 7) was published in the No-
vember/December 2009 issue of *The Gilbert & Sullivan Society
of Austin Newsletter* (*GSSANL*), p. 3.

**William Harrison Ainsworth's popular and oft' re-
printed 1840 novel *The Tower of London*** is readily available
from the used-book market. See abe.com.

**Edward Fitzball's libretto for William Vincent Wal-
lace's opera *Maritana*** is readily available online.

Auditions for *The Yeomen of the Guard* (p. 8) was published in the January 2010 issue of *GSSANL*, p. 3. (When I started the pre-audi-
tions columns, I based them on similar articles by James Ellis and
his musical colleagues before they cast Savoy Operas for the Valley Light Opera of Amherst, Massachusetts.)

Some Musical Rarities from *The Yeomen of the Guard* (p. 10) was published in the February/March 2010 issue of *GSSANL*, p. 2, under
the title "March Musicale Preview: Some Musical Rarities from
The Yeomen of the Guard."

This production included Shadbolt's song, Sergeant Meryll's song, and "Rapture, rapture" but not the "couplets" for the
Third and Fourth Yeomen.

Sum Up Some History—Clear Up Some Mysteries (p. 13) was published in the April 2010 issue of *GSSANL*, p. 2 with the byline "by
Ralph MacPhail, Jr.—and Harry Benford!"

That source is *The Gilbert & Sullivan Lexicon* **of Harry
Benford.** In the 3d edition, Chapter XI, *The Yeomen of the Guard*
runs pp. 147-50, which is also available online: gsopera.com/lexicon.

"We, Gilbert and Sullivan, Have A Song to Sing, O!" (p. 15) was published in the May 2010 issue of *GSSANL*, p. 2.

In *the Complete Annotated Gilbert and Sullivan,* **Ian
Bradley notes:** his note is on page 778 of the 1996 edition; page
848 of the 2016 edition.

**William Archer first quoted Gilbert's recollection of
how this well-loved duet came about:** Arthur Robinson told me
that Gilbert's recollection first appeared in 1901 [in William
Archer's "Real Conversation" with W. S. Gilbert in *Pall Mall
Magazine*]; this is the version I've reproduced.

Three years later, Archer collected his "real conversations" into book form, and the Gilbert quotation was included
though slightly edited. Arthur added, "But later sources, such as
Dark & Grey (1923)" on page 108 changed it further, if slightly.

As I struggled with which version to transcribe, Arthur
advised: "Personally, I'd quote the earliest (1901) source."

So that's what I've done.

The quotation in Archer's book *Real Conversations* appears on pp. 123-25; in Dark & Grey it appears on p. 108. Bradley
apparently reprints this version.

I have a song to sing, O! (p. 18) was published in the program for the production presented at the Travis High School Performing Arts Center, Austin, June 10-20, 2010, pp. [10-12].

It is not generally recognized that, as Ian Bradley noted in his *Complete Annotated Gilbert & Sullivan*, Gilbert also tapped into a 'wave of patriotism and nostalgia which swept Britain in the wake of Queen Victoria's golden jubilee' in 1887. Ian Bradley's very interesting note is on p. [755] in the 1996 edition; on p. [825] in the 2016 edition.

The Mikado (2011)

The Mikado: **The Masterpiece** (p. 23) was published in the November/December 2010 issue of *GSSANL*, p. 5.

This and the following columns were written, of course, before the work came under the cloud of "cultural appropriation."

The Mikado's **Secrets** (p. 24) was published in the January 2011 issue of *GSSANL*, p. 5.

D'Oyly Carte copyrighted a work in America called *Titipu; or, The Lord High Executioner*, according to records at the Library of Congress. See "Library of Congress Copyright Office" in list of references below.
In an interview in the *Pall Mall Gazette* published in 1889, Gilbert explained that "It is easy enough to get a title, but very hard to get a good one. For instance 'The Mikado' was a fluke. We had almost settled on 'Titipu.'"

Onward to Titipu! Auditions for *The Mikado* (p. 26) was published in the February/March 2011 issue of *GSSANL*, p. 4.

The Mikado: **Several Secrets in Sullivan's Score** (p. 29) was published in the April 2011 issue of GSSANL, p. 4.

Here's the third verse of Russell's song: See "Fine Old English Gentleman" in the references below for an online source for these lyrics.

The lyrics to **the well-known English war-song, "The Girl I Left Behind Me"** are also online. See "Girl I Left Behind Me, The," in the references below.

Lexicographic Gleanings for *The Mikado* (p. 31) was published in the May 2011 issue of *GSSANL*, pp. 4-5.

These gleanings from **the invaluable *Gilbert and Sullivan Lexicon*** come from Chapter IX, *The Mikado*, pp. 113-25, in the 3rd edition or online at gsopera.com/lexicon.

Our Object All Sublime . . . (p. 35) was published in the program for the production presented at the Travis High School Performing Arts Center, Austin, June 9-19, 2011, [pp. 9-10].

It is rather ironic that this note, proclaiming a traditional production, has the longest "pedigree" of any of the program notes printed in this book. It was first used in July 1977 for a production at Oak Grove Theatre in Verona, Virginia; then twice for productions at Barksdale Theatre in Hanover, Virginia (July-October 1980 and June-September 1989); for Gilbert & Sullivan Austin (in June 1998 and June 2005); and for the Virginia Commonwealth University Opera Theatre (April 2008). Doubly ironic is that the traditional staging concepts proclaimed in this note have passed from favor due to sensitivity to the concept of "cultural appropriation."

Patience (2012)

An Introduction to *Patience* (p. 39) was published in the November/December 2011 issue of *GSSANL*, p. 4.

"Short Article by Rafe on *Patience*" (p. 41) was published in the January 2012 issue of *GSSANL*, p. 3.

I'm going to . . . make this something of a take-home quiz—and I'll leave it that way by not supplying most of the answers back here. But many answers can be found in subsequent articles, and those that are not are worthy of your further research!

2. In the original production, the aesthetic poet Bunthorne was made up and costumed with elements reflecting a well-known painter and a well-known poet: See articles by Alan Fischler, William D. Jenkins, John Bush Jones, Jane W. Stedman, and Carolyn Williams for discussions of Bunthorne's "antecedents." John Bush Jones, in his article "In Search of Archibald Grosvenor," sums up prior thought on the subject and concludes that "Swinburne [is] the most likely candidate for the primary, though not sole, source of the person and poetry of Reginald Bunthorne" (p. 247 in Jones, *W. S. Gilbert*).

Alan Fischler, writing nearly a half-century later, however, makes a convincing case that Bunthorne "is, after all, an ad hominem portrait, and . . . the model was the single prominent artist whose work was both Pre-Raphaelite and aesthetic: Dante Gabriel Rossetti" ("It Proves that Aestheticism Ought to Be Discarded," p. 366).

See Carolyn Williams' article, "Parody and Poetic Tradition" (pp. 379ff) for further discussion on the topic and an analysis of specific poets' works targeted in Bunthorne's dialogue, lyrics, and poem. (Ms. Williams also discusses this in her book, *Gilbert and Sullivan: Gender, Genre, Parody,* pp. 177-81.)

4. Bunthorne's poem in Act I, "Oh, Hollow! Hollow! Hollow!" is *not* a hunting song. In fact, it might be regarded as a rather (for Gilbert in the Savoy operas) scatological poem! What supports this analysis? Carolyn Williams offers lots of support on this interesting topic in her article "Parody and Poetic Tradition: Gilbert and Sullivan's 'Patience'," pp. 382ff and in her book *Gilbert and Sullivan*, pp. 179-81.

5. A seldom appreciated and surprising theme runs through *Patience* equating love with pain: See Jenkins, "Swinburne, Robert Buchanan, and W. S. Gilbert: The Pain that Was All but a Pleasure" for an excellent discussion of this motif.

Audition Notes on *Patience* (p. 42) was published in the February/March 2012 issue of *GSSANL*, p. 4.

Mr. Bunthorne's Solicitor (silent role). For this production, Jeffrey and I cast Gilbert & Sullivan Austin favorite Russell Gregory and also gave him a solo in the Act I Finale: the eight lines starting "Come walk up and purchase with avidity," originally written for Bunthorne.

Spring Fever in Far-Off Bridgewater (p. 44) was published in the April
2012 issue of *GSSANL*, p. 4.

Patience **and Oscar** (p. 46) was published in the May/June 2012 issue of
GSSANL, p. 4.

> **But as Gilbert worked, he felt "hampered" (his word)
> by the idea of clergymen, concerned that such a plot might
> lead to a "charge of irreverence" (also his words).** Gilbert dis-
> cusses this at some length in his "Author's Note" to *Patience, pp.*
> v-vii.

> **Gilbert's original idea for his plot had its "genesis."**
> See Jane W. Stedman's article, "The Genesis of *Patience*" for a
> full description of Gilbert's earlier ideas for the comic opera,
> along with extracts from his early drafts. Carolyn Williams dives
> more deeply into "The Clerical Version" (375) and its influence
> on the final work in "Parody and Poetic Tradition," pp. 375-79.
> Ms. Williams also discusses this in her book, *Gilbert and Sullivan*,
> pp. 175-77.

> Oscar Wilde **went to America on a lecture tour as *Pa-*
> *tience* ran in London.** This tour has been covered by a number
> of books on the poet, recently in a book devoted to this tour by
> Roy Morris, Jr., in *Declaring his Genius: Oscar Wilde in North
> America.*

> **But as Gilbert himself wrote, "The old opera woke up
> splendidly."** Gilbert letter, November 17, 1900, to Sullivan,
> quoted in Reginald Allen's *The First Night Gilbert & Sullivan, p.*
> 461. The quotation is actually the postscript to the letter, which is
> printed in full in Hesketh Pearson, *Gilbert: His Life and Strife, p.*
> 187.

Patience **in Perspective** (p. 49) was published in the program for the pro-
duction presented at the Brentwood Christian School Performing
Arts Center, June 7-17, 2012, pp. [9-10]. It was based on earlier
program notes for productions by Barksdale Theatre, Hanover,
Virginia (June-September 1983) and Gilbert & Sullivan Austin
(June 1999).

**Grosvenor represented another poet, they thought—
Algernon Swinburne.** However, John Bush Jones, "In Search of
Archibald Grosvenor" concluded that Grosvenor's physical char-
acteristics suggest William Morris as Gilbert's inspiration, while
Grosvenor's poetry bears a strong resemblance to that of Coventry
Patmore (pp. 250-55 in Jones, ed., *W. S. Gilbert*).

Alan Fischler makes the interesting case "that the real
real-life model for Archibald Grosvenor [SPOILER ALERT] was
none other than W. S. Gilbert himself"! (See "It Proves that Aestheticism Ought to Be Discarded," pp. 374-81.)

Carolyn Williams' "Parody and Poetic Tradition" ana-
lyzes Grosvenor's poetry in terms of Gilbert's satiric targets (pp.
388ff). Ms. Williams also discusses this topic in *Gilbert and Sullivan*, pp. 181-85.

**Patience's dress was based on Luke Fildes' painting,
"Where Are You Going, My Pretty Maid?"** ... The influences
of these paintings on Gilbert's costumes for *Patience* and his staging were listed by Townley Searle in *Sir William Schwenck Gilbert: A Topsy-Turvy Adventure*, pp. 47-48.

**"When it was revived after a lapse of nineteen years,"
he wrote in 1902, "the 'æsthetic craze' was as dead as Queen
Anne..."** See Gilbert, "Author's Note," p. vii.

*How to Write Your Own
Gilbert & Sullivan Opera* (2012)

"I'm Not Making This Up, You Know!" (p. 53) was published in the
November/December 2012 issue of *GSSANL*, p. 4.

**... the routine Miss Russell recorded in Baltimore in
1984:** The recording was originally released as a videocassette
and then as a DVD under the title *Anna Russell: The (First) Farewell Concert*.

Since receiving this envelope: The envelope, letter, and
autograph quotation are in my "Savoyard Scrapbook," Volume 21
(1983-84).

Princess Ida (2013)

Princess Ida: **Mighty Maiden with a Mission—and A Mighty Melodic Comic Opera, Too** (p. 59) was published in the January 2013 issue of *GSSANL*, p. 4.

> **In my library I have a book entitled** *Castle Adamant in Hampstead: A History of Westfield College 1882-1982*: *Castle Adamant in Hampstead* was written by Janet Sondheimer; publication information can be found in the References following.

> **. . . an incredibly lovely sequence of musical numbers that is frequently called "the string of pearls."** I believe I learned from Michael P. Walters years ago that this description of musical numbers from Act II of *Princess Ida* was first used by H. M. Walbrook in his *Gilbert & Sullivan Opera: A History and A Comment* (1922). Chapter IX, devoted to *Princess Ida*, is headed "A String of Pearls" (p. 73).
>
> Arthur Robinson adds that "Walbrook's is the earliest book I know of to use this phrase of *Princess Ida*, but Sterling Mackinlay, in his book *Light Opera* (London: Hutchinson, 1926), p. 219, seems to claim the *Pall Mall Gazette* used the term in 1913 ('that string of pearls, the second Act'), though he doesn't give a precise citation."

> **Which character in *Princess Ida* is often considered to be a Gilbertian self-portrait?** I resist the temptation to answer this and the following questions. (Many of them, however, are answered in the following columns.)

An Introduction to the Characters and Audition Notes on *Princess Ida* (p. 61) was published in the February/March issue of *GSSANL*, pp. 2-3.

Deadlines—Deadlines—Deadlines! (p. 65) was published in the April 2013 issue of G*SSANL*, p. 4.

> **The resourceful Bill has also managed to rent some interesting props for the Girl Graduates to use in their studies in Act II from our friends at the Gilbert & Sullivan Society of Seattle:** These props included "scientific paraphernalia" such as measuring protractors, chemistry laboratory equipment, biological specimens, etc.

"Useful Knowledge Everywhere One Finds" [1] (p. 68) was published in the May/June issue of *GSSANL*, pp. 4-5.

> **. . . in the end affirms that universal influence, "the sway of love," in a final finale that is unique in the Savoy operas:** We also used, with this permission, Albert Bergeret's rearrangement of lines in the final dialogue sequence which he devised for his company, the New York Gilbert & Sullivan Players. No one seemed to notice, I was *very* pleased, and it certainly did give Ida more dignity going into the resolution.

"Useful Knowledge Everywhere One Finds" [2] (p. 71) was published in the program for the production presented at the Worley Barton Theater at Brentwood Christian School, Austin, June 13-23, 2013, pp 8-9.

Trial by Jury (2014)

Trial by Jury (p. 77) and **The Story** (p. 77) were published in the program for the production presented at First Presbyterian Church, Austin, February 23, 2014, p. 4.

H.M.S. Pinafore (2014)

What's in a Name? (Sometimes, a lot, actually . . .) (p. 81) was published in the November/December 2013 issue of *GSSANL*, p. 4.

> **Sir Joseph is 1) a male and 2) of highest professional rank among the characters (though not the highest in social rank; this topsy-turvy state of things needs a column devoted to it alone).** He almost got it—in the column that follows, "Saluting Sir Joseph," pp. 83ff.

> **I did an online search on "cripps"—and found this definition**—at urbandictionary.com.

> **[And the *West Side Story* gang is called the Crips—with but one p.]** But see the end of "Saluting Sir Joseph," p. 85.

W. S. Gilbert originally called his work *H.M.S. Semaphore*: In the original appearance of this article, I called this a "legend"; in several presentations titled "The Secrets of *H.M.S. Pinafore*" early in this century I suggested doubt that this was true and once even (again) called it a "legend"; however, on a recent reading of Ian Bradley's latest (and "more complete") edition of *The Complete Annotated Gilbert & Sullivan* (2016) I was reminded (on page 198) that in an 1880 Gilbert interview published in *The World* the librettist had indeed admitted that he originally christened his ship H.M.S. *Semaphore* and the change to *Pinafore* was indeed the result of Sullivan's suggestion. *Mea culpa!*

But *did* Sullivan make the suggestion? Arthur Robinson responded to the above, suggesting that the jury may still be out on the matter: "Gilbert referred to *Pinafore*'s originally being called the *Semaphore* not only in the 1880 *World* but in the 1889 *Pall Mall Gazette*. In neither of these sources, however, does he state that it was Sullivan's idea to change the title. But neither does he say explicitly that it was his idea; and I'm sure I've read that he credited Sullivan with rechristening the ship, though I can't locate the source. So again, feel free to leave your note as it is."

I didn't.

Saluting Sir Joseph (p. 83) was published in the January 2014 issue of *GSSANL*, p. 4.

My friend Bill Hyder cautioned me years ago to beware of Sir Josephs wearing epaulettes: On reflection, I think I should have credited William Hyder with more input to this column than I did. Three years earlier he had given a paper titled "*H.M.S. Pinafore* in American Waters" at a symposium I organized for the second Gilbert & Sullivan Festival in Gettysburg. Bill's points concerning Sir Joseph's social v. political status were fresh in my mind, especially after editing the proceedings, which were published as *Papers, Presentations and Patter*.

Audition Notes on *H.M.S. Pinafore* (p. 85) was published in the February/March 2014 issue of *GSSANL*, pp. 2-3.

***Pinafore*an Roots in Bab** (p. 89) was published in the April 2014 issue of *GSSANL*, pp. 2-3.

"That Ole *Pinafore* Magic" (p. 93) was published in the May/June 2014 issue of *GSSANL*, p. 4.

This Saucy Ship's a (Topsy-Turvy) Beauty! (p. 96) was published in the program for the production presented at the Worley Barton Theater at Brentwood Christian School, Austin, June 12-22, 2014, pp. 8-9. It was based on earlier notes for productions presented by Gilbert & Sullivan Austin (June-July 2000 and June-July 2006); and The Pinion Players of Bridgewater College (Virginia) (November 2001). Another antecedent of this note can be found in the program note for the production at Barksdale Theatre, Hanover, Virginia (June-October 1981).

. . . **a reviewer from *The Daily Telegraph* characterized the show as a "frothy production destined soon to subside into nothingness."** This "prescient" review is quoted at length by H. M. Walbrook in his *Gilbert and Sullivan Opera: A History and A Comment* (p. 48): "Messrs. Gilbert and Sullivan have a splendid opportunity of building up a stage for this type of English lyric drama, and it is to be hoped that neither the one nor the other will treat the matter lightly and rest satisfied with the momentary recompense gained by frothy productions destined soon to subside into nothingness."

The Zoo (2015)

[**The illustration on the program cover** (p. 99) was drawn by Geoffrey Shovelton for Harry Benford's *The Gilbert & Sullivan Lexicon* (GSOpera.com/lexicon).]

The Zoo: **The Story** (p. 101) and **The Story Behind the Story** (p. 103) were published in the program for the production presented at the Worley Barton Theater at Brentwood Christian School, Austin, February 15, 2015, pp. 4 and 7.

The work was recorded in 1978 on LP by the D'Oyly Carte Opera Company: This recording was subsequently (in 1993) released on CD in this country on the London label, paired with *The Sorcerer*, according to Marc Shepherd's *Gilbert & Sullivan Discography*

> . . . **while preparing for this production I was reminded of evidence that work had begun on a two-act version of what became *The Zoo* before *Trial by Jury* opened:** See George C. McElroy, "Whose *Zoo*; or, When Did the *Trial* Begin?"

The Sorcerer (2015)

Looking Ahead to *The Sorcerer* (p. 105) was published in the November/December 2014 issue of *GSSANL*, p. 4.

> **First, it was based on earlier work by Gilbert (in this case, a short-story called "An Elixir of Love" published the previous Christmas.** It was published in the Christmas Number of *The Graphic* for 1876. Gilbert subsequently included it in his 1890 collection of short stories, and it has occasionally been reprinted since. See References, below.

> **Reginald Allen, in his *First Night Gilbert & Sullivan*, quotes a number of press reports** on page 48.

The Source of *The Sorcerer* (p. 107) was published in the January 2015 issue of *GSSANL*, p. 4.

> **Gilbert himself, late in life, expressed his "indebtedness to the author of the Bab Ballads . . . from whom I have unblushingly cribbed:** These words are from Gilbert's speech to the O. P. Club in 1906, which was published under the title "Savoy Memories."

> **[Gilbert] went to his own short story, "An Elixir of Love," which had been published in the Christmas issue of *The Graphic* the year before:** See References for to various print appearances of Gilbert's "An Elixir of Love."

Audition Notes on *The Sorcerer* (p. 108) was published in the February/March 2015 issue of *GSSANL*, pp. 2-3.

The "Two" *Sorcerer*s (p. 112) was published in the April 2015 issue of *GSSANL*, p. 4.

Communicating through *The Sorcerer* (p. 115) was published in the May/June issue of *GSSANL*, p. 4.

With Heart and with Voice Let Us Welcome this Mating! (p. 117) was published in the program for the production presented at the Worley Barton Theater at Brentwood Christian School, Austin, June 18-28, 2015, pp. 8-9.

      . . . in a context Gilbert called "a grave and quasi-respectful treatment of the ludicrous." This famous Gilbert quote was cited in the Master's entry by Edward Abbott Parry in the 1912 Supplement to the *Dictionary of National Biography.* "His humour consists mainly in logical topsy-turveydom [*sic*] in a vein so peculiar to Gilbert as to justify the bestowal on it of the epithet 'Gilbertian.' He himself disclaimed any knowledge of Gilbertian humour, stating that 'all humour properly so called is based upon a grave and quasi-respectful treatment of the ludicrous.'"

      But did Gilbert write "ludicrous"? Andrew Crowther led me to Parry's probable source (it's listed in his *DNB* bibliography), Percy Fitzgerald's *The Savoy Opera and The Savoyards.* Fitzgerald quotes Gilbert as writing, in a letter, "I have no notion what Gilbertian humour may be. It seems to me that all humour, properly so called, is based upon a grave and quasi-respectful treatment of the ridiculous and absurd" (p. 14).

Very Truly Yours, Gilbert & Sullivan (2016)

A New Play on an Old Subject (p. 123) was published in the program for the production presented at First Presbyterian Church, Austin, February 21, 2016, pp. 4-5.

      The play was written by Gayden Wren who controls the performing rights and to whom application can be made for further information on possible production:

gaslocoli.wren@gmail.com

      Gayden Wren has written that too often the story of the Gilbert-Sullivan collaboration is defined in popular understanding by their quarrels: Gayden Wren's comments on many retellings of the Gilbert & Sullivan story can be found in his article, "Emphasis on the 'Truly'."

Cox and Box (2017)

Cox and Box: **Another Austin Première** (p. 127) was published in the December 2016/January 2017 issue of *GSSANL,* p. 6.

For me, working on *Cox and Box* in Austin completed a circle. I directed the full-length version in 1972 as a part of my Master of Fine Arts thesis production. . . : It was the full-length version that formed a part of my Master of Fine Arts Thesis production, along with Gilbert's Shakespearean burlesque, *Rosencrantz and Guildenstern.* The plays were presented under the umbrella title *Victoria's World* at Virginia Commonwealth University in Richmond, Virginia, in 1-5 March 1972.

Research on the history of the comic opera for the thesis led, in 1974, to publication of a bit of juvenilia, *Additional Adventures of Messrs. Box and Cox,* which contains F. C. Burnand's "sequel" to *Box and Cox, Penelope Anne,* and W. S. Gilbert's brief prose contribution to *Fun,* "Continuations of Dramatic Histories: *Box and Cox.*"

Must Have a Beginning, You Know! (p. 129) was published in the program for the production presented at Worley Barton Theater at Brentwood Christian School, Austin, March 4 & 5, 2017, p. 5.

Sullivan **sighed, "A cobbler should stick to his last."** Again, I am grateful to Arthur Robinson for his careful reading of this book when it was in the final stages of preparation. He wrote: "You may want to qualify this with something like 'he allegedly sighed . . .'. The source for this is Reginald De Koven, but his account is suspect (he claims that he sat next to Sullivan 'at the first performance in Covent Garden of "Ivanhoe"'[in 1910]— something unlikely since Sullivan had been dead several years; nor could he have sat next to Sullivan at the first night in 1891 since Sullivan was conducting.) I posted about this on Savoynet in 2008, and later found David Eden had already disputed this story; see Sullivan Society *Magazine* No. 62, p. 15 (<sullivansociety.org.uk/wp-content/uploads/2018/12/Magazine-62.pdf>). It's possible that Sullivan said these words at some point, but I think it's safer to qualify unsupported anecdotes like this one."

So do I. Especially when confronted by evidence—or the lack thereof.

The Pirates of Penzance **(2017)**

Why I Love *The Pirates of Penzance***: It's Personal!** (p. 133) was published in the October/November 2016 issue of *GSSANL*, p. 4.

I discovered what Sullivan meant when he wrote to his mother from New York in 1879, ". . . it is exquisitely funny, and the music is strikingly tuneful and catching. It's more humorous and operatic, too": Michael Ainger reprints the first part of this quotation from Sullivan's 10 Dec. 1879 letter to his mother (the original is at the Morgan Library) on p. 177. But I've been unable to find the source from which *I* reprinted the fuller quotation including the second sentence.

Elsewhere the composer noted that the musical situations were more highly developed than in *H.M.S. Pinafore***:** For more from Sullivan's 2 January 1880 letter, see Jacobs, *Arthur Sullivan: A Victorian Musician,* p. 138.

The Illustrations:

The National Theatre's *Playbill* **for** *The Pirates of Penzance* **and the photographs of Ralph MacPhail, Sr., as a pirate and as a policeman:** From MacPhail, Comp., "Savoyard Scrapbook," Vol. 1 (1943-68).

The Richmond Opera Company's program for *The Pirates of Penzance***:** From MacPhail, Comp., "Savoyard Scrapbook," Vol. 7 (1978).

Alexander MacPhail as Major-General Stanley: From MacPhail, Comp., "Adventures with Gilbert & Sullivan" [scrapbook], Vol. 1 (1962-85). The production was presented by the Pinion Players of Bridgewater College (Virginia), 19-22 Oct. 1995.

The plaque on East 20th Street: this photograph is from the Gilbert & Sullivan Archive.

(More about the circumstances of writing the show in The Big Apple in a future column.): See "Fighting Piracy with The Pirates," pp. 140ff.

I can't wait to see (and hear) their show. I wasn't disappointed!

Audition Notes on *The Pirates of Penzance* (p. 136) was published in the February/March 2017 issue of *GSSANL*, pp. 4-5.

Fighting Piracy with *The Pirates* (p. 140) was published in the April-May 2017 issue of *GSSANL,* pp. 4-5.

. . . all without a dollar being returned to the Englishmen across the pond. "It's not that I miss the money," Gilbert snorted. "It upsets my digestion." I slightly misquoted Gilbert from memory (or quoted from an elusive source). Hesketh Pearson, in *Gilbert and Sullivan: A Biography* (p. 112) quotes Gilbert as complaining, "'I will not have another libretto of mine produced if the Americans are going to steal it,' he declared: 'not that I need the money so much, but it upsets my digestion.'"

. . . the Gilbert dictum that "All humour, so-called, is based upon a grave and quasi-respectful treatment of the ludicrous." See the note on Gilbert's definition of humor under "With Heart and with Voice Let Us Welcome this Mating" above, p. 228

If Gilbert called the work "only burlesque of the lowest possible kind . . ." I may have misquoted Gilbert again—or quoted from still another elusive source. In Hesketh Pearson's telling of this story (in *Gilbert and Sullivan: A Biography*, p. 107), the librettist described *H.M.S. Pinafore* (to an operatic diva rehearsing the role of Josephine) as "only a low burlesque of the worst possible kind."

Gilbert & Sullivan pulled off another remarkable coup during their busy stay: they rehearsed and sent out on tour *four complete companies* of *The Pirates of Penzance* in an attempt to reap their rewards before their work could be pirated: Reginald Allen told this fascinating story and more in his booklet, *Gilbert & Sullivan in America: The Story of the First D'Oyly Carte Opera Company American Tour.*

To learn more, find a copy of Reginald Allen's wonderful *First Night Gilbert and Sullivan* and turn to pages 134-38.

A Pass Examination on *The Pirates of Penzance* (p. 142) was published in the June 2017 issue of *GSSANL*, pp. 4-5. It was adapted from material shared for years with Gilbert & Sullivan Road Scholar (Elderhostel) classes in New York, Connecticut, and Virginia.

This particular "exam" was actually put together for an Elderhostel class on *The Pirates of Penzance* offered at Incarnation Center, Ivoryton, CT, in 2004 (and referred to above in "Why I Love *The Pirates of Penzance*: It's *Personal!*", p. 134f).

. . . **decades after Frederic turned 21 (in 1940):** Savoyards have for years discussed the fact that Gilbert forgot (or ignored) the fact that 1900 was not a leap-year, and so Frederic could not to be free of his indentures until 1944. The *New York Times* thought that February 29, 1940, was worthy of a lengthy discussion of the matter. See "Frederic Goes Free."

***The Pirates of Penzance* (1880):** 1880 was indeed the year of the première in London (on April 3rd), but the work was presented in Paignton, England (in a "scratch" copyright performance) on December 30, 1879 and in New York on the last day of that year.

Gilbert and Sullivan: The Very Model of a Merry Musical Partnership (p. 147) was published in the program for the production presented at Worley Barton Theater at Brentwood Christian School, June 15-25, 2017. pp. 10-11. Antecedents of this note can be found in programs for productions for the Richmond (Virginia) Opera Company (July 14-15, 1978); Barksdale Theatre, Hanover, Virginia (June-October 1982); the Pinion Players of Bridgewater College, Virginia (October 1995); and Gilbert & Sullivan Austin (June 2003 and June 2008).

. . . **the critic from *The Sun* reflected on whether the new work was successful:** Reginald Allen reprints this review *The First Night Gilbert & Sullivan*, pp. 102-03.

" . . . Well, hardly ever!" Pedantic note: This line invariably appears in libretti and scores as "Hardly ever!" The performance tradition of adding the "Well," probably dates back to the earliest of days.

Trial by Jury (2018)

Richard D'Oyly Carte: He Had a Dream (p. 153) was published in the December 2017/January 2018 issue of *GSSANL*, pp. 4-5.

Trial by Jury (p. 156) and **The Story** (p. 157) were published in the program for the production presented at Worley Barton Theater at Brentwood Christian School, Austin, March 3 and 4, 2018, p. 4. Alert readers of this book will note that they were also used in the program for the 2014 Austin production.

Ruddigore (2018)

SFX in G&S (p. 161) was published in the October/November issue of *GSSANL*, p. 4.

Audition Notes on *Ruddigore* (p. 163) was published in the February/March 2018 issue of *GASSANL*, pp. 4-5.

> **Something of the "black sheep" of the Savoy opera family:** Since the purpose of this article was to create interest and encourage actor/singers to audition, I rather skipped over *Ruddigore*'s problematic opening-night history. Some of this history, however, can be found in "'Curtain Up' on *Ruddigore*," pp. 174ff. This was the program note for the production, and by the time it was read, the show had been cast and rehearsed, and most readers had purchased their tickets and were in their seats!
> Gilbert and Sullivan and their stage crew had, early in the initial run, fixed many of the problems experienced by the first-night audience, which are also briefly discussed, pp. 174ff.

A Unique Gilbert Lyric (p. 167) was also published in the February/March 2018 issue of *GSSANL*, p. 5.

As noted in the text, "Only Roses" originally appeared in the December 10, 1881, issue of *The Illustrated Sporting and Dramatic News* [on p. 323].

A Genealogical Fantasy (p. 169) was published in the April/May 2018 issue of *GSSANL*, p. 4. "TRIAL BY JURY—A Sequel to *H.M.S. Pinafore*" was originally published in *The Savoyard*, The Magazine of the D'Oyly Carte Opera Trust, 8.3 (January 1970), 17-18. It is reprinted here by kind permission of Ian Martin, General Manager of the D'Oyly Carte Opera Trust.

Setting Contrasts (p. 171) was published in the June 2018 issue of *GSSANL*, p. 4.

As the Master himself said, "All humour so-called is based upon a grave and quasi-respectful treatment of the ludicrous": See the note on Gilbert's definition of humor under "With Heart and with Voice Let Us Welcome this Mating" above, p. 228

"Curtain Up" on *Ruddigore* (p. 174) was published in the program for the production presented at the Worley Barton Theater at Brentwood Christian School, Austin, June 14-24, 2018. Its antecedent was in the program for the Gilbert & Sullivan Austin production of June 2007.

"Well, it put 7,000 pounds into my pocket, and I could do with a few other such failures." I may have been writing from memory or quoting from a now-elusive source. I cannot find a source for this exact quote, but in Gilbert's famous O. P. Club speech (1906) he wrote, "We are credited—or discredited—with one conspicuous failure, 'Ruddigore; or, the Witch's Curse.' Well, it ran eight months, and, with the sale of the libretto, put £7,000 into my pocket. In the blackness of my heart the worst I wish to my rival dramatists is that they may each have a dozen such failures, and retire upon the profits" (p. 12).

The indefatigable Arthur Robinson located this in the first volume of Rutland Barrington's reminiscences: *The Mikado* "achieved a run of some twelve months, a thing that many modern managers would consider quite good enough; but it so impressed me as a kind of failure that I once alluded to it as such in conversation with Gilbert, who remarked, 'I could do with a few more such failures . . .'" (pp. 59-60).

Perhaps my source, which remains a mystery, combined the two?

H.M.S. Pinafore in Concert (2019)

Welcome Aboard! (p. 179) was published in the program for the production presented at the Worley Barton Theater at Brentwood Christian School, Austin, March 2and 3, 2019, p. 5. Alert readers will note that it was adapted and condensed from the program note for the 2014 Austin production (see pp. 96ff).

Gilbert intended to call his ship *H.M.S. Semaphore*, but his composer-colleague Arthur Sullivan suggested christening the vessel with the name of a child's smock. See the note on this name change under "*H.M.S Pinafore*: 'What's in a Name? (Sometimes, a lot, actually . . .)'," above, p. 225. By the time this program note appeared, I'd come to believe that this change at Sullivan's suggestion was not a legend, but, in fact, a *fact*.

. . . a reviewer characterized the show as a "frothy production destined soon to subside into nothingness." This appeared in *The Daily Telegraph*. See the note under "This Saucy Ship's a (Topsy-Turvy) Beauty!" on p. 226, above.

Iolanthe (2019)

***Iolanthe*an Babs** (p. 183) was published in the October/November 2018 issue of *GSSANL*, p. 4. It was an expansion of an earlier article published in the November/December 2008 issue, p. 3, titled "*Iolanthe*'s Background: *The Bab Ballads*."

Another "Lost Lyric" from *Iolanthe* (p. 186) was published in the December 2018/January 2019 issue of *GSSANL*, p. 2. It was a slight expansion of an earlier article published in the January 2009 issue, p. 3, titled "A Little-Known Lyric from *Iolanthe*."

Dickens was one of Gilbert's favorite authors; in fact, the librettist once admitted that he never traveled without a volume of Dickens in his luggage: For a study of Gilbert and Dickens, see Jane W. Stedman's article, "Boz and Bab."

Audition Notes on *Iolanthe* (p. 188) was published in the February/March 2019 issue of *GSSANL*, pp. 4-5. It was an expansion of an earlier article published in the February/March 2009 issue, p. 2, titled "Audition Parts for *Iolanthe*."

> *Now* **you can see why I remembered this after all these years.** If you've noticed the irony of this appearing after so many other similar articles on auditions that built on the idea of but did not quote the Ellis/Venman ones in Amherst, it's because this was originally used for the 2009 production of *Iolanthe*, cited above.

A Ten-Question Quiz on *Iolanthe* (p. 192) and **Answers to The Ten-Question Quiz on *Iolanthe*** (p. 193) were published in the April/May 2019 issue of *GSSANL*, pp. 4 and 5. The quiz was an expansion of an earlier version in the April 2009 issue, p. 7, which appeared with the same title. (The answers appeared in the June 2009 issue, p. 3.)

> **The doyenne of Gilbert studies, the late Jane W. Stedman, wrote about what she called Gilbert's "invasion plot":** See her dissertation, "William S. Gilbert: His Comic Techniques and Their Development," p. 285 and Chapter V, pp. 317-397.

> **. . . but see Ian Bradley's *Annotated Gilbert & Sullivan* for the juicy details:** They're on page 422 in the 1996 edition and page 492 in the 2016 edition.

What's So Great about *Iolanthe*? (p. 194) was published in the June 2019 issue of *GSSANL*, p. 4. It was an expansion of an earlier article in the May 2009 issue, p. 3, titled "What's So Great About *Iolanthe*?"

A Postscript Concerning the Quiz in the Last Newsletter

> **. . . the first person who sends email . . . with the name of that third Gilbert & Sullivan opera with an Act II that begins with a male solo will receive from this careless test maker a Gilbert & Sullivan gift.** I hereby withdraw this offer by revealing the answer: Captain Fitzbattleaxe opens Act II of *Utopia Limited* (1893) with the recitative, "Oh, Zara, my beloved one" and then sings of the travails of singing while in love with "A tenor, all singers above. . . ."

Welcome to Our Hearts Again, *Iolanthe* (p. 196) was published in the
program for the production presented at the Worley Barton Theater at Brentwood Christian School, Austin, June 13-23, 2019. It is
a slightly expanded version of the note that appeared in the program for the June 2009 Austin production.

A Day at the Savoy Theatre with *Mr. Jericho* (2020)

Mr. Jericho: **A "Curtain-Raiser"** (p. 201) was published in the January
2020 issue of *The Austin Savoyard* (*TAS*), p. 1. (This was the first
newsletter issued under its new name.)

A Day at the Savoy Theatre; or, Who is Mr. Jericho? (p. 202) was published in the February 2020 issue of *TAS*, p. 1.

> ***Mr. Jericho*** **was briefly in print, but for decades lan-
guished in obscurity until a recent republication in a scholarly
edition:** It was edited by Christopher O'Brien and published in
London by Stainer and Bell in 2018. I referred to this edition
while writing these three articles on *Mr. Jericho.*
> A nineteenth-century score containing the libretto and a
contemporary re-setting of the libretto (and more) are available at
the Gilbert & Sullivan Archive: https://gsarchive.net/compan-
ions/jericho/index.html.

Mr. Jericho! (p. 204) was published in the program for the production
presented at the Worley Barton Theater at Brentwood Christian
School, Austin, March 7 and 8, 2020.

Appendix:
Two Productions for
The Gilbert & Sullivan Society
of Northwest Louisiana:

Rosencrantz and Guildenstern (2007)

Bab and the Bard: A Short History of *Rosencrantz and Guildenstern*
(p. 209) was published in the program for the production, which

was presented with The Carl Rosa Opera's production of *The Pirates of Penzance* at the Strand Theatre, Shreveport, on April 16, 2007. This and the following production were produced by Dr. John Goddard, President of the Gilbert and Sullivan Society of Northwest Louisiana.

Sweethearts (2009 & 2010)

W. S. Gilbert's *Sweethearts* (p. 213) was published in the programs for the productions which were presented at the LSU-S Black Box Theatre, Shreveport, March 19-22, 2009; then at the Anderson Auditorium, Centenary College, Shreveport, June 18-19, 2010 and at the Kline Theatre, Gettysburg College, Gettysburg, Pennsylvania, June 20, 2010.

Gilbert was paying homage to his theatrical mentor Tom Robertson: I recall consulting Andrew Crowther's article on *Sweethearts* when preparing this article.

A lovely new recording of this song: I asked John Goddard to review what I've written of these two productions, and his replies included this information: ". . . the recording of 'Sweethearts' can be listened to on Apple Music. . . ."

The Apple Music search engine does indeed respond to "'Sweethearts' (Sullivan)" by providing links to both "'Sweethearts' (Song)" and "'Sweethearts' (Album)" by The Gilbert and Sullivan Society of Northwest Louisiana.

Also from John Goddard: "Interesting tidbit: Another recording from that 'Sweethearts' album was used for an independent movie that used a Gilbert and Sullivan play production as part of the plot."

The movie, *She Lights Up Well*, was released in 2014. The producers licensed Sullivan's song "The Long Day Closes" from the "Sweethearts" CD. The film tells the story (according to the IMDb [Internet Movie Database] of "[a]n out-of-work actress [who] moves back in with her parents and directs a production of Gilbert and Sullivan's 'The Mikado' to try and save the community theater," which helps to explain the title.

I have not seen *She Lights Up Well* on a large or smaller screen, nor does it seem to have been released on DVD. Dr. Goddard saw the film "on either YouTube Movies or Amazon Prime.

. . . 'The Long Day Closes' did make the final cut—deployed at the crisis part of the Narrative."

References and Further Reading

This list contains references specifically referred to in the texts included in this book (in detail or in passing) and in the preceding notes. It also lists general references consulted to confirm "common knowledge" as well as suggestions for further reading.

Ainger, Michael. *Gilbert and Sullivan: A Dual Biography.* Oxford: Oxford UP, 2002. Print.

Ainsworth, William Harrison. *The Tower of London.* London & Glasgow: Collins' Clear-Type Press, n.d. Print.

Apple Music. "'Sweethearts' (Sullivan)." Web. 8 Nov. 2013. <https://music.apple.com/us/search?term=Sweethearts%20(Sullivan)>.

Archer, William. *Real Conversations.* London: Heinemann, 1904. Print.

_____. "Real Conversations. Conversation VI.—with Mr. W. S. Gilbert." *Pall Mall Magazine* 25 (1901): 88-98. Print.

Allen, Reginald. *The First Night Gilbert & Sullivan.* New York: Heritage, 1958. Centennial Ed. London: Chappell, [1975]. Print.

_____. *Gilbert & Sullivan in America: The Story of the First D'Oyly Carte Opera Company American Tour.* New York: Morgan Library/Gallery Assn. of NY State, 1979. Print.

Baily, Leslie. *The Gilbert & Sullivan Book.* [Revised Edition.] London: Spring Books, 1966. Print.

Barrington, Rutland. *Rutland Barrington by Himself.* London: Grant Richards, 1908. Print.

Benford, Harry. *The Gilbert & Sullivan Lexicon.* 2nd ed. Ann Arbor: Jennings, 1991. 3rd ed. Houston: Queensbury, 1999. Print. Online Edition: Web. 24 Aug. 2023 <https://gsopera.com/lexicon>.

Bergeret, Albert. "Final Dialogue in Act III of PRINCESS IDA." Messages to the author. 21 & 22 August 2012. E-mail.

"'Blank, Blank!' The New Opera at the Savoy. A Chat with Mr. Gilbert." *Pall Mall Gazette* (3 Dec. 1889); rpt. *Chicago Tribune* (29 Dec. 1889): p. 17. Web. 20 Nov. 2023 https://gsarchive.net/gilbert/interviews/blank_blank.html.

Bordman, Gerald. *American Operetta: from* H.M.S. Pinafore *to* Sweeney Todd. New York: Oxford UP, 1981. Print.

Bradley, Ian. *The Complete Annotated Gilbert & Sullivan*. Oxford: Oxford UP, 1996 and 2016. Print.

Brooke, William J. "Princess Ida Children's Matinee" [reproduced t.s. for a production of *Princess Ida* by the Village Light Opera Group in NY City, date uncertain]. Print.

Burnand, F. C. *Penelope Anne.* See MacPhail, *Additional Adventures of Messrs. Box and Cox.*

"Celebrities at Home. No CXCV. Mr. W. S. Gilbert at the Boltons." *The World.* (19 May 1880): 4-5. Print. Also here: Web. 20 Nov. 2023 <https://gsarchive.net/gilbert/cel_home/index.html>.

Cevasco, G. A. "Gilbert and Sullivan and the Brooklyn Bridge: Two Newly Discovered Letters." *Studies in English, New Series*: Vol. 10, Article 20 (1992): [173]-76. Print

Cox-Ife, William. *How to Sing Both Gilbert and Sullivan*. London: Chappell, 1961. Print.

_____. *Training the Gilbert & Sullivan Chorus*. London: Chappell, 1955. Print.

"Cripps" <urbandictionary.com/define.php?term=cripps%20it>. Web. 1 Oct. 2023.

Crowther, Andrew. *Sweethearts*. The Gilbert & Sullivan Archive. <https://gsarchive.net/gilbert/plays/sweethearts/swethearts_home.html->. Web. 24 Aug. 2023.

Dark, Sidney, and Rowland Grey. *W. S. Gilbert: His Life and Letters.* London: Methuen, 1923. Print.

Der Vampyre. See *Vampyre, Der.*

D'Oyly Carte Opera Company. *The Sorcerer* (Gilbert & Sullivan) with *The Zoo* (Rowe & Sullivan). Royal Philharmonic Orchestra. Cond. Isidore Godfrey and Royston Nash. London. 1993. CD.

Eden, David. "The Cobbler and His Last. *Sir Arthur Sullivan Society Magazine* No. 62 (Summer 2006): 15-18. Print. And here. Web. 16 Nov. 2023 <sullivansociety.org.uk/wp-content/uploads/2018/-12/Magazine-62.pdf>.

"Fine Old English Gentleman" (Henry Russell version) <ingeb.org/-songs/illsinga.html>. Web. 1 Oct. 2023.

Fischler, Alan. "It Proves that Aestheticism Ought to Be Discarded: W. S. Gilbert and the Poets of *Patience*." *Nineteenth Century Literature* 66.3 (2011): 355-82. Print

Fitzgerald, Percy. *The Savoy Opera and The Savoyards*. London: Chatto, 1894. Print.

"Frederic Goes Free." *New York Times* 29 Feb. 1940: 18. Print.

Gilbert, W. S. "Author's Note" in *Patience; or, Bunthorne's Bride*. Doubleday, Page, 1902. Print.

———. *The Bab Ballads*. Ed. James Ellis. Cambridge: Belknap/ Harvard UP, 1970. Print.

———. *The Bab Ballads with which are included Songs of a Savoyard*. 6th ed. London: Macmillan, 1910. Print.

———. "Continuations of Dramatic Histories: *Box and Cox*." See MacPhail, *Additional Adventures of Messrs. Box and Cox*.

———. "An Elixir of Love." In *The Graphic*. Christmas Number 25 Dec. 1876, pp. 24-26. (Also in Gilbert's *Foggerty's Fairy and Other Tales* [pp. 43-68] but without Gilbert's "Bab" illustrations, which were restored in Andrew Crowther's recent compilation of some of Gilbert's short fiction, *The Triumph of Vice and Other Stories* [pp. 151-76]) Print.

———. *Foggerty's Fairy and Other Tales*. London: Routledge, 1890. Print.

———. *The Mikado; or, The Town of Titipu* [Lord Chamberlain's Licensed Deposit Copy, 1885]. Add. Ms. 53334. British Lib., London. Print.

———. *New and Original Extravaganzas*. Ed. Isaac Goldberg. Boston: Luce, 1931. Print.

———. "Only Roses." *Illustrated Sporting and Dramatic News* 10 Dec. 1881: 323. Print.

———. "Rosencrantz and Guildenstern." In *Foggerty's Fairy and Other Tales* (pp.349-66).

———. "Rosencrantz and Guildenstern." *Fun,* 12, 19, 26 Dec. 1874, pp. 238-39, 256-57, 261. Print.

———. *Rosencrantz and Guildenstern*. In *Original Plays*, 3rd Series. London: Chatto, 1920 (pp. 75-89). Print.

[———]. "Savoy Memories." See "Savoy Memories."

———. *The Savoy Operas*. 2 vols. London: Oxford UP, 1962-63. Print.

———. *The Triumph of Vice and Other Stories*. Ed. Andrew Crowther. Richmond, Surrey: Alma Classics, 2018. Print.

"Gilbert, William Schwenck." *Dictionary of National Biography*. See Parry, Edward Abbot.

Gilbert & Sullivan Archive, The. <gsarchive.net>. Web. 20 Oct. 2023.

Gilbert & Sullivan Austin. *The [Gilbert & Sullivan Society of Austin] Newsletter* and (starting in Jan. 2020) *The Austin Savoyard, passim.* (The entire archive can be accessed online <www.gilbertsullivan.org/newsletter-archive/>. Web. 24 Aug. 2023.

"Girl I Left Behind Me, The." <en.wikipedia.org/wiki/The_Girl_I_Left_ Behind>. Web. 1 Oct. 2023.

Goddard, John. Personal Communication. 23 October, 17 November 2023. Email.

Gordon, Ann Marie. Renderings for the settings for *Ruddigore* for Gilbert & Sullivan Austin, 2018. MacPhail Gilbert & Sullivan Collection, Lawrence and Lee Theatre Research Institute, Columbus: Ohio SU. Drawings.

Green, Martyn. *Martyn Green's Treasury of Gilbert & Sullivan.* New York: Simon & Schuster, 1961. Print.

Greenbank, Harry. *Mr. Jericho.* Comp. Ernest Ford. Web. 8 Nov. 2023. https://gsarchive.net/companions/jericho/index.html. (See also "O'Brien," below.)

Hyder, William. "*H.M.S. Pinafore* in American Waters: Reflections, Corrections, and a Startling Revelation." In *Papers, Presentations and Patter: A Savoyards' Symposium.* Ed. Ralph MacPhail, Jr.

_____. Personal communications 1977 and ca. 2011. MS and E-mail.

Internet Movie Database [IMDb], The. *She Lights Up Well.* Web. 17 Nov. 2023.https://www.imdb.com/title/tt3231686/?ref_=fn_al_tt_1.

Jacobs, Arthur. *Arthur Sullivan: A Victorian Musician.* 2nd ed. Portland, OR: Amadeus, 1992. Print.

Jenkins, William D. "Swinburne, Robert Buchanan, and W. S. Gilbert: The Pain that Was All but a Pleasure." *Studies in Philology* 69.3 (1972): 369-87. Print.

Jones, John Bush. "In Search of Archibald Grosvenor: A New Look at Gilbert's *Patience.*" *Victorian Poetry* 3.1 (1965): 45-53. Print. Rpt. Jones, ed. *W. S. Gilbert: A Century of Scholarship and Commentary*, pp. 243-56.

Jones, John Bush. Ed. *W. S. Gilbert: A Century of Scholarship and Commentary.* New York: NY UP, 1970. Print.

Library of Congress Copyright Office. *Dramatic Compositions Copyrighted in the United States 1870 to 1916.* Vol 2 O to Z. Washington: GPO, 1918. Print.

Mackinlay, Sterling. *Light Opera.* London: Hutchinson, 1926. Print.

MacPhail, Ralph, Jr. *Additional Adventures of Messrs. Box and Cox.* [Includes Gilbert's "Continuations of Dramatic Histories: *Cox and*

Box" and F. C. Burnand's *Penelope Anne.*] Bridgewater, Va.: Parenthesis, 1974. Print.

_____. "Bab and the Bard: Gilbert's *Rosencrantz and Guildenstern.*" Paper presented at the W. S. Gilbert Sesquicentennial Symposium, Cambridge, MA, 20 Nov. 1986. MacPhail Gilbert & Sullivan Collection, Bridgewater, VA. TS.

_____. "The Secrets of *H.M.S. Pinafore.*" A Lecture Given for the Bridgewater Retirement Community Village Assn., 3 Apr. 2006; for the Gilbert & Sullivan Opera Company, University of Chicago, 6 March 2014; and for Gilbert & Sullivan Soc. of Austin, 18 May 2014. TS Notes and Mss. MacPhail Gilbert & Sullivan Collection, Lawrence and Lee Theatre Research Institute, Ohio SU. Print.

[MacPhail, Ralph, Jr., comp.] "Adventures with Gilbert & Sullivan," Volume I: 1962-1995. MacPhail Gilbert & Sullivan Collection, Bridgewater, VA. Scrapbook.

[_____.] "Savoyard Scrapbook" Volumes 1 (1943-68), 7 (1978), and 21 (1983-84). MacPhail Gilbert & Sullivan Collection, Lawrence and Lee Theatre Research Institute, Columbus: Ohio SU. Scrapbooks.

MacPhail, Ralph, Jr., ed. *Papers, Presentations and Patter: A Savoyards' Symposium.* York, PA: International Gilbert & Sullivan Association, 2012. Print.

MacPhail, Ralph C., Jr. "TRIAL BY JURY: A Sequel to *H.M.S. Pinafore.*" *The Savoyard*, 8.3 (January 1970), 17-18. Print.

MacPhail, Ralph Cordiner, Jr., *A Production of Victoria's World* [*Rosencrantz and Guildenstern* and *Cox and Box*]. MFA Thesis. VA Commonwealth U., 1972. Print.

McElroy, George C. "Whose *Zoo*; or, When Did the *Trial* Begin?" *Nineteenth Century Theatre Research* 12 (1984) 39-54. Print.

"Miya Sama." Google yields many sources with translations, including familiar Gilbert & Sullivan sites. Web. 1 Oct. 2023.

Morris, Roy, Jr. *Declaring His Genius: Oscar Wilde in North America.* Cambridge & London: Belknap/Harvard, 2013. Print.

O'Brien, Christopher, Ed. *Mr[.] Jericho. An Operetta in One Act.* 1893. Words by Harry Greenbank. Music by Ernest Ford. Vocal Score. London: Stainer & Bell, 2018. Print. (See "Greenbank," above.)

Pall Mall Gazette, The. 1889. See "'Blank, Blank!' The New Opera at the Savoy. A Chat with Mr. Gilbert."

Parry, Edward Abbot. "Gilbert, William Schwenck." *Dictionary of National Biography*, 1912 Supplement, Volume 2. Web. 7 Nov.

2023.   <https://en.wikisource.org/wiki/Dictionary_of_National-_Biography,_1912_supplement/Gilbert,_William_Schwenck>. Web. 7 Nov. 2023.

Pearson, Hesketh. *Gilbert and Sullivan: A Biography.* London: Hamish Hamilton, 1935. Print.

_____. *Gilbert: His Life and Strife.* London: Methuen, 1957. Print.

[Plaque on East 20th Street commemorating the site of the hotel at which Sullivan composed most of *The Pirates of Penzance* in 1879]. Gilbert & Sullivan Archive. <https://gsarchive.net/pirates/html/-plaque.html>. Photograph. Web. 5 Nov. 2023.

Robinson, Arthur. Personal Communication. 4, 5, 15, 17-20 Nov. 2023. Email.

"'*Ruddygore*' and Savoy Operas: An Interview with Mr. W. S. Gilbert." In *Pall Mall Gazette*, 21 Jan. 1887, pp. 1-2; rpt. *Pall Mall Budget*, 27 Jan. 1887, pp. 10-11 Print; and here: <gsarchive.net/gilbert/interviews/ruddygore.html>. Web. 1 Oct. 2023.

Russell, Anna. *Anna Russell: The (First) Farewell Concert.* VAI, 1984. DVD.

_____. *Anna Russell Sings! Again?* Columbia, 1953. LP.

_____. *The Anna Russell Songbook.* New York: Citadel, 1960. Print.

_____. *I'm Not Making This Up, You Know! The Autobiography of the Queen of Musical Parody.* Ed. Janet Vickers. New York: Continuum, 1985. Print.

_____. Letter to the Author. 25 Aug. 1984. MS.

"Savoy Memories. Interesting Speech by Mr. W. S. Gilbert." *Daily Telegraph* 31 Dec. 1906: 12. Print.

Searle, Townley. *Sir William Schwenck Gilbert: A Topsy-Turvy Adventure.* London: Alexander-Ouseley, 1931. Print.

Shepherd, Marc. *Gilbert and Sullivan Discography.* Web. 1 Nov. 2023. <http://gasdisc.oakapplepress.com/>.

Sondheimer, Janet. *Castle Adamant in Hampstead: A History of Westfield College, 1882-1982.* London: Westfield College, U. London, 1983. Print.

Stedman, Jane W. "Boz and Bab." *The Dickensian* 58:3 (1962): 171-78. Print.

_____. "The Genesis of *Patience*." *Modern Philology* 66 (1968): 45-53. Print. Rpt. Jones, *W. S. Gilbert: A Century of Scholarship and Commentary*, pp. 285-318.

_____. "William S. Gilbert: His Comic Techniques and Their Development." Diss. U. Chicago, 1955.

Sullivan, Arthur. *Ivanhoe.* Lib. Julian Sturgis. BBC Nat. Orch. of Wales. Cond. David Lloyd-Jones. Chandos, 2010. CD.

Topsy-Turvy. Dir. Mike Leigh. October Films. 1999. DVD.

VLO News [Newsletter of Valley Light Opera, Amherst, MA]. Audition
    Notes by James Ellis and his musical collaborators, *passim.* Print.

Vampyr, Der. Opera composed by Heinrich Marschner. *Wikipedia.* Web.
    7 Nov. 2023. < https://en.wikipedia.org/wiki/Der_Vampyr>.

Walbrook, H. M. *Gilbert & Sullivan Opera: A History and A Comment.*
    2nd ed. London: White, 1922. Print.

Williams, Carolyn. *Gilbert and Sullivan: Gender, Genre, Parody.* New
    York: Columbia UP, 2011. Print.

————. "Parody and Poetic Tradition: Gilbert and Sullivan's 'Pa-
    tience.'" *Victorian Poetry* 46.4 (Winter 2008): 375-403. Print.

World, The. 1880. See "Celebrities at Home."

Wren, Gayden. "Emphasis on the '*Truly*'." *The Gilbert & Sullivan Society
    of Austin Newsletter*, Feb. 2016, p. 2. Print.

R alph MacPhail, Jr., is Professor *emeritus* of Theatre, Communication Studies, and English, Bridgewater College of Virginia, where he taught and directed theatre for 33 years.

He staged productions for Gilbert & Sullivan Austin starting in 1998, was named the company's first Artistic Director in 2005, and became Artistic Director *emeritus* in 2021. He continues to write for *The Austin Savoyard*, consult with GSA, and treasure his Austin friendships.

In "retirement," he and his very patient and loving wife Alice live in the Bridgewater Retirement Community, where he pursues research and publishes articles on the Savoy operas, collects anything and everything relating to those remarkable works, and enjoys corresponding with fellow Savoyards. His email address is RafeMacPhail@Yahoo.com.

He is in the process of giving his collection of books, media, memorabilia, and papers to the Lawrence and Lee Theatre Research Institute at the Ohio State University, where most of it already resides: <https://library.osu.edu/collections/spec.tri.mgs/summary-information>.